INTERNATIONAL SERIES OF MONOGRAPHS IN
LIBRARY AND INFORMATION SCIENCE
GENERAL EDITOR: G. CHANDLER

VOLUME 10

Automation in Libraries

Automation in Libraries

SECOND EDITION

R. T. KIMBER

PERGAMON PRESS
Oxford · New York · Toronto · Sydney

Pergamon Press Ltd., Headington Hill Hall, Oxford
Pergamon Press Inc., Maxwell House, Fairview Park, Elmsford,
New York 10523
Pergamon of Canada Ltd., 207 Queen's Quay West, Toronto 1
Pergamon Press (Aust.) Pty. Ltd., 19a Boundary Street,
Rushcutters Bay, N.S.W. 2011, Australia

Copyright © 1974 Richard Kimber

All Rights Reserved. No part of this publication may be reproduced, stored in a retrieval system, or transmitted, in any form or by any means, electronic, mechanical, photocopying, recording or otherwise, without the prior permission of Pergamon Press Ltd.

First edition 1968
Reprinted 1970
Second edition 1974

Library of Congress Cataloging in Publication Data

Kimber, Richard T
Automation in libraries.
(International series of monographs in library and information science, v. 10)
Bibliography: p.
1. Libraries—Automation. I. Title.
Z678.9.K55   1975   025.2′028′54   74–13847
ISBN 0-08-017969-X

Printed in Great Britain by A. Wheaton & Co., Exeter

Contents

PREFACE vii

1. Libraries and Automation — 1
2. Reasons for Automating — 17
3. Planning an Automated System — 28
4. Implementing an Automated System — 38
5. Bibliographic Record Structures — 61
6. Listing and Accounting Systems — 97
7. Serials Accessioning Systems — 124
8. Circulation Control — 144
9. Ordering and Acquisitions — 174
10. Catalogues and Bibliographies — 196

INDEX — 237

Preface

THIS second edition of *Automation in Libraries* represents a complete restructuring of my original approach to the subject, with the addition of a substantial amount of new material on the systems analysis side. The text has been entirely rewritten to take account of the great expansion in the use of computers in libraries since the publication of the first edition 6 years ago.

The new approach, however, retains the original emphasis on methodology. It is my belief that in this way it is possible to see beyond many of the superficial differences between individual systems, to understand the fundamental principles of the subject, and to some extent, to find a stable foundation for a rapidly changing subject. Throughout the book, principles are linked to practice, and while examples tend to be taken from British libraries, the work of libraries in the United States, France and Germany is frequently mentioned, in order both to give as broad a basis as possible to the book, and, in many cases, to illustrate particular points of principle.

The last chapter in the first edition attempted a résumé of the then present state of automation in libraries. It was felt that it would not be appropriate, or even possible, to attempt to repeat this task in the second edition. Accordingly, the work of individual libraries in connection with particular systems is discussed throughout the body of the book. No attempt has been made to be comprehensive in this respect: libraries mentioned are those known personally to the author and with the exception of a number of systems that are quite unique, libraries have been chosen simply to illustrate and provide examples of the systems under discussion.

A major omission has been the chapter on computers themselves. It is felt that it is no longer realistic for every textbook on computer applications in a specific area to introduce its readers to the basic principles of computers. A textbook on the basic principles of computers can do this more effectively, and there are many such texts.

The first edition of *Automation in Libraries* was somewhat deficient in respect of illustrative material, and an attempt has now been made to rectify this. The flow charts of the first edition have been redrawn and extended, but in addition, many illustrations of the products of computer systems are now reproduced. Most of these are in the nature of typical samples of what particular systems can produce, for it is in the area of their outputs that the greatest differences between systems are found.

It has naturally not been possible to provide this illustrative material without the willing help and kind co-operation of a large number of librarians. I want to acknowledge here the assistance and permission to reproduce material given by Mr. H. J. Heaney, Queen's University Library, Belfast; Marcel Dekker Inc., New York; Mr. V. Fox, The City University Library, London; Dr. C. J. Aslin, University of East Anglia Library; Mr. J. F. Stirling, University of Exeter Library; Mr. H. F. Dammers, Sittingbourne Laboratories, Sittingbourne, Kent; Messrs. Routledge & Kegan Paul Ltd.; Mr. J. M. Smethurst, Aberdeen University Library; the Librarians of Institutes and Schools of Education group; Miss L. M. Morris, Oak Ridge National Laboratory Library; Miss L. Santoro, San Francisco Public Library; Mr. E. Balch, University of California San Diego Library; Dr. R. A. Wall, Loughborough University of Technology Library; Dr. J. Fayollat, University of California Los Angeles, Biomedical Library; Mr. R. G. Woods, University of Southampton Library; Dr. G. Pflug, University of Bochum Library; Mr. A. A. Thomas, Plessey Telecommunications Ltd.; Mr. W. A. J. Davie, Automated Library Systems Ltd.; Mr. F. W. Brown, Cheshire County Libraries; Mr. C. J. Hunt, University of Manchester Library; Mr. R. Adam, The City University Library, London; Miss J. M. Voegle, The Oklahoma Department of Libraries; Mr. C. Earl, Kent County Libraries; Mr. R. E. Coward and Mr. R. Butcher, The British Library; Mr. R. Bregzis, University of Toronto Library; Mr. P. Brown, Trinity College Library, Dublin; Mr. F. G. Kilgour, The Ohio College Library Center; Mr. Wm. R. Maidment, London Borough of Camden Libraries; Mr. A. R. Hall, University of Birmingham Library; Mr. J. W. Jolliffe, the Bodleian Library; Mr.

R. J. Huse, West Sussex County Library; Mr. P. D. Friend, AWRE Library, Aldermaston; Mr. J. N. Allen, Brighton Public Libraries; Miss J. Plaister, LASER; Mr. B. Gallivan, University of Lancaster Library; Mr. J. P. Wells, Oxfordshire County Libraries.

In particular I should like to express my thanks to Dr. Anne H. Boyd, Mr. A. Maltby and Dr. R. C. Young, who have read the manuscript and made a number of helpful suggestions.

CHAPTER 1

Libraries and Automation

THE human mind has an infinite capacity for invention and an insatiable desire for discovery and exploration. The human spirit is creative and cannot but write, paint, fashion and build. As the inheritors of several millenia of civilization, and more particularly of three or four centuries of very intense and rapid growth and expansion of knowledge, we today are confronted with an intricate and constantly developing network of knowledge, and live in a world where the discovery and application of new technology has become essential, not just to enable us to stand still—for therein lies stagnation and economic disaster—but to progress to even higher and better civilization along an exponential scientific–technical–industrial growth curve.

Because of his ability to plan ahead, coupled with his real power to influence the course of events in the Universe, inventive man has learned to control his environment and to harness natural resources for his own benefit, convenience and enjoyment. A new discovery in chemistry may have pharmacological implications; a new drug is successfully tested and a former "killer" disease can now be cured. Medical services must be expanded and financed to put the new cure into practice. The rate of growth of the world's population is thereby increased with consequential effects on requirements for food, housing and social services.

A small advance in physics can have practical applications in telecommunications engineering, perhaps making possible significant reductions in the cost of transmitting messages over long distances. New telephone, telex and data-transmission business is generated, with social, business, industrial and scientific implications. The building of the first stored program electronic computer in the 1940s and the successful marketing of such machines from the 1950s onwards, has led in the 1960s and 1970s to such an innumerable host of applications in almost every facet of life that it is no exaggeration to say that we are now witnessing a revolution in data processing, storing and transmitting, commensurate in its likely effects with the Industrial Revolution that was sparked off in the eighteenth and nineteenth centuries by the then newly harnessed power of steam.

This book is concerned with the use of computers in libraries, and more particularly the routine clerical (housekeeping) tasks which form the essential foundation upon which library services must be built. But it is important to remember that this, like all new inventions, discoveries, and applications, has implications in many other directions. Some of these are already apparent; others may not be obvious for many years or decades still to come. One thing is clear, the quality of library service that can be provided is increasing steadily as computer methods become more and more widely adopted in libraries. While problems remain, associated for example with the cost of mechanized systems, and some human problems of running them, very few librarians can afford, now, not to be seriously involved in library automation.

OBJECTIVES

In the first instance, librarians' objectives in automating any library activity were strictly limited. Regardless of the size or complexity of the task to be mechanized (whether it was the production of a list of current periodicals or a complex integrated system embracing most of a library's operations) the goal of the mechanized system was essentially the same as that of the conventional system it replaced. On this basis all the major areas of library housekeeping have been successfully mechanized. Since the first viable systems became operational, roughly between 1963 and 1966, the basic principles underlying their operation have been understood and to a large extent become standardized. This means that any library seeking to mechanize a particular system has available to it now a knowledge of standard procedure for that system, so that its own task reduces to building in the divergences from those standard procedures that are necessitated by its own individual non-standard requirements.

But these limited objectives are beginning slowly to change. Just as has been the case with other discoveries and inventions, human ingenuity has perceived that it is possible not only for new types of library services to be developed, but that an automated library system can monitor and report on its own performance and on the changing behaviour of the library's public. The human librarian thus has a tool by means of which he can make changes to the operation of his library system, based on reliable quantitative data, and so bring about real improvements in his library's services.

The old adage remains true, that the systems designer should not allow the machine to dictate his requirements—in some of the earliest specifications for mechanized library systems, failure to adhere to this principle resulted in catalogue entries being sorted on the first five letters only of the author's surname, because this was then standard data-processing practice. But it is not true that we should continue to force each succeeding generation of computer hardware and each new concept in file-handling software into the old traditional library moulds. Why, for example, should subject indexes to library book collections continue to be quite different in kind from subject indexes to annual volumes of abstracting journals? Why should individual libraries have individual catalogues; why not go much further in the direction of union catalogues? Why should we continue to think in terms of the library user travelling to the library building to transact his library business? It is comparatively expensive to transport human beings but comparatively inexpensive to transport books and other library materials and to transmit data. The stage has been reached when the technology and perhaps also the economic incentive exist for a radical long-term appraisal of the nature of the library and information services that should be an integral part of a highly organized and scientifically and industrially advanced society. In computer-based library and information systems we have both the reason for making such an appraisal and the means for achieving the goals that may emerge from it.

CHANGE AND PRODUCTIVITY

In a primitive society life changes but little, and an effective balance is maintained between the size of a human population in a given locality and the ability of that locality to support it. Human fertility tends to increase the population, disease tends to reduce it. If more food is required, farmers and hunters must work harder. If more land is required for cultivation, then in all likelihood more land exists for the taking, for the wresting from a neighbouring people, or perhaps for the cost of clearing it of scrub or forest.

But once inventive man interferes in this natural cycle, in order to achieve some good purpose, then he sets up an unending chain of cause and effect. Having taken a hand in changing a natural equilibrium, he thereby assumes, perhaps unwittingly, responsibility for the continued successful functioning of those natural processes with whose operation he has become involved. Because a change in one part of nature leads to change in another, man is forever saddled with the responsibility of making changes, inventions, applications and improvements, consequent upon one primordial change, which has long since passed from the memory of the race.

But not only is continual effort required of man because of this. One change is likely, on average, to affect or have implications for not just one other aspect of life or part of nature, but more than one. Thus, there is a growing requirement for man's involvement in the control of and responsibility for his environment. This requirement is growing geometrically. Consider a simple example of this kind of geometrical growth. Imagine an environment in which one original action produces, after 10 years, results which necessitate further action in two areas. Then 20 years after the original action, four new actions are directly attributable to its operation, after 30 years, eight, and so on.

So today we can observe, particularly in the fields of technology, medicine, agriculture, science and the social sciences, the vast network of cause and effect for which man is responsible, and which has raised society to its present high level of civilization. Libraries are one link in this network, and a constantly active link at that. Not only did the first library have some immediate effect on society or knowledge, but all succeeding libraries, information centres and the rest, have continued to affect the whole course of human endeavour and experience. The library is as a continuing catalyst in this whole chain of development.

Now a change or invention of this kind clearly has a much more important influence on the future course of human life than something like the discovery of a new drug, even if that drug be penicillin. Other inventions have been of a similar nature; writing, printing with movable type, the extraction of mechanical energy from fossil fuels, computing machines. Such key inventions have the effect of increasing the whole pace of development and change.

A further possibility is open to man. If a constant and interrelated sequence of changes, applications and inventions has resulted in material improvement to his whole way of life, and if to continue this process will yield still further betterments, the enjoyment of those benefits can be hastened by a speeding up of the rate of invention. This can relate to either economic or to scientific, medical, or to any other kind of development. And at the present time, in the last third of the twentieth century, this possibility of speeding up the application of new discoveries is part of the whole ethos of scientific and industrial research and development.

We live, therefore, in a world of change, from which, by and large, we all benefit. And so, we all bear an obligation to contribute to future benefits by making appropriate improvements in our own areas of professional competence and responsibility. And where a man's profession lies in a key area, such as medicine, computer science, or librarianship, where change is likely to be much more productive than average, then his obligation to contribute to the future benefit of the human race is the greater.

Automation in libraries, the subject of this book, is thus seen as an especially critical area from which future benefits will emerge. Research effort in library automation should therefore be directed towards improving existing services, and developing new services, rather than just mechanizing a *status quo*. There is a real need to consider the costs of library systems and it is greatly to the credit of those librarians who have been involved in programmes of library automation that it is now the accepted practice to cost a new computer-based system. But cost must not be the overriding criterion in estimating the worth of mechanized library systems. Service is a more important criterion, and estimating the value of a library service (a difficult task) is more important than putting a figure to its price.

Despite their key role in the processes of research and development, libraries, like any human activity, have been critically dependent on their appropriate technologies. While contributing materially to the development of civilization, they have themselves been dependent on the state of civilization, expressed in technological terms, for their ability to contribute to it. Libraries deal essentially in recorded knowledge, which, in our world is expressed in terms of alphabetic and numeric characters written on some suitable medium. The technology pertinent to library function and development has therefore been that dealing with characters and their manipulation, their storage and transmission. In other words, alphabets and writing, ink, stone, clay, papyrus, vellum, paper, film, type and other storage media, printing, photography, postal, telephone and telex services, data-processing machinery, computers and data transmission.

This list of library technology is quite crucial to an understanding both of the historical pace of library development and to an appreciation of what is now happening to libraries through the influence of the computer. Absent from the list are the key inventions which made possible the Western world's rapid technological and economic progress over the past two centuries. These are concerned with mechanical energy, its generation, transmission and application. Libraries are concerned only very indirectly with mechanical energy—printing presses are driven by electric motors, internal combustion engines are employed during the erection of a library building and enable a mobile library service to be provided in rural areas, and motors of various kinds are found in typewriters, stencil duplicators, photocopying machinery, and the like. But these apart, and excepting also the very important developments in library service resulting from the application of photographic technology, there has been no major breakthrough in library technology since the invention of printing by movable type. Instead, since the days of clay tablets and the library of Assurbanipal in Nineveh, there has been a slow and continuous development of libraries and their services. With the advent of printed books, libraries became larger and more numerous, and the growth of libraries has paralleled the world growth of knowledge and wealth.[1]

Libraries and Automation

But where a new invention has direct relevance to library services, as, for example, in the case of automatic photocopying machines, then the growth of library services and of their contribution to society is suddenly enhanced. Figure 1.1 contrasts the comparatively slow growth of a conventional library service (loans within the Library of Congress) with the very rapid growth of electrostatic photocopying in the same library. In Fig. 1.2 the latter curve has been redrawn on semi-logarithmic graph paper. The curve of Fig. 1.1 has become a straight line, indicating that the electrostatic photocopying service is growing exponentially with a doubling period of just over 2 years.

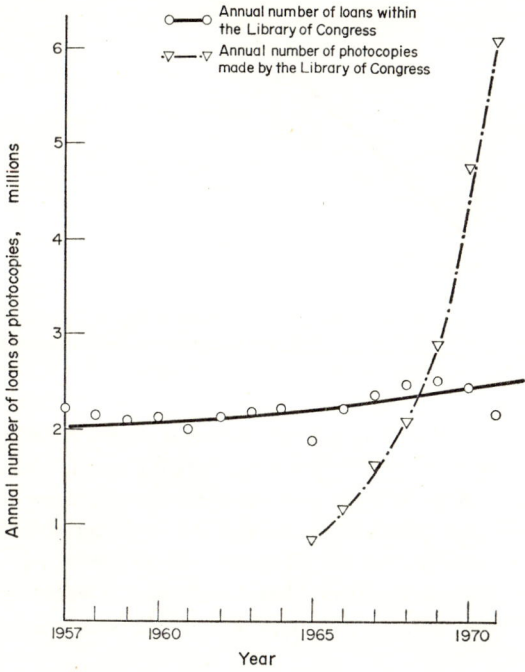

FIG. 1.1. Comparative growth curves for conventional library services and photocopying services. For the Library of Congress, the slowly growing curve plots the total number of loans each year for use within the Library; the rapidly growing curve shows the number of electrostatic prints (excluding catalogue cards) made by the Library's Photoduplication Service. (Source of statistics: Annual Report of the Librarian of Congress.)

8 *Automation in Libraries*

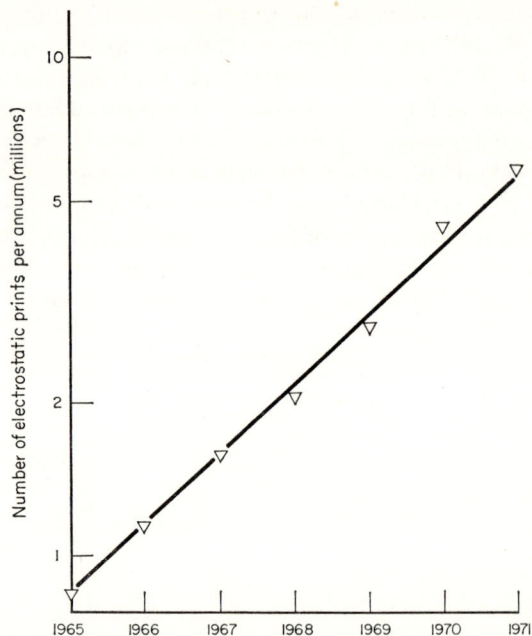

Fig. 1.2. The growth curve for electrostatic prints of Fig. 1.1 plotted on semi-logarithmic paper. This straight-line plot denotes exponential growth with a doubling period of just over 2 years.

The computer, which in general terms is a machine not just for performing mathematical computations but for manipulating characters and storing them, is an invention of direct relevance to libraries' prime concern—the acquisition, storage and exploitation of knowledge as recorded in documents of all kinds—in other words, character manipulation. We must expect, therefore, to see a very rapid growth in the use of computers in libraries and in the services provided by those libraries.

Figure 1.3 illustrates this growth of the use of computers in libraries. The periodical *Program* has, since its inception in 1966, provided reasonably full coverage of library automation activity in the British Isles, and the number of papers published in *Program* each year can therefore be taken as an indication of the extent to which computers

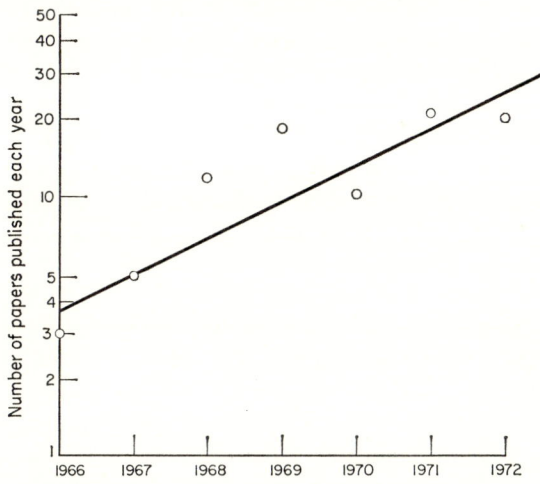

FIG. 1.3. Growth of library automation in the UK as indicated by the number of papers describing operational computer systems published each year in *Program*. Exponential growth is indicated with a doubling period of about 2 years.

are being used in Britain and Ireland. When the numbers of papers describing operational systems published each year is plotted against the year, an exponential curve is again obtained (a straight-line graph on semi-logarithmic paper). The yearly number of papers published has tended to double approximately every 2 years, suggesting a corresponding growth rate for library automation in the UK.

CHANGE IN LIBRARY AUTOMATION

Perhaps because the electronic computer has appeared on the scene at this late stage in the history of scientific and technological development, when its potentialities have been very rapidly appreciated, and when the rate of development in science and technology as a whole is greater than it has ever been before, it is not surprising that computers themselves have been improved and developed technically very rapidly indeed. Their rate of development can be measured by the size of their internal memory or central processing unit (cpu), or by the number of basic arithmetical operations that can be performed each second. The latter is probably a better measure of the state of fundamental computing technology at any moment in time, and over the past 30 years has been growing exponentially, doubling once every 1.8 years approximately.[2]

When a library uses a computer in one or more of its housekeeping routines it becomes linked thereby to this rapidly growing and rapidly changing technology, with some important implications for the future planning of its library services.

The first is that once a particular library function has been automated, it is likely to remain automated. There have been cases of gross failure of newly designed systems that have reverted to manual procedures, but such instances are rare. This means that when planning and budgeting for library mechanization programmes, long-term maintenance and development must be allowed for. In particular there is a need for senior library staff able to devote time to systems work and to planning and organizing the library side of the computer–library interface.

The second relates to the timescale of the development of a particular library system. For a typical application, such as circulation control or book ordering and acquisitions, a period of not less than 2 years is likely to elapse between the start of planning for the project and the time when the system becomes fully operational. During this period, equipment may become available with significantly faster processing speeds and with hardware logic doubling the capabilities of central processing units. So that there is some justification for the common belief that any system is obsolete by the time that it is fully operational.

However, one must ask the question, "obsolete with respect to what?" If it is with respect to the very latest developments in computing, then the belief may be well founded. But if the comparison is with other newly introduced computer systems, and if performance is measured against existing manual systems and not against the ultimate in sophisticated computer systems, then, if the new system compares satisfactorily, it is not obsolete.

But any given computing laboratory will change its computer from time to time to gain advantage from cumulated progress in computing technology. And all systems run on the old machine will have to be changed so as to enable them to be run on the new equipment. In general terms, this means that a library committed to one or more mechanized systems will be involved in a change of computer hardware roughly once every 5 years or so. This may entail reprogramming to a greater or lesser extent, and may require certain changes to the overall structure of a program suite, as, for example, is the case when magnetic tape based systems are rewritten to use magnetic disc stores. In all such cases, however, the effort involved in rewriting or redesigning can be regarded as an investment for the future which will be repaid many times over by virtue of the greater operating efficiency of the new system.

So the problem of the rapid advance of computer science and technology boils down to this. Considering the field as a whole, or in isolation from any local computer laboratories, development is continuous. But in local terms, development is discontinuous, proceeding in a series of large steps, one step every 5 years or so. In this way each local computer laboratory maintains a relatively stable technology between such "steps", which makes it possible for individual applications, such as library systems, to take place in an effectively stable technological environment.

The third implication for planning that results from the rapid rate of growth of computer science concerns the planning and development of library automation on the national and international level. It concerns the development and adoption of standards of all kinds relevant to library mechanization. No one today seriously questions the value of standards for all kinds of activities; indeed the concept of standardization has been crucial to the acceleration of scientific and technological advance and the good material benefits accruing to mankind therefrom.

The existence of a standard implies a plateau or stable state in the development of the object or procedure concerned. And while standardization brings acknowledged benefits, the price paid is in terms of a reduced rate of development. For example, there is a draft International Standards Organization standard for the exchange of bibliographic records on magnetic tape. The worldwide adoption of this standard could revolutionize the bibliographic services available to libraries, but the idea of transmitting data by the physical distribution of magnetic tapes is based on already obsolete technology—before the standard has been adopted even by a handful of different countries.

The best approach to this problem is probably to emphasize the very great benefits which accrue from standardization, for example, an efficient bibliographic information exchange network among western European nations and the United States will almost certainly be based on the ISO standard mentioned above. But because of the rapid development of computer science, it will be necessary to recognize that such standards will have a limited useful life span, which is the same as acknowledging the international validity of the stepwise approach to development in the local situation. But internationally, the steps will be larger and new standards will be less up to date because of the difficulty and complexity of the negotiations required before an international standard can be specified. These differences are illustrated diagrammatically in Fig. 1.4.

LIBRARY AUTOMATION AND PEOPLE

Beginning in the early 1940s and gathering momentum at the turn of the decade into the 1950s, there was considerable interest in Britain and the United States in the use of punched cards for a variety of library housekeeping tasks. It is interesting to note that among the disadvantages of these early mechanized systems, their designers included adverse reaction from library users. Whether designers of computer-based systems 25 years later need take the same possibility of adverse public reaction into account is open to debate, but library users' attitudes do vary, and they are worth examining briefly.

A safe starting point is to assert that the public at large dislike change in general, and computers in particular. Witness the standard joke-form based upon a computer error, or a supposed similarity between human behaviour and computer "behaviour". Consequently, human error, in whatever sphere that error may take place and with whatever consequences, is always more readily pardoned than computer error. The serious systems designer must set aside any irrational public preferences such as this, and put himself in the position of one who is able to, and has the responsibility to, give the public what is in their own best interests. And where this comes into conflict with

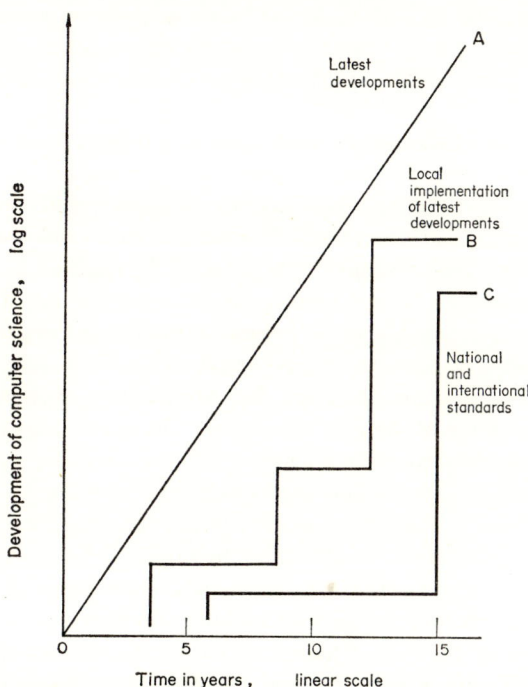

Fig. 1.4. Development of computer science. Curve A represents the latest available knowledge at any one time—the frontier of research work in the field. Curve B illustrates how an individual computing laboratory keeps pace with developments, while Curve C shows how national and international standards progress in the same stepwise manner, but always behind the (reasonably progressive) laboratory of Curve B.

prejudice and ignorance, his task resolves into that of the honest educator or salesman.

The attitude of the machine enthusiast is equally unsatisfactory. He is over-eager to accept computer-based systems just because they make use of a piece of modern electronic machinery. The safest approach therefore, avoiding both of these unsatisfactory extremes, is to concentrate not on the methods of operating a system, but on the end products of its operation. In one respect, this is no more than sound common sense, in another, it is also good librarianship. It is possible to go further and say that it should be a stated objective in the design of new computer-based systems, that when viewing their end products, it should not be possible to infer that a computer was involved in the system.

The reaction of the people who work in a library must also be considered by the systems designer. Part of his professional philosophy is to replace routine clerical chores performed slowly and expensively by human beings by routine clerical chores performed quickly and cheaply by a computer. And therein lie the fears of the routine clerk.

It is necessary to be completely honest when facing this problem. Fortunately it is possible to be honest in the library situation, and at the same time to reassure library clerks that their jobs are not in danger of disappearing, although they are likely to change.

From the point of view of the library clerical assistant, the introduction of automated methods has as its objective the minimizing of human clerical routines; and this is quite definitely in his or her own interest. There is a danger, however, that mechanization will serve merely to replace one type of routine by another, for example, replace the manual filing of loan slips by the manual insertion of punched book and reader cards into the maw of a data-collection device, and who is to say which of the two is more routine or the greater chore? Some routines will always remain (and routine can serve as a valuable respite from more demanding tasks), and chores can and should be minimized by intelligent planning of duty rotas so that library assistants move from job to job during the course of the day.

One of the basic purposes of library mechanization is to make library clerical staff more productive; in other words, to do a given job with less effort, and more particularly with less staff. This is the ground of the fear on the part of clerical assistants that their jobs will disappear consequent upon mechanization. But it has been fairly common experience in libraries that when they automate, staff requirements are not reduced. In other words, the clerical assistant has not lost his or her job. Why?

The answer may well lie in the nature of much of the work associated with library housekeeping. Figure 1.5 illustrates in generalized form the nature of such work. It can be broken down into a large number of unit operations, each consisting of three sections. Each unit is initiated

Libraries and Automation

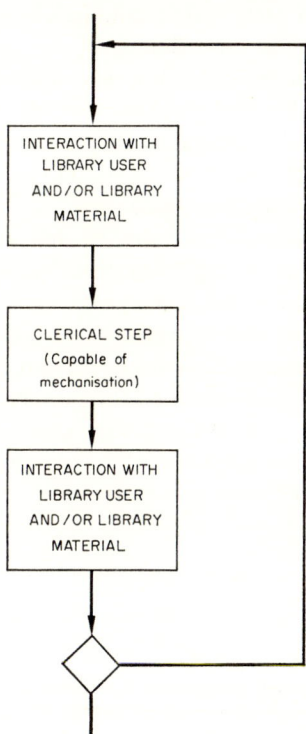

Fig. 1.5. The nature of library housekeeping.

by contact with a library user (e.g. as in a loans system) or a piece of library material (e.g. as in an acquisitions or cataloguing system). In some cases both a human being and library materials are involved. A clerical processing step follows, which is capable of automation, and this in turn is succeeded by some form of interaction with the library user (receiving back a book returned from loan) or library material (shelving the newly catalogued book). Work of this nature, even when mechanized, is still comparatively labour intensive, with the result that staff savings consequent upon library mechanization are not large. In other words, the library assistant is unlikely to lose her job when her work is mechanized.

It has been found, however, that although comparatively few staff savings are made possible immediately upon mechanization, library business is thereafter able to grow quite rapidly with only a small increase in library staff effort. In other words, staff productivity is enabled to increase. This is probably due as much to a higher degree of organization of the flow of work in the library as due to the direct influence of any computer procedures.

But this simple illustration provides an indication of the direction in which library automation should move in future. It shows an existing manual procedure largely unchanged except that part of it has been mechanized. Better library services and higher staff productivity will result when the machine has been enabled to play a larger part in the overall process, and when human intervention has been still further reduced by a closer correlation and integration of all the processes which together comprise the basic housekeeping routines upon which the library's services may be built.

REFERENCES

1. For a further and more detailed discussion of library growth rates see Chapter 1 of DOLBY, J. L., FORSYTH, V. J. and RESNIKOFF, H. L., *Computerized library catalogs: their growth, cost and utility.* MIT Press, 1969.
2. Graphs of the rate of growth of cpu size and processing speed in operations per second, from which this figure was derived, are given on page 245 of HAYES, R. M. and BECKER, J., *Handbook of data processing for libraries.* Wiley–Becker–Hayes, 1970.

CHAPTER 2

Reasons for Automating

IN AN ideal world, a newly installed computer-based library system would, typically, be the end result of the following chain of events. Over a period of time it would have become clear that the existing system (probably a manual, but possibly a simple mechanized one, e.g. using edge-notched cards) was performing with decreasing efficiency as the volume of library business increased steadily from year to year. This would have manifested itself through delays, backlogs, errors, staff dissatisfaction and perhaps a high rate of staff turnover. Library users would probably be suffering through the library's failure to provide needed material on time, although they might gain in other ways—for example, when no attempt was made to enforce loans regulations.

In an ideal world, the textbook solution to this problem would have been followed. The librarian, seeing that something serious was amiss, would have taken the correct textbook approach and called in a work-study consultant. This man, or more probably this team, would have studied the offending system thoroughly, costed it, assessed the service it was providing, and then considered the range of alternative systems which could give the same service or more for the same cost or less. Because they would have found that a computer-based system gave the best combination of good service and low cost, this was recommended, designed and installed.

But this is not an ideal world. Nor are libraries and librarians identical. One finds therefore a wide range of problems in libraries which could lead to the introduction of mechanized systems; one finds a wide range of attitudes on the part of librarians, and a broad spectrum of reasons for the adoption of computer methods. But although the textbook approach, as outlined above, is rarely followed in its entirety, the symptoms of clumsy and inefficient systems are everywhere in evidence, and the various stages of systems analysis and design cannot really be bypassed. So that where there are departures from the ideal or textbook approach, they will be mainly concerned with the reasons for automating. We must, therefore, consider the following question: given a system that is unsatisfactory, or less than the best possible, why should it be changed, at great expense, for a computer-based system doing the same job?

At this point it is necessary to make three points. The first is that, by and large, most conventional libraries and most normal library systems operate fairly satisfactorily. Given an average degree of competence on the part of the library assistants, and a modicum of vision, tact and persuasiveness on the part of the chief librarian, no really serious problems should mar the day-to-day operation of traditional manual library systems.

The second is that so far, in the historical development of library automation, computer systems have tended to do the same jobs as their manual counterparts and produce largely the same products and services. There are exceptions, and the MARC bibliographical services are a good example of the kind of innovation that is possible by switching to the new technology—the kind of service that really cannot be offered with conventional library procedures. But until the differences are emphasized between manual and mechanized systems, ostensibly doing the same job but with the latter capable of a much wider variety of products, then librarians will continue to think of one as a replacement for the other, rather than as an extension and development as well.

The third point concerns costs. Where developments, improvements, new services and lower unit costs are sought through the utilization of new technology, then it is always necessary to make an investment in terms of effort and money beforehand. In the world of business it is a fairly straightforward matter to show, by standard accounting procedures, the increased profits arising from the introduction of new technology. But libraries are not in business, they do not show profits, and no good way is known of setting a value on the services which result from their working. And so a librarian contemplating mechanization is faced with the need to make substantial investments with no hope of being able subsequently to recover them through increased profits, and with no ability to measure their value to his customers, the library's public.

In these circumstances it is possible to understand why library decision makers depart from textbook procedures at the point of justifying a decision for automation and that when they do stick rigidly to the rules, then the decision is likely to be against automation.[1]

RESEARCH

During the past 10 years or so, the development of computer-based library housekeeping systems has been essentially a process of research and development. Not fundamental or "pure" research, but very much a breaking of new ground and paving the way for others to follow. In such circumstances it is not realistic to expect new systems to be adopted only where they can be shown to be cost effective. Only by the actual development and operation of real systems in real library environments can mechanized systems be tested effectively. If, then, 10 years' research and development have already gone into the use of computers in libraries, what has been learned as a result? Firstly, that it is a perfectly feasible proposition to mechanize library housekeeping procedures, although some problems still exist and the goal of the totally automated library with linked and integrated housekeeping systems has not yet been achieved. (Incidentally, while this is still regarded as the ultimate goal for mechanized housekeeping systems, it is less often mentioned now than formerly, perhaps because it has been more difficult to achieve than was at first realized.)

Further, there has been a growing realization that automation of individual systems in individual libraries has important implications for the structure and organization of library services on a national and international scale. Questions of standardization arise and the extent to which libraries should and can differ. In these areas much remains unclear and, indeed, dependent on particular technological developments and the extent to which mechanized systems are introduced in individual libraries.

Another category of problem areas which require further research for their resolution, includes such detailed topics as record and file structures for library systems, filing rules, character sets and typesetting technology for catalogues and bibliographies, and the whole field of evaluating and costing automated library systems.

In other words, although much that is basic has been learned, fundamental problems solved and standard procedures developed, there remain many areas where research and development remain to be done, which alone is a good reason for some libraries to be heavily committed to the mechanization of their housekeeping systems.

PRESTIGE

It is a fact that those libraries which have initiated a mechanization programme have attracted attention within the library profession and have enhanced their reputation accordingly. So much so that to be involved with computers can be regarded as being as meritorious an activity as assembling a large and well-balanced collection suited to the needs of one's users. There is no harm in acquiring prestige in this way. The library profession will not be permanently dazzled by technology, and for every librarian who is temporarily carried away by enthusiasm for the big machine there are a score who are not and never will be. In fact the achievements of the libraries which are involved in using computers are monitored and evaluated quite closely. This is exactly as it should be.

Not only with reference to the national and international scene, but also within its own organization or institution is prestige to be acquired by the library which automates. It is doubtful if prestige would ever be the factor which alone made for a decision in favour of automation. But it must always be present and can be admitted as a valid argument in support of other reasons. Provided that the odds are not too heavily weighed against automation on other counts, and provided always that those factors are expected to swing in favour of automation in the near future, then the enhancement of the prestige of the library within the institution is a valid reason for automating.

MEASUREMENT AND STATISTICAL ANALYSIS

Reference has already been made to the difficulty of measuring and evaluating library services in the sense of placing a value on an individual unit of service. For example, what is the value, in quantitative terms, of a textbook borrowed by a student from his college or university library? What would he miss if he did not borrow that particular book but borrowed another one instead? What if he didn't borrow any books at all, but read only one basic text which he purchased? What if he read no books at all but confined his studies to his lecture notes? Would he still pass in his examinations? Would he suffer any loss, or would his future employers suffer any loss, and what would be the "value" of that loss, expressed quantitatively?

We can give no answer to questions of this kind, save to affirm our belief in the real and lasting value of reading books, and, in a general sort of way, we feel that the more books our hypothetical student reads the better for him. In the industrial sphere we know that the information contained in books and other documents can be of vital importance to a business or firm (and because a business exists to make a profit for its owners it begins to be possible to put a figure on the value of the information its library provides). And in the field of public librarianship we know that it is intrinsically good for people to read. And so we support public libraries with our money. We know what it costs to support them, yet we know nothing of their value. Are we getting good value for our money or bad?

Now automating a library is not going to change all this in a dramatic way, but in a very real sense computer-based library systems have the ability to monitor and report on their operations in a way that no manual system ever can. They can provide the librarian with information of a kind never possible before. He can use this to optimize the working of his systems, to assist in forward planning, to study the behaviour of his users, and possibly also as data from which theoretical models of library operations can be derived.

When operating manual systems it is a relatively straightforward matter to count the total number of units handled, the total amount of work done, the total numbers of readers served or of questions answered. In so far as these statistics can be seen to change with time, a picture is also obtained of the way a library's overall service is changing. Theoretically, there are no limits to the statistics that can be derived from the operation of conventional systems, provided always that the raw data is there for analysis in the first place. But in practical terms, such statistics can be obtained only through extra work. Library staff must count and categorize the units of work they do and then perform the statistical calculations on this data. Manual systems do not themselves do the counting and the calculating, and the number of statistical measures derived is directly proportional to the amount of extra work involved.

The situation is quite different with computer-based systems in which the extra work of counting and analysing can be included in the computer program which controls the working of the system itself. The production of statistics is still extra work but it is so little extra as to make it worth while deriving quite detailed analyses of the system's operations. The point to emphasize is that mathematical and statistical calculations are ideal work for the electronic digital computer, and that while a computer is engaged on the comparatively tedious and laborious tasks that are necessary to work the library system, it is relatively easy to categorize and count the work as it progresses, tot up some figures on the way and calculate all kinds of means, percentages, coefficients, indices and parameters descriptive of the library's working. The data from which such statistical measures are derived is simply that which is needed for the operation of the system, and no extra human effort is involved.

The number and kinds of measures of a library's activity that can be obtained in this way are limited only by human ingenuity in devising useful measures. It will suffice here to mention the kinds of measures that are practicable and useful.

Straightforward totals are necessary as a matter of course; money spent, books bought, borrowed, bound and lost, and readers who borrow. Next come sub-totals; money spent and books bought and borrowed, etc., month by month, week by week, day by day. This gives the information from which a detailed picture of the amount of work done by the library can be built up, and how it fluctuates throughout the year. Looking at these figures over a longer period of time enables growth rates to be derived. Totals may next be subdivided by category;

money spent by subject, by type of publication, by language of publication, books bought by subject, type, price, language, etc.; readers who borrow, by subject specialization, by status; length of borrowing by reader category, etc. Correlations and comparisons can be made; for example, between the mean prices of books in various subjects, the money devoted to those subjects, and the numbers of readers interested in them; between the kinds of books that are borrowed from the library and the kinds of books that are bought for the library. And finally the effect can be studied of changes in library policy and activity; the way borrowing activity and the performance of the circulation system change when changes are made in the loan regulations; the way in which the level of service and degree of user satisfaction given by the library are related to the pattern of allocating funds or to the proportions of different kinds of materials that are added to the library's collections.

To date, even in the case of those libraries with operational computer systems, statistical measures and correlations of this kind have not been derived or used to their fullest extent. No library has yet demonstrated the possibilities or the difficulties involved in this kind of work. But clearly they point to an entirely new dimension in the realm of monitoring a library's performance. Here is one area where computer-based systems, with virtually no extra effort beyond the programming involved, and little extra cost, can break new ground and open up fresh possibilities quite outside the scope of manual systems.

It is important that such differences between conventional systems and their computer-based counterparts be fully emphasized. They constitute important and valuable reasons for mechanization.

THE ECONOMIC ARGUMENT

In our brief look at an imaginary world where a librarian followed textbook procedures and introduced automated procedures for theoretically correct reasons, he did so because the unit cost of the proposed computer-based system was lower than that of his old manual system and lower also than that of any improved manual system that would meet his needs adequately. If in the real world a librarian finds this to be true for his library, if he will, in fact, save money by using a computer, then almost certainly, he ought to do so. The only reasons that might restrain him would be associated with the long-term planning of his library service or of the long-term technological development of the particular system or systems he was interested in. In other words, he might make even greater savings, or perhaps be able to provide significantly better services, by waiting a few years before mechanizing.

Things are rarely so simple in the real world, and rarely is it possible to say with any degree of generality that the unit cost of a computer system is lower than that of its cheapest manual counterpart. There are a number of reasons for this.

Libraries differ greatly in the way they perform basic housekeeping tasks, and the tasks themselves, and their products differ also. There is therefore little agreement as to what a particular unit of work consists of, even before it is costed. Such agreement is badly needed as librarians perforce must be more concerned in future with the costs of their operations.

Then there is little agreement on how to assign costs to a given task. In most libraries, labour will be the major constituent, and materials and equipment will be minor components of the total unit cost. But how is labour charged for; is it the cost of the person actually doing the job or of some notional person always at the mid-point of their salary scale? Normally the latter, but to what extent are fringe benefits and personnel taxes allowed for? And what of the cost of providing a building for the staff to work in? Does one assume that the library has to be there anyway to hold the books, does one calculate rigorously the floor area occupied by each assistant and multiply by the rate per square foot or square metre of building, heating, lighting and servicing the library building, or does one alternatively just add an extra 10 per cent or so on top of the assistant's salary? Any one of these alternatives is perfectly appropriate: the point is that there is no agreement on any one as a suitable basis for the costing of systems in different libraries.

And when it comes to deriving the unit costs of computer-based systems the situation is still further complicated by the need to cost the work done by the computer. The unit cost in a computer-based system is made up of contributions from the following; labour, materials, system development, programming, computer time and computer and other ancillary equipment. Are systems development and programming costs to be charged to the system or are they to be written off as research costs? How is computer time to be charged; is it free, available only at the full commercial rate, or perhaps at some concessionary rate to institutional users? And over what period of time is the cost of ancillary equipment to be amortized? Once again any of these alternatives constitutes a valid means of costing a mechanized system. Agreement is needed on one method which can be adopted as a standard.

There is little or no problem if one library needs to compare its own costs before and after mechanization; all that is necessary is to use the same costing method and to cost the same things each time. The problems really only become significant when it is necessary to compare costs in two or more libraries.

Therefore it is not possible to make generalized statements such as "automated systems have higher unit costs than their manual counterparts", or "automated circulation systems are cheaper than manual ones". Unit costs are quoted in the literature but they vary quite widely. However, it is possible to give some very general indications of how costs compare in situations where salaries and computing costs are similar to those of western European countries.

Basic off-line computerized circulation systems begin to have lower unit costs than manual systems in academic libraries issuing something in the region of 250 or more items daily. In public libraries, where photo charging is often appropriate, much lower unit costs are possible using this very simple microfilm system. Unit costs for on-line systems range from $1\frac{1}{2}$ to 2 times those of off-line systems.

Costs are quoted from time to time for the computer production of library catalogues. Occasionally a lower unit cost is claimed, but in general, computer system costs will be up to 50 per cent higher than manual system costs. It should be remembered, however, that computer-produced catalogues have the capability of providing a greatly enhanced reader service, so that it is not usually possible to compare like with like in this field.

Unit costs, however, do not remain static but tend to change slowly in favour of computer-based systems. This is because labour costs tend to rise steeply while computer costs tend to drop in real terms. There is a larger labour component in manual systems than in mechanized ones and so the passage of time favours the latter. The rate of swing, however, has been slower than was at first predicted, possibly because of the large labour component still remaining in computer systems. Nevertheless, there is a swing in favour of automated systems, so that despite their slightly higher unit costs at present, because it takes a number of years to develop and install a mechanized system, the economic argument is one for mechanizing sooner rather than later.

IMPROVEMENTS TO READER SERVICES

It is through their improved services to library users, however, that computer-based library systems find their greatest justification. Returning to the problem of how to set a value on the work of a library, it is clear that if a library were in business it would sell its services. The investment in books and staff time would hopefully be less than the money brought in from the sales of services, so making a profit. The fact that few libraries charge for their services must not be allowed to conceal the fact that service is the library's prime end product.

Almost without exception computer-based library systems make for new and better reader services. Because of the nature of housekeeping systems (which are essentially concerned with the library's internal operations) their services to readers are not always directly obvious (unlike the services provided by an information storage and retrieval system, for example). Cataloguing systems based on computer methods can make library catalogues of improved type more widely available; circulation systems, through the stricter control of lending that they provide for, improve reader services by means of a generally fairer sharing of the available stock among those users who need to have access to it. Printed lists of serial holdings, like catalogues, can easily be made available to many potential users, but accounting, ordering and accessioning systems tend to be of most value to the library staff themselves, although some of their products, such as periodic reports on the balance in special subject book funds, and lists of new books received are of interest to certain categories of users. The MARC bibliographic service makes it possible for a library to supply its readers with an entirely new service—selective dissemination of information on newly published books.

The reader service aspects of individual systems are stressed in the chapters where the systems themselves are discussed. It is of interest to note here in conclusion that those library-like organizations such as book wholesalers and jobbers, which must make a profit from their services, are generally further ahead than libraries in their adoption of computer-based systems.

REFERENCE

1. See, for example, OWEN, D. G., A computer circulation system feasibility study. *Program*, vol. 5, no. 1, pp. 16–18 (Jan. 1971).

CHAPTER 3

Planning an Automated System

No LIBRARY exists and operates on its own in isolation from other libraries. It is at one and the same time a part of local, regional, national and international networks of organizations providing bibliographic, library and information services to all sections of the community.

No library system exists and operates on its own in isolation from other systems. It has relationships with other systems within the same library and in other libraries, probably (though not necessarily) of the same type and in the same locality.

Therefore the automation of one system in one individual library cannot be undertaken in isolation. It must be planned and introduced as an integral part of a large-scale and ideally a long-term plan, or concept for the local, regional and perhaps national and international networks of which the library is a part. This is so partly because of interlibrary relationships, but also because of the very nature of mechanized systems and the means used for creating them. It is not a matter of issuing a directive to an existing staff member, group or department, and leaving them to carry it out within the existing management framework of supervision and control. Rather, a totally new kind of management is required, with its own staff structure and its own particular brand of reporting and control. Accordingly, effective planning is required for automation if the new system is to run smoothly, if the library's professional and clerical library staff are to continue to enjoy a high degree of job satisfaction, and if the library's public is to benefit from the automated system to the fullest possible extent.

STAFFING FOR AN AUTOMATED SYSTEM

The quality of service given by a conventional library system depends quite clearly on the abilities of the staff who do the work from day to day. Their professional skills, their resourcefulness in overcoming the obstacles and solving the problems that arise from day to day, their tact and charm in dealing with the public all contribute to the success of their library's service. In exactly the same way, it is the skills of human beings which go to make for a successful computer-based library service. A reliable computer is also required, of course, together with a variety of other pieces of equipment which must all function smoothly. But ultimately, even a computer system is conceived in the minds of human beings, and is brought into being through their efforts. And the measure of their ability in designing, programming and planning is the measure of the success of their system.

Perhaps the first requirement is for permanent staffing. During the stages of actively specifying, designing, programming, testing and installing a computer-based system, staff are clearly needed on a permanent, and probably a full-time basis. But after that, once the new system is successfully installed and operating satisfactorily, it is not possible to manage without assistance from the kind of people who designed the system in the first place.

No system is static; but every system is constantly adapting to the changing needs of those whom it serves and to the changing environment and conditions in which it functions. In manual systems, changes are brought about by giving verbal instructions and practical demonstrations to the people who do the work. In mechanized systems, similar changes are brought about only through the same processes of designing, programming, testing and implementing that were necessary when the system was first installed. And the same kind of human skills are needed to effect the changes as were required in the first instance.

But what are those necessary skills? Library automation is the application of a new technology to a field of professional activity and so both technical and professional knowledge, skills and abilities are required. It is therefore necessary to include in the team responsible for a particular automation project, experts both in computer science and in librarianship. What sort of people are these? Sometimes one finds individuals with a wide knowledge of librarianship who also possess the requisite abilities in systems analysis and design and in programming, but more usually the twin skills will only be obtained from two or more persons.

Consider firstly the expert in the librarianship aspects of the programme. He must be able to act as a means of communication between the full-time library staff and the computer experts who will design the computer systems and write and test the programs. Clearly, therefore, he must speak both "languages". He must be sufficiently mature and must possess a broad knowledge and understanding of library aims, objectives and methods, to command the respect and ensure the cooperation of the library's department heads. His task will be to determine the library's requirements expressed in librarians' vocabulary, to determine necessary quantitative measures of the systems in question, and to translate them into requirements for the computer system, expressed in computing terms. Often bibliographical factors are quite crucial in determining major aspects of the design of an automated library system (this is as it should be) and the task of this librarian member of the automation team is correspondingly important.

Depending upon the scale and extent of the planned automation activity, of course, this library "expert" may be a single person, or may consist of a small committee possibly of library department heads. In the latter case, it is desirable that there should be at least one full-time librarian member of the automation team, to provide a balance of expertise and to carry out the many essentially librarianship tasks of the project. In the interests of speeding the progress of the work, it is undesirable for more than a few segments of the automation programme to be done part-time by otherwise full-time librarians.

The skills and abilities of the computer experts in the library automation team are exactly the same as those required in most other data-processing applications. Essentially they relate to the two main divisions of the work on the computing side; systems analysis and design, including the specification of file structures, record formats, the overall system logic and operating procedures; and programming, the translation of these requirements into a sequence of program instructions. It is therefore likely that at least two persons will be required on the computer side, a systems analyst and a programmer.

Perhaps the only major question relating to these computer experts is whether or not they should be employed as members of the library's own staff. If the planned programme for automation is anything more than one or two very simple systems, the library will need the full-time services of at least two data-processing experts for several years. And since they will be devoting all their time to automation work in the library it makes sense administratively for them to be employed by the library. This also makes for good communications, a vital aspect of their task.

But where a library is not a separate organization (and most libraries nowadays are associated with a larger body, whether it be a local authority, an educational institution or an industrial firm), then there is every likelihood that the larger organization of which it is a part will own or have access to a computer, and will therefore have established a computing or data-processing department. This department will be familiar with recruiting and employing programmers and systems analysts. In all probability its basic purpose will be to provide an expert computing service precisely in order to avoid the need for other departments to employ their own computer experts.

It may therefore be a matter of policy for the library's institution or organization not to employ data-processing experts in any department other than the data-processing department. But even if this is not so explicitly stated, such a policy has one other major advantage. It is that a central group of experts, working together and on one machine, build up a degree of communal expertise far greater than would be the case were those experts to be scattered throughout a number of separate departments. If this is so, then it is more advantageous for a library not to employ its own computer staff, but to rely on the expertise of a central computing or data-processing department.

The one major problem arising from such a policy of reliance on outside experts is that of ensuring good communications between the automation expert in the library and those members of the computing department working on library systems. But this problem of communicating effectively across departmental boundaries is not confined to the activities associated with the automation of libraries. Nor is it incapable of satisfactory solution by any one of a number of well-tried methods.

FINANCING AN AUTOMATED SYSTEM

An inefficient system readily gives rise to a vicious circle. Because of its inefficiency, the people who work the system are too busy to be able to improve it. And because they do not improve the system, the inefficiency grows as the pressure of work grows, and so the situation gets worse. What is needed is an injection of time, and therefore money to pay for the time, to work out ways of improving the system. After improvements have been made, the resulting gains in efficiency, leading to lower unit costs for the product, will hopefully more than pay for the initial investment.

This is the essence of the reasoning behind the work study or O & M approach to improving the efficiency of systems, whether they be in libraries or in factories. Well-proven methods exist for making the improvements and by and large they are to be commended. In general terms, the introduction of computer methods should be viewed in the same way (for the computer is simply another machine that the O & M practitioner will seek to use in appropriate circumstances), that is, an initial investment will lead to long-term gains.

Financing an automated system is thus seen in terms of making an investment for future library services. As has already been discussed, the gains from that investment will not be wholly financial, but there should be some financial advantage.

It is desirable in the first instance, that a new post be established within the library, for the library automation expert who will work with the systems analyst and programmer. This will be a continuing commitment, of course, for it is just not realistic to think of the need for this kind of expert existing for just a few years only. Invariably, once a system has been automated, automated it will stay, and the only question will be as to how long it will be before one suite of programs or one system design is replaced by another newer and better one. Far from seeing a library automation expert as a temporary addition to a library's normal strength, it is more realistic to view him as the first member of a new department within the library. And that new department is going to cut right across existing departmental boundaries, for it will have functional relationships with all of them.

This places the thoughtful librarian in a dilemma. Libraries grow.

Their growth can be thought of in two parts; the new part, comprising an ever-increasing volume of newly published material and expressed, for example, in the rate of increase of annual accessions; and the old part, which is essentially the sum total of the library's stock, which grows each year as the new accessions are added to the old. As the stock grows, so it becomes increasingly more expensive to store it and make it available to the public. And the cost of each year's new purchases is compounded not only by there being more books to buy each year, but also by the price of those books rising faster than the going rate of inflation. Because of external financial constraints, e.g. a limitation to a prescribed percentage of total institutional expenditure, many libraries nowadays are actually losing ground as time passes. Although they are getting bigger, and that rapidly, they are stocking an increasingly smaller proportion of the world's new literature relevant to their users' needs. In such circumstances it is not reasonable to expect a librarian to attempt to make out a case for more staff.

But therein lies the fallacy. It is only through such extra investment, through such "unreasonable" requests for experts in library automation to be added to the library staff that any hope of a solution to this impasse may be entertained.

One must make it clear straight away, that no librarian has yet seen his way through to the end; no one has yet provided a solution to this universal problem. Because so far computers have only been used in the most elementary ways in libraries, to mechanize existing manual systems. Changes will come in many directions, and indeed are already to be seen. A new generation of catalogues, printed on microform, and probably by a central agency, has just begun to make its appearance. They will make radical changes to the practicability of library cooperation and to the extent of interlibrary lending. And secondly, the largely mathematical and statistical problems of library growth rates, cost and effectiveness have begun to be tackled through the use of descriptive and predictive mathematical models. Automated library systems will provide data necessary for the further development and refinement of such models, and the ability to monitor their activity and performance constantly, so as to enable the librarian to maximize the effectiveness of his library.

THE APPROACH TO AUTOMATION

It is likely that at some future date a number of larger libraries may well be very largely automated. But practical experience over the past 8 or 9 years has served to emphasize the problems of integrating separate functional systems within one library, without, however, suggesting that there are any aspects of library housekeeping which are unsuited to computer application. Thus a library about to embark upon its first mechanization project will probably have some basic conception of a future highly mechanized state, of which the current venture will constitute one small segment.

So any individual system, for producing a printed list of serials holdings for example, is seen to exist not alone, but in relation to other closely related systems. Systems which are related to a serials listing system might include procedures for handling subscriptions and for accessioning new parts of periodicals. In the wider sphere, a serials holdings list is related to other catalogues produced by the library, other acquisitions systems, etc.

A library's approach to automation then, recognizing such relationships, should enable one automated system to stand on the shoulders of a previously installed and closely related one. It might, for example, use machine readable output from a former system directly as input to its own procedures. Record structures and data fields might be common in the two systems, or else be related closely.

This evolutionary approach to mechanization is of value not only from the systems viewpoint. There is a definite educational element in designing and installing a mechanized library system. If one assumes that most libraries will learn the hard way (i.e. by making mistakes) despite the valuable body of cumulated expertise, then it is desirable that the first mistakes should be made in some not-too-important backwater of the library's activities. Only later should a system in the mainstream of the housekeeping procedures be attempted.

But the requirements also hold that maximum gain should be derived from any automated system, including the first, and that library users should benefit as much as possible.

With these requirements in mind then, and always allowing that many libraries have special problems and operate in special circumstances which demand special action, the following four systems are relatively simple, result in significant benefits to library users or library staff, and can be considered in isolation quite readily. In order of increasing complication and sophistication they are: a system to print a list of serials holdings; a system to print an authority file, possibly an alphabetical subject index to a classification scheme; a monograph or periodicals accounting system; a selective dissemination of information system using MARC tapes.

These systems are discussed in detail in subsequent chapters, where their record and file formats, processing procedures and outputs are described. Perhaps the prime argument against each one of them is that they do not (by and large) get to the heart of the major problems that libraries face from day to day. This is true, but each one demands that the library staff begin to think and work in the logical, accurate and systematic way that is necessary with automated procedures. This is valuable training for further work with automated systems in more crucial areas of the library's activity.

For many libraries, circulation control is the one major housekeeping activity which seems to cry out for some final "solution". Computer-based circulation or issue systems now seem to have provided an acceptable solution, and because librarians appear to be more than averagely interested in circulation "systems", it is not surprising that there have been many computer applications in this area. Add to this the fact that with the ready availability of hardware packages to handle data collection, and with no major problems remaining on the software side, it is apparent that circulation systems can be bought virtually "off the shelf".

Circulation systems are discussed in detail in Chapter 8. Suffice it to mention here that on-line real-time systems, which alone can provide a truly "final" solution, are still only in their infancy, although standard off-line packages can readily be given a measure of real-time performance, specifically to enable them to recognize flagged books and readers, e.g. reserved books or recalcitrant borrowers. Eventually also, some real solution will be found to the problem of linking the issue file with the file of catalogue records—the other area in which many present-day circulation systems leave something to be desired.

Book ordering and acquisition is an area of library activity which can fairly readily be considered in isolation. A considerable amount of clerical activity is associated with this function which is accordingly a good candidate for mechanization. Bibliographical record structures for acquisitions systems can be comparatively simple and need not necessarily conform to any external standards since order records have a limited life span.

Cataloguing and circulation systems can make use of output from an acquisition system, and if the latter is mechanized, it can in time build up useful machine readable files which may be put to good use on the subsequent mechanization of circulation or cataloguing routines.

But it is the library's catalogue which is central to all other activities and services. Its mechanization therefore is of the greatest importance, not only because of the catalogue's direct relationships with other peripheral functions and files, but also because it is the key to the most important public services offered by the library. Also, it is through its catalogue and the bibliographical records contained in it that an individual library has links with other libraries and their collections, and the wider spheres of national and international bibliography.

Many libraries have successfully mechanized the production and printing of their catalogues, but the problems to be faced in this task are probably greater than in any other area; problems of record formats and their standardization, forms of catalogue and keeping it up to date, typesetting for the catalogue, its bulk and legibility, and finally costs. These are all very real and as a result many librarians are content to wait for a few years, perhaps even a decade or so, until some major trends become apparent. It is likely also that national developments will strongly influence the activities of individual libraries in this area. For example, although centralized catalogue card printing services have been available for many years, their value has been limited by sheer problems of supply and acquisition and integrating the cards into a local catalogue. In future, it is likely that flexible national computer-based catalogue printing services will be available at attractive prices. This alone will have a radical effect on individual libraries' attitudes to catalogue mechanization, and through this to the mechanization of other library functions.

If there is any general conclusion that can be derived from the present state of the art of mechanized housekeeping systems, it is this. That individual libraries should begin to be involved in this field sooner rather than later. That a stepwise approach towards eventually integrated systems is the only practical method of proceeding, and that unless there are strong local needs or pressures, catalogue mechanization, in particular the retrospective conversion of catalogue records, should not receive highest priority at the present time.

CHAPTER 4

Implementing an Automated System

THIS chapter deals with the crucial stages in the long chain of events leading from existing conventional manual procedures to a successfully operating automated or computer-based system. Library management have already decided that a change is necessary, having taken all considerations into account. They have determined the general nature of the work that must be performed, have sketched in outline what the final system should look like, and have delineated a staff structure which is appropriate to the task. Now the work proper begins.

Essentially, we are here concerned with systems analysis and design; the analysis of existing systems and the design of new ones. The emphasis is on the general principles, techniques, and methodology of the work. A detailed consideration of the design of individual systems, that is, the application of the general methodology to specific areas of library work, follows in subsequent chapters.

STUDYING THE EXISTING SYSTEM—SYSTEMS ANALYSIS

There is nothing particularly esoteric, or even difficult, about systems analysis. Although the two words, when combined together, can convey a certain something that is more than the sum of the parts, this is no more than an impression in the mind of the reader or listener. Systems analysis is simply the work of analyzing systems.

Implementing an Automated System

To analyze means to study carefully, seeking out the essential components, and to set down and describe the results of this work in an orderly and intelligible fashion.

Systems are the object of this study. Now the word "system", in either its singular or plural form, is used very loosely nowadays, probably because we live in a highly developed technological society. (The word "automated" is used in a similarly lax way.) But if we use the word "procedure" to mean the way in which a given task is carried out, a particular job of work done, or the steps involved in making a particular artefact—with an emphasis on and an interest in the methodology— then a "system" is a group of procedures, interrelated and interdependent, which together perform, act upon, or result in, a larger unit of work.

Systems analysis therefore is concerned with methodology. The way people work; the way specific tasks are performed. It is necessarily closely related to work study and O & M. These latter terms, however, refer to activities whose final objective is the specification and description of improved procedures, normally within the context of manual methods, and using conventional office machinery such as typewriters, duplicators, etc. Systems analysis almost always implies the eventual use of data-processing machinery and generally refers to the first part of the work of the O & M practitioner. The second part of his work, the development of improved manual procedures, corresponds, in the context of a computer system, to the term system design.

There is nothing particularly esoteric about systems analysis and design, or even O & M and work study. But it is necessary when doing this kind of work to be able to think clearly and logically, both with regard to the overall structure of the task or procedure in hand and also with respect to fine points of detail. Complex logical interrelationships are frequently involved, but fundamentally nothing more is needed than clear and straightforward thinking.

A number and variety of special techniques have been developed and are practised widely to assist in this process of clear thinking. They can be fascinating in themselves as methodology or as tools, and a great deal of pleasure can be derived from using a powerful tool skilfully. But in a sense such techniques serve to obscure the essential objective and simple nature of systems analysis.

Procedures

In the careful description of operational systems, the systems analyst is very largely concerned with procedures—the way individual tasks or jobs are carried out. The tool he uses in his study of procedures is the flow chart (which is sometimes given its fuller name of flow process chart). This is a very simple tool, neither mysterious nor esoteric, but very powerful in its ability to describe operations and procedures and to communicate them to others. Very little training is needed either to draw flow charts or to read and interpret them. And as with all systems work, the best way to learn about flow charts is to practise using them.

The underlying approach behind the use of flow charts is to divide and conquer. A system is broken down into its constituent procedures. Each procedure is broken down into its component parts. Each part is broken down into a number of steps. Each step is further subdivided. And so on, until a sufficiently detailed breakdown or sufficiently small steps are reached. Flow charts not only show the steps and what they consist of, but also the order in which they are performed, and the logical relationship between them. Examples will be found in later chapters of this book, illustrating the component parts and method of operation of computerized library systems.

During the process of analyzing and describing existing procedures, a systems analyst will draw many flow charts. The first ones will show the relationships between the system being studied and other systems in the library. Subsequent charts will go into more detail, showing the main components of the chosen system, parts of the components, and so on. A good working rule when drawing flow charts is to use A4 size paper. This limits the sheer quantity of information that can be squeezed on to one sheet of paper, forcing the systems analyst to divide a large chart into one or more smaller ones, roughly at the point where the large chart becomes too difficult to comprehend easily.

Staff Structure

Every organization, or department within an organization, employing people to perform tasks to achieve a desired objective or goal,

Implementing an Automated System

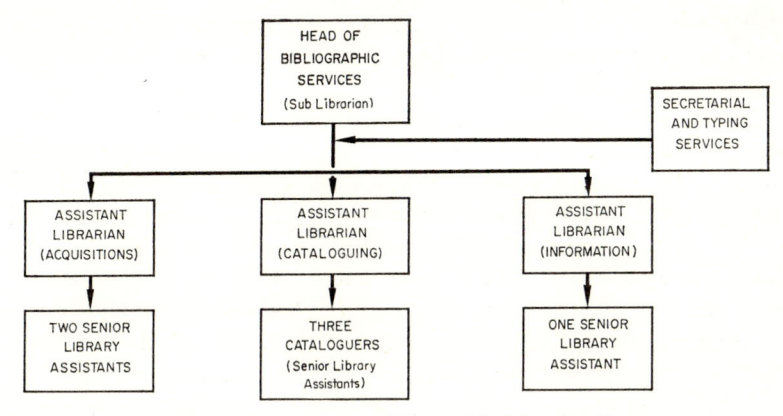

```
                    ┌─────────────────┐
                    │     HEAD OF     │
                    │  BIBLIOGRAPHIC  │
                    │     SERVICES    │         ┌──────────────┐
                    │  (Sub Librarian)│◄────────│ SECRETARIAL  │
                    └────────┬────────┘         │  AND TYPING  │
                             │                  │   SERVICES   │
          ┌──────────────────┼──────────────────┐└──────────────┘
          ▼                  ▼                  ▼
   ┌─────────────┐    ┌─────────────┐    ┌─────────────┐
   │  ASSISTANT  │    │  ASSISTANT  │    │  ASSISTANT  │
   │  LIBRARIAN  │    │  LIBRARIAN  │    │  LIBRARIAN  │
   │(ACQUISITIONS)│   │(CATALOGUING)│    │(INFORMATION)│
   └──────┬──────┘    └──────┬──────┘    └──────┬──────┘
          ▼                  ▼                  ▼
   ┌─────────────┐    ┌─────────────┐    ┌─────────────┐
   │ TWO SENIOR  │    │    THREE    │    │ ONE SENIOR  │
   │   LIBRARY   │    │ CATALOGUERS │    │   LIBRARY   │
   │  ASSISTANTS │    │(Senior Library│  │  ASSISTANT  │
   │             │    │  Assistants)│    │             │
   └─────────────┘    └─────────────┘    └─────────────┘
```

FIG. 4.1. Staff structure: Library Bibliographical Services Department.

will create a hierarchy or structure among its staff, and will assign tasks to individuals on the basis of their own particular skills and their position in the hierarchy. One of the systems analyst's first tasks is to discover what the staff structure is in the department or organization being studied. It is a straightforward task to illustrate this by means of a chart, as in Fig. 4.1, which shows the staff structure of the bibliographical services department of a typical library.

The analyst's next and straightforward task is to indicate on his flow charts the status of the person who performs each unit of work that he has identified.

Quantities

So far only qualitative factors have been considered, but for the successful specification of a design for any system (and more especially so for an automated system) it is necessary to know how much work it will have to handle. This involves measuring how much work is done now and making intelligent estimates of how it will change in future.

This is a good example of the kind of careful planning that is needed for an automated system (systems analysis is just part of the planning) as compared with conventional systems. With the latter, experience built up gradually over the years greatly reduces the need for detailed quantitative planning and, of course, human beings are very flexible;

they can be persuaded to work harder for short periods if necessary, and can always be asked to tackle a new job on a temporary basis if a situation becomes desperate.

Not so with a mechanized system. In the first case it is probably new, so that there is no helpful past experience to guide the systems analyst, apart from the figures that will be obtained from the existing manual system. In the second, because of the need to define beforehand such things as record and file sizes and structures, numbers of units handled or processed, and to have detailed statements of the output required with print formats, number and size of records and frequency of printing, the systems analyst, with the active help of the library staff, must obtain reliable figures for all these and other parameters.

Firstly, the numbers of items handled must be obtained: books bought, catalogued or borrowed each day, week, month, etc. Library housekeeping systems deal with records of stock and activity, so the kinds of records that are needed must be specified, their size and structure indicated. Output from the computer system will concern librarians and the public most of all; this constitutes the interface between the user and the system. What medium is to be specified for output, paper or film, full size or micro? The character set, founts, total number of characters to be printed, layout of the printed output, and so on, must all be defined. All this demands a lot of painstaking work.

Times

Time is really just one more parameter, values of which must be obtained to complete the detailed quantitative planning that is part of the process of systems analysis. But time, whether thought of as the duration of a particular task or process identified in a flow chart, or as the interval between two operations, is fundamentally different in nature from the simple numerical counts of books bought, processed, or lent, so that it merits separate treatment.

A knowledge of elapsed time together with counts of the amount or volume of work done enables the rate of working to be calculated. This is a more immediately useful figure than simple totals. For example, the rate at which books are borrowed from a library must be determined before data-collection equipment for a circulation system can be specified. In particular, the maximum rate must be found, so that this can be handled without causing queues to form. Because a computer-based circulation system, for example, must have data-collection machinery of some kind at the issue counter or charging desk, because each book borrowed must be recorded by the data-collection equipment, and because that equipment will have a maximum rate of working, it becomes necessary (though quite straightforward) to calculate how many data-collection units will be needed to cope with anticipated maximum rates of working.

In the same way, times for each operation, and from them rates of working, must be obtained for all aspects of the system under study. In particular also, the intervals between doing a job and repeating it must be known. For example, how often are batches of new book orders sent to booksellers? How frequently should the library's list of serials holdings be updated?

Costs

A reliable figure for the cost of operating the existing system is necessary if the decision for or against automation is to be made on objective grounds. For this purpose the cost of performing one unit of work is quoted. This is termed the unit cost. In a furniture factory, for example, the unit cost is the cost of making one piece of furniture of stated type, and it is made up of contributions from the raw materials, labour, machinery used in its manufacture and overheads, such as insurances and fringe benefits for staff, the need to provide a suitable building for the factory, heat, clean and maintain it, etc.

Similarly, in a library, there will be a unit cost for adding one book to the collection, for lending one book, etc. And in a library, unit costs are broken down in very much the same way as in the furniture factory. Labour, of course, is the major part, but machines such as typewriters, duplicators, etc., make a small contribution. Materials consist of nothing more than stationery in most cases, and are virtually negligible. Library "materials" themselves, in the sense of books and journals, etc., are so variable in price that it is usually not helpful to include their contribution towards unit costs.

There is a temptation to use cost as the most important or even the sole criterion in deciding between two courses of action. As was discussed at length in Chapter 2, this has not often been the case with automated library systems. If cost had been the overriding factor, there would be few operational computer systems in libraries today. What is required is to make an intelligent decision on the basis of reliable data on all aspects of a system, of which cost is only one.

This means, therefore, that no particularly high degree of accuracy is needed in deriving unit costs. If the accuracy of the final quoted figure is within ± 20 per cent, this should be perfectly satisfactory. There are two reasons for this. Firstly, cost is only one factor among many to be taken into account. Secondly, the cost of the proposed system can only be estimated, and it does not make sense, when comparing an existing system with a proposed new one, to measure one accurately and the other only approximately. What is important is to have some idea of the accuracy, and therefore the reliability, of both figures, and to make the comparison accordingly. Furthermore, when proposed systems are put into operation actual unit costs have a habit of rising above estimated unit costs, sometimes quite considerably.

DESIGNING THE NEW SYSTEM—SYSTEM DESIGN

A preliminary systems study, or feasibility study, will have sketched in broad outline the overall structure of a computer-based system which could replace an existing system and provide additional benefits and services. It may go into detail on some aspects of the proposed system, and will probably give some indication of the likely unit costs to be expected. The decision to proceed with an automated system must be made on the basis of the information provided in the feasibility study. The task then is to develop, expand and act upon the original suggestions, to give the desired end product of an operational system that has been fully tested and proven. There are a number of inter-related tasks in this work, of which system design is a part. Figure 4.2 shows schematically what is involved.

The overall development task can be divided into four parallel streams of work as indicated by the four parallel horizontal streams of operations in Fig. 4.2. They concern equipment, system design, file

Implementing an Automated System 45

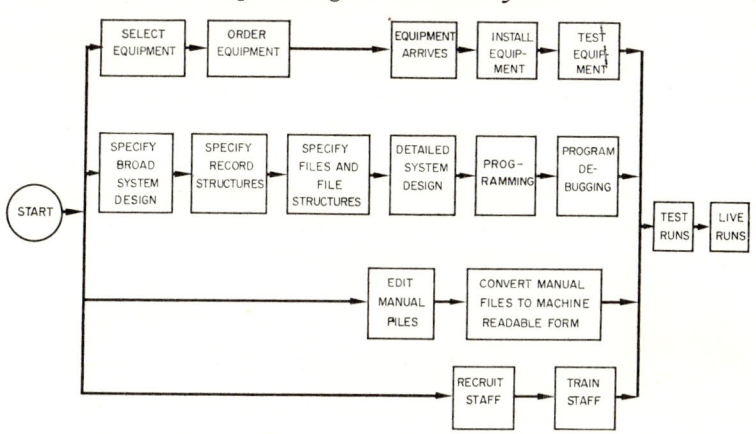

Fig. 4.2. Implementing a computer-based system.

conversion and staffing respectively. System design is usually the critical task in this diagram in that the minimum time required for this work is greater than the minimum time required for the work in any other area. In some cases selecting and procuring equipment may become the critical task because of long delivery dates. In others, where large manual files are to be converted, this may be the critical task. But in most cases, the system design and programming work will take longest and must be tackled first.

The several stages of system design follow each other in logical sequence. Starting with a broad system specification, which will probably be taken over with only minor changes, if any, from the preliminary feasibility study, the first step is to define the necessary record structures for the system.

The next stage is to determine the format and structure of the main files the system will use, in conjunction with a decision on the auxiliary storage medium which will hold the files—punched cards or tape, magnetic tape, magnetic disc stores. The overall system design sketched out in the preliminary study must be elaborated upon and broken down into program modules of manageable size. Programs can then be written and tested.

While this systems and programming work is progressing, any necessary equipment must be selected, ordered, received and tested, so as to be ready for use in time for the system to commence operation at the planned time. Existing manual files must be converted to machine readable form. Additional staff may be needed to operate the new system, to assist in the changeover, and existing staff may need to be retrained for their new work. It cannot be emphasized too strongly that the success of a computer system depends very largely on the staff who design and operate it. This side of the work, therefore, is just as important as the more technical aspects.

Record Structures

Record structures are considered in more detail in Chapter 5, but at this stage, the analogy can be drawn between the record structure in a computer system and the layout of a form in a manual system. Figure 4.3 represents schematically a loan form which would be appropriate for a typical small-to-medium-sized library. The important thing to notice is the way in which such a form specifies the various pieces of information necessary for a full and accurate record of a particular loan. The layout of the form is not itself important, nor is the fact that a form is a piece of paper. Some circulation control systems record the same data on to card, or microfilm, but the data remains essentially the same.

A computer-based loans system must obviously handle at least the same data as the manual system, and will probably include additional information as well. The purpose of defining a record structure for the computer system is firstly to specify those categories of data that must and can be present, and secondly to say how much data there will be in each category. For a manual system, this latter requirement simply means making the form large enough to record the loan of a typical book in normal sized handwriting. If a complicated item is to be borrowed, for example, with an involved or unduly long author or title, then human common sense will decide at the time of loan, either to abbreviate some categories of data, or to give the data in full, but in a minuscule script. But in a computer system, the existence of such unusual items must be foreseen, and the record structure so designed to accommodate them either in full, or to accept suitable abbreviations.

Implementing an Automated System

AUTHOR'S NAME	BOOK NO.
TITLE	DATE BORROWED
BORROWER NAME	RETURN DATE
BORROWER ADDRESS	
BORROWER STATUS	

FIG. 4.3. Loan form for manual system.

File Structures

While record structures for computer systems are not difficult for librarians to comprehend, because of their close similarity to the manual records librarians have long been familiar with, file structures seem more remote and abstruse because of their closer association with programming details. But this need not be so, because conventional libraries contain many manual files, some of which have a quite complicated structure.

The simplest file structure is one in which records are arranged in order by one item of data in each record. Thus records may be arranged in numerical, alphabetical, or chronological order. A file whose records are ordered in this way is termed a serial file and is, of course, quite common in manual library systems. In computer systems, serial files are normally found in connection with the use of magnetic tape for storage. Records are stored on the magnetic tape in much the same way as pages of a book are photographed onto a roll of microfilm. And similarly, when the time comes for the computer to perform some action on the records in the file, it must deal with each one sequentially, in turn, just as it is necessary, when viewing microfilm, to scan sequentially from page to page.

The use of serial files and magnetic tape storage demands that as high a proportion as possible of the records in the file are acted upon in some way each time the program is run. This leads to batching the work for the computer, and running the programs with a frequency which gives an acceptable compromise between reducing the overall cost of running the system (run the program seldom) and giving quick or frequent service (run the program often).

The structure of a serial file on magnetic tape is illustrated in Fig. 4.4, and the method of updating records in such a file is indicated in Fig. 4.5.

The other common storage medium for library files is magnetic disc. Physically, a magnetic disc store resembles a rapidly spinning stack of gramophone records or phonodiscs, each separated from its neighbour by about an inch. A number of reading and writing heads move radially over each surface of each disc. This, in conjunction with the rotation of the discs, enables the computer to read or write at any position on any surface with very little delay. This gives the name "direct access" to such directly accessible stores.

Direct access storage devices (which include magnetic discs, drums, cards and the IBM "data cell" which consists of strips of magnetic tape) may hold serial files which can, of course, be processed sequentially, just as with magnetic-tape stores. But there is no need to be limited in this way, and use is often made of other more flexible file structures. Rather than just arrange records in order, it is possible to adopt a strategy which places records in specified and known locations in the direct-access memory store on the basis of one or more data fields in each record.

Figure 4.6 represents part of a bibliographic file in a direct-access store. Nine storage locations are shown in the store, each of which has a two-digit address which indicates its position. The address of the bottom left-hand location is 3–5; the address of the top right-hand location is 5–7. Each location may hold up to four bibliographical records, and records are assigned to locations in the memory on the basis of the last two digits of their identification numbers—the same number that was used to arrange them in order in Figs. 4.4 and 4.5. Thus, record No. 4135 is stored in location 3–5, along with other records whose identification numbers also have 35 as their last two digits.

Implementing an Automated System 49

FIG. 4.4. Serial file structure on magnetic tape. Records are arranged in order by one item of data in the record (the *sort key*), in this instance a numerical identification number.

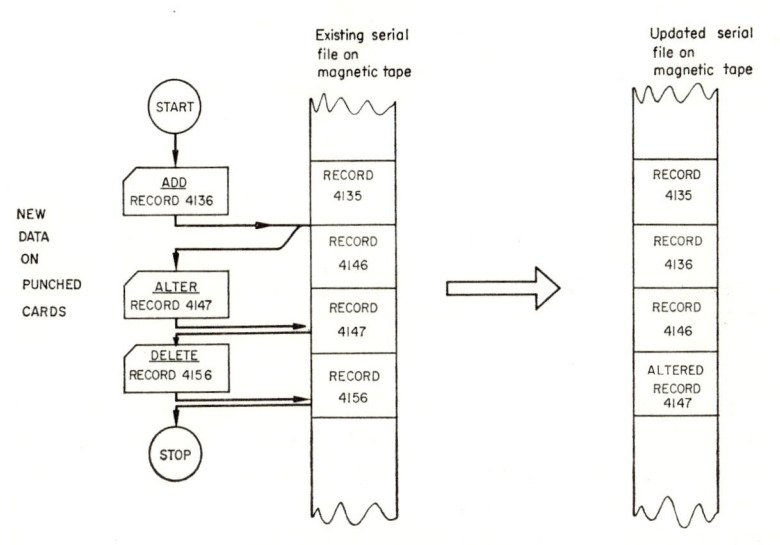

FIG. 4.5. Updating a serial file.

50   *Automation in Libraries*

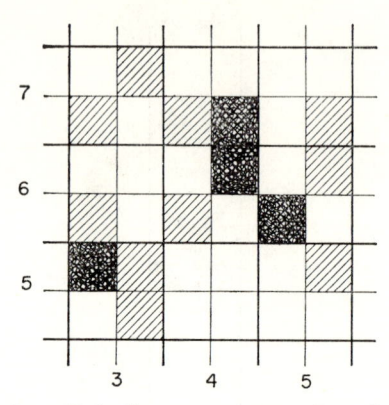

Fig. 4.6 (i). Updating a file in direct-access storage. Records 4135, 4146, 4147, 4156 (indicated by double hatching) and others, in direct-access store.

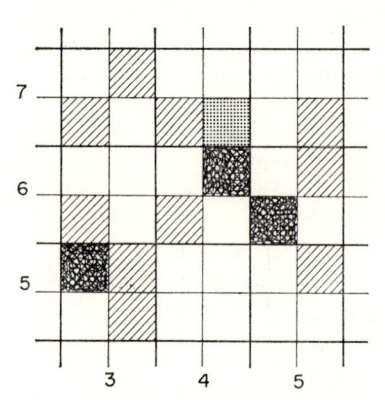

Fig. 4.6 (ii). Updating a file in direct-access storage. Following an instruction to ALTER Record 4147, location 4–7 has been accessed and Record 4147 altered in accordance with the instruction given.

Unlike the situation with the serial file, operations on records in the file on direct-access storage need not be performed in sequential order of identification number. Chronological order is usually more convenient, especially if, as is the case with a real-time computer system, the operation must be carried out immediately so that any necessary response from the system can be obtained at once.

Implementing an Automated System 51

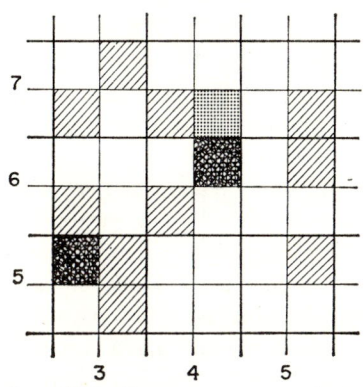

Fig. 4.6 (iii). Updating a file in direct-access storage. An instruction is received to delete Record 4156, location 5–6 is accessed and Record 4156 deleted.

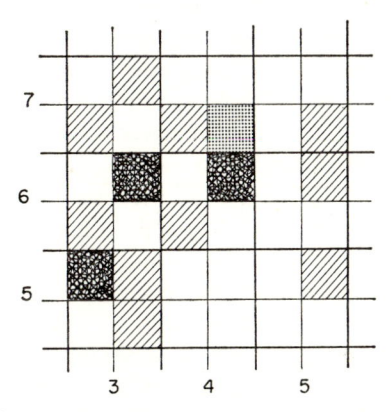

Fig. 4.6 (iv). Updating a file in direct-access storage. An instruction is received to add Record 4136, location 3–6 is accessed and Record 4136 is written to a vacant position there.

Figure 4.6 illustrates how the records in the direct-access memory store are affected by three pieces of updating information—the same information as that which served as an illustration of batch processing in Fig. 4.5.

A.L.—C

Programming

The one word "programming" serves to group together under one convenient and generally intelligible term a series of interrelated, logical steps. It is easy to understand these steps by thinking along the lines suggested in Fig. 4.7.

The work proceeds in stages, each stage covering a smaller part of the overall task in greater detail than the one before. The overall data-processing task is divided into a number of separate programs, each of which has a specific task to accomplish. Each program is given a structure when it is broken into separate sections or modules. At this stage, one program module has a straightforward task to do. This is then charted at the level of detail where one box in the flow chart corresponds roughly to one program instruction in the language chosen. The job of coding, or translating flow chart instructions into program instructions, then becomes a fairly straightforward procedure.

At every stage of this work careful written records are kept which form the program documentation. This serves as an introduction to the programs for newcomers who may either be joining the systems and programming team, or may simply want to use the program. Program documentation may include flow charts showing detailed working of the system, record and file structures, input and output formats, together with a complete listing of all the instructions in the program.

The inevitable errors in the coding and the logic of the system design must be corrected before the system is put into operation. To do this, a small dummy file is created, and a series of test runs is made to simulate all possible circumstances liable to crop up in real life.

The choice of language in which programs are to be written is normally a matter for an individual computer laboratory to decide. Essentially the decision on a programming language is whether to use one of the standard high-level languages or to use a low-level language specially designed for the computer which will be used for running the system.

High-level languages should be machine independent, so that programs written in a high-level language for one make of computer could be run on another manufacturer's machine. But in practice, different computers tend to "understand" different "dialects" of the

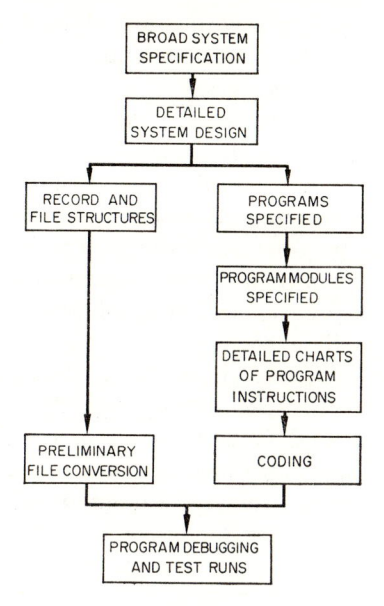

```
        BROAD SYSTEM
        SPECIFICATION
              ↓
         DETAILED
        SYSTEM DESIGN
         ↓        ↓
  RECORD AND    PROGRAMS
 FILE STRUCTURES  SPECIFIED
     │             ↓
     │       PROGRAM MODULES
     │         SPECIFIED
     │             ↓
     │       DETAILED CHARTS
     │        OF PROGRAM
     │        INSTRUCTIONS
     ↓             ↓
  PRELIMINARY   CODING
 FILE CONVERSION
     └──────┬──────┘
            ↓
    PROGRAM DEBUGGING
      AND TEST RUNS
```

Fig. 4.7. Programming.

standard high-level languages, and additional factors such as the way in which character strings are handled, and in particular the problems of using auxiliary storage devices efficiently, mean that sharing high-level language programs and cooperating in their development tend to be limited to groups working with the machines of one particular manufacturer.

Low-level languages, in which one program instruction normally corresponds to one machine operation, clearly involve more work for the programmer. High-level languages, on the other hand, simplify the task of programming and speed it up by making it possible for one program instruction to instigate a series of machine operations. This is done by a translating program, or compiler, which translates the high-level language program (the source program) into its equivalent in the binary language that the machine itself obeys (the object program). Because the compiler is exceedingly complex, it cannot always translate source program into object program with maximum effectiveness. So that programs written in high-level languages tend to take longer for the machine to execute than programs written (more laboriously) in low-level languages.

On the other hand, an experienced programmer can write more efficient programs than one with less experience, and this differential can be greater than that due to inefficiencies arising from the operation of compilers. So really, this discussion boils down to the simple conclusion that good programmers write good programs.

The high-level commercial- and business-orientated language COBOL enjoys some favour for bibliographical programs because of its facilities for handling textural data, although quite complex character-handling programs have been successfully written in FORTRAN, an essentially scientific language. PL/1 combines features of both FORTRAN and COBOL, and, of course, the machine-dependent low-level languages handle character manipulation in the context of complex record structures without difficulty.

Equipment

For many computer-based library housekeeping systems, the library will find it necessary to purchase one or more items of computing equipment or "hardware". In most cases such equipment will be needed for data capture; for converting records of library activity into a form that the computer can accept. In some instances special printing or display equipment may be required, and occasionally special storage facilities must be purchased. For some types of application, notably some on-line systems, the library might even consider the purchase of a small central processor.

DATA INPUT EQUIPMENT

As a general rule, if a computer-based system handles sufficient library business as to require one clerical assistant working full time to convert raw data into machine-readable form, then the library should purchase (or lease) the necessary equipment for its own use and should employ the clerk who will do the keyboarding. A number of factors must be considered in relation to this. If the work is not urgent by nature, or if it occurs spasmodically, then there is less need for the library to handle the work of data conversion. But if the volume of work is large, if it must be handled rapidly and on schedule, and if there are any peculiarities in the data (for example, where keypunching must be done from incomplete or only partially edited manual records), then library-owned equipment operated by members of the library staff is indicated.

Such manual keyboarding of conventional library records may produce punched eighty-column cards, punched paper tape, magnetic tape, or may write the data directly on to magnetic-disc storage through teletype or visual display terminals connected on-line to a computer. The last alternatives can handle large volumes of data conveniently and, if suitable software is available, enable errors to be found and corrected easily. As computing costs fall steadily, they are also being adopted more widely. Otherwise the choice between input media will largely be influenced by the forms in which the computer laboratory can accept input data.

Over and above this it can be said that since punched cards are unit records, to punch data onto cards makes the task of correcting errors particularly simple—replace the cards containing errors with correct ones. Paper tape is convenient where the library records are in variable field format, though it can involve clumsy procedures for making corrections. The advantages of keyboarding directly onto magnetic tape is that the tape can be read by the computer at high speed; at roughly 5 times the rate of reading punched cards or paper tape.

If large quantities of data are to be converted into machine readable form then optical character recognition (OCR) techniques are indicated if the original data already exists in a fairly "clean" form. That is, clearly typed or printed, and in a typeface that can be "recognized" by one of the various makes of OCR scanning equipment. This method does not achieve 100 per cent accuracy in recognizing characters so that a further proof reading stage will be necessary just as with conventional keyboarding. But used in conjunction with programs to parse and label the bibliographical records in printed library catalogues, OCR methods are an attractive possibility for the large-scale conversion of catalogues to machine-readable form.

In many computerized systems, and library circulation control systems are a good example, the data necessary to create the record of an event (e.g. the loan of a book) already exist, and the new record is created by bringing this existing data together into one place. If the prior records can themselves be converted into machine-readable form, then it is possible to build up the new record mechanically, without resort to error-prone human keyboarding procedures. Such mechanical data-collection procedures are particularly attractive in circumstances where the new records have to be made quickly and accurately. All these conditions apply in the case of circulation control. Data-collection equipment for library loans systems is discussed in Chapter 8. Suffice it to say here that such machinery may scan punched cards or tape, may read strips of magnetic tape, or may use a light pen to read suitably coded data in source documents. Many permit additional data to be inserted manually by keyboard or through variable dials, and others can be supplied with small core storage units, which effectively transform them into tiny computers, albeit with strictly limited processing power.

OUTPUT PRINTING EQUIPMENT

For most library systems there is simply no choice in the matter of the output printing equipment that is to be used. The computer centre uses a standard line printer for printing, and that is that. The librarian must accept the limited character set (usually not more than fifty characters are available) and make the best of it that he can.

It is possible to do a lot with a standard line printer. Good design and high legibility in any printed document depend not only on the quality of the type, but also on layout. With white space and good layout, the humble line printer can work wonders, especially if it is well adjusted and perhaps not run at its highest printing speed. If a line printer is to be used for the output from the library system then, of course, the librarian will simply use the printer in his computing laboratory.

But the range of available alternatives to the line printer is increasing. It remains possible, of course, to have the system output punched onto paper tape which is subsequently used to drive a tape typewriter. But this is a very slow option, is impracticable for anything other than small quantities of data, and produces nothing better than typescript in the end. A better alternative is to try to use a line printer with an extended character set. For example, a set of 120 different characters is specified for use with MARC bibliographical records. This is an improvement over the standard "upper case only" line printer character set, but retains the rectangular appearance of the standard output.

The big breakthrough in computer output printing methods is associated with the use of photo-typesetting equipment. This can be quite readily controlled by a computer-prepared magnetic tape, and offers the two alternatives of setting type full size for normal reading, or in micro size to produce microfilm or microfiche. Equipment for printing computer output onto microfilm has been given the acronym COM.

Such computer-controlled typesetting techniques were pioneered in the library field by the US National Library of Medicine for its monthly *Index Medicus*, and have produced improvements in all parameters associated with typesetting, in a way that is quite unusual. Normally an improvement in one aspect of design or performance is obtained only at the expense of a corresponding deterioration in another aspect. But here, improvements are obtained in speed and quality of printing, legibility, a very much larger character set is possible, less space is required for the same text, and unit costs are lower. Large versatile computer-controlled typesetters will not be available in every computing laboratory, so that their use will in all probability be restricted to the centralized production of the catalogues of large libraries.

Data storage equipment

Modern computer systems can have access to a wide range of storage devices. Some are appropriate for small files to which frequent and rapid access is required (discs and drums) while magnetic tape can accommodate very large files at low cost, but with the disadvantage of a rather long access time. This is why large files which must be consulted frequently, such as library catalogues, are made available to users in printed form. Problems can arise when a large file requires frequent updating and is also consulted frequently for up-to-date information. Some library catalogues possess these characteristics. Large, costly, direct-access stores which can be updated and interrogated in the on-line mode are appropriate in such cases, but if rapid and reliable response is needed over long periods of time then the discs and the disc-handling equipment and probably also the central processor must be dedicated to the sole use of the library.

This is really the only circumstance in which library storage needs would exceed the capabilities of a typical modern medium-to-large-sized computer installation. If such a system design for an on-line catalogue were shown to be economically justified, then it might be necessary to augment the direct-access storage capacity and perhaps also the processing power of the computer to be used for the system.

PURCHASE, INSTALLATION AND SERVICING

The main requirement here is to order any necessary equipment in good time. Delivery dates of up to a year after the order date are not uncommon for computer equipment. This need be no disadvantage, provided that this potential source of delay is recognized and a decision on equipment made early in the development of the system. While the delivery of equipment is awaited, programming and the work of editing and converting existing manual files can proceed.

Installing, testing and servicing equipment are the responsibility of the manufacturer or supplier. The librarian's task is to ensure that the supplier is in a position to service the equipment reliably and, in the event of breakdown, be able to send an engineer quickly to effect repairs. Even the best machinery breaks down occasionally, and not even the most efficient of service engineers can be on the spot immediately, so that it is always necessary for alternative manual procedures to be available for use in the event of machine failure.

Manual File Conversion

Library files may either be permanent records or inventories of stock or may contain information of a transitory nature about library materials undergoing a particular process. The library's catalogue is the prime example of the first kind of file. A binding list, or list of books on order, is a typical example of the second. Individual records in files of the second kind have only a limited lifetime, and the introduction of computer methods does not normally require them to be converted to machine-readable form. When the new system starts functioning, it creates its own machine-readable records, and through time, there

Implementing an Automated System 59

will increasingly be more of the new records and fewer of the old. Thus existing transitory files can be allowed to shrink through the normal procedures of withdrawing records.

But a library's permanent files cannot normally be treated in this way. Sometimes, especially if the file is large, the manual file may be retained and used alongside the new system and its new file. As time passes, since activity tends to centre on the new records in any file, the old manual file will be used less, although it will never be totally superseded. But if the existing file is not too large, and especially if the file-handling ability of the computer system is to be fully exploited (remember that only very limited processing is possible with manual files), then there are many advantages to be gained from converting the existing file to machine-readable form *in toto*.

Such conversion of manual files relates mainly to catalogues, which may be of books, or serials, or may include several kinds of library materials. The general principles of file conversion are discussed here while detailed consideration of converting bibliographic records for books are given in Chapter 10 on Cataloguing.

When in computer-readable form, a record from the manual file will have been changed in two ways. Firstly, all the characters in the original record will have been translated into their equivalent patterns of holes or magnetic dots on some suitable computer-readable medium. Secondly, the record will have been given a structure, corresponding to the various sections of the manual record. The former task is a straightforward keyboarding operation, although because of its large-scale nature it may require careful organization. The latter will require the attention of skilled librarians and probably a large amount of editorial work. So if a library file is to be converted into machine-readable form as the basis of a new mechanized system, then its records must be scrutinized carefully for content and structure.

Manual records are notoriously inaccurate when it comes to details, and a major portion of the editing effort prior to conversion will be devoted to verifying their accuracy. This in itself, the production of reliable library records, is one of the more valuable by-products of library automation.

The structure of each record, as is discussed in detail in Chapter 5, may be indicated implicitly, or more usually by a series of labels. It is the task of the file editor to make clear what labels are to be inserted into the record and where. Given an intelligent keyboard operator, able to learn the basic structure of the records in hand, such pre-labelling of manual records can be limited to minor details, and any exceptions to the general rules. A proof-reading stage is, of course, necessary as with any keyboarding operation.

Recruiting and Training Staff

In Chapter 3 the requirements for staff were discussed in connection with the work of systems analysis and design. Here, it is necessary to point out that staff will be needed to operate the system once it has been installed.

Senior library staff, department heads within whose span of responsibility the system will operate, must be thoroughly acquainted with the system. They need to know especially the procedures to be followed in case of human error or system failure. Junior library staff will be concerned with the system as it affects the interface between the library and the library users. In many cases, as, for example, with a circulation control system, it is they who will normally operate the system.

Clerical assistants will have the task of keyboarding data for input to the system. Ordinary typing skills are needed here, together with further training in operating the particular machine used to convert input data to machine-readable form. Since no computerized library systems should require extra staff, the only circumstances when it may be necessary to recruit additional staff will be when large manual files must be converted.

CHAPTER 5

Bibliographic Record Structures

It is an almost intuitive process for an educated person, reading the bibliographic record reproduced below as Fig. 5.1, firstly to appreciate that the whole consists of a number of parts, and secondly to assign names to the parts. Or, at least, to most of the parts. Although some may be unfamiliar to non-librarians, most people are able to distinguish an author from a publisher, a price from a date. The ISBN will puzzle many, but few will bother to find out what it is, nor will it matter. Students and teachers, as well as librarians, are familiar with the need to write standardized descriptions of books and other documents. The purpose of such descriptions (and Fig. 5.1 is a fairly complete description) is to identify one publication uniquely, either in a bibliography or library catalogue, and standardization assists in this task.

Exactly the same requirements obtain in computer systems which deal with bibliographic records. Except for one vital difference. The computer is not an "educated person" nor can it intuitively understand the structure of even the simplest bibliographic record. The purpose of this chapter is to show how bibliographic record structures are interpreted for the purpose of computerized library systems which must handle them.

The objectives in this process of interpretation are to identify the various parts of the record, distinguishing them from each other sufficiently for the purposes of the system that is being designed. Due regard must also be had for the possibly greater needs of any future system that may use the same records. But note that whereas a human understands "author" to be the name of the person who wrote a particular book, the computer takes "author" to be the string

Patterson, Edward Mervyn
The County Donegal railways, by Edward M.
Patterson. 2nd ed. Newton Abbot, David &
Charles, 1969. £2.50. ISBN 0 7153 4376 9.
208p. 22 plates (1 fold); (incl 1 col),
facsims, maps. 23 cm. bibl p200–201;
index. (a history of the narrow-gauge railways of North-West Ireland, part 1)
Previous ed. (B63–3939) 1962
B69–10037
385.5094163

FIG. 5.1. A bibliographic record.

of characters positioned on the first line of the printed record. It is also the key by which a file of similar records may be arranged in order. In other words, the identification of parts of the record is strictly related to the needs of the system under consideration.

This chapter examines record structures appropriate to three different computer-based library systems, and then considers a complex record structure (the MARC format) in detail. It shows how the above principles work out in practice, and provides a basis for later chapters which consider how bibliographic records are processed in different computer-based library systems.

1. A SERIALS HOLDINGS LIST SYSTEM

The details of a system to produce a printed list of a library's serials holdings are discussed in Chapter 6. But typically, the machine-readable file from which such a list is printed is held on magnetic tape. Each record on the tape is of a predetermined fixed size, and contains the information about one serial. It contains, typically, the following information:

>   Title
>   Holdings
>   Call Number
>   Location
>   Unique Identification Number

Each of these five units of data in the record is called a data field. For simplicity in programming, each data field is assigned a certain fixed size or length, so determined as to enable as many as possible of the library's records to fit within the space available. The system designer is free to choose field lengths which suit the data. If he makes the fields too long a lot of storage space will be wasted, whereas if he makes the fields too short many long records will have to be abbreviated to fit the limited space available.

The medium to be used for data input has a bearing on the lengths that are determined for data fields. Punched cards are convenient for inputting relatively simple records, and they are used in this example. It will be helpful, therefore, to think in terms of the eighty characters, one per column, that each punched card can contain.

For example, the record for one serial can be punched onto two eighty-column cards if fields are given fixed lengths as follows:

Title	60 characters
Holdings	60 ,,
Call Number	10 ,,
Location	20 ,,
Unique Identification Number	10 ,,

The title, call number and unique identification number can be contained in one card; the location and holdings in a second. Since each field now has a fixed length, it becomes a simple matter to place each field in a fixed position on a card and to identify the field, and the data it contains, in terms of that position. This is normally expressed as a range of column numbers on a stated card. Our record structure can now be defined in the following way:

Unique Identification Number	Card 1	Columns 1–10
Call Number	Card 1	Columns 11–20
Title	Card 1	Columns 21–80
Location	Card 2	Columns 1–20
Holdings	Card 2	Columns 21–80

The data fields are identified in terms of their position. Thus, as far as the computer is concerned, the periodical's title is the string of characters running from column 21 to column 80 on card 1. The location is not understood in geographical terms, but simply as those characters punched in columns 1 to 20 on card 2.

Figure 5.2 gives an example of this format, with data for a real periodical in an imaginary library, punched onto two cards. Notice

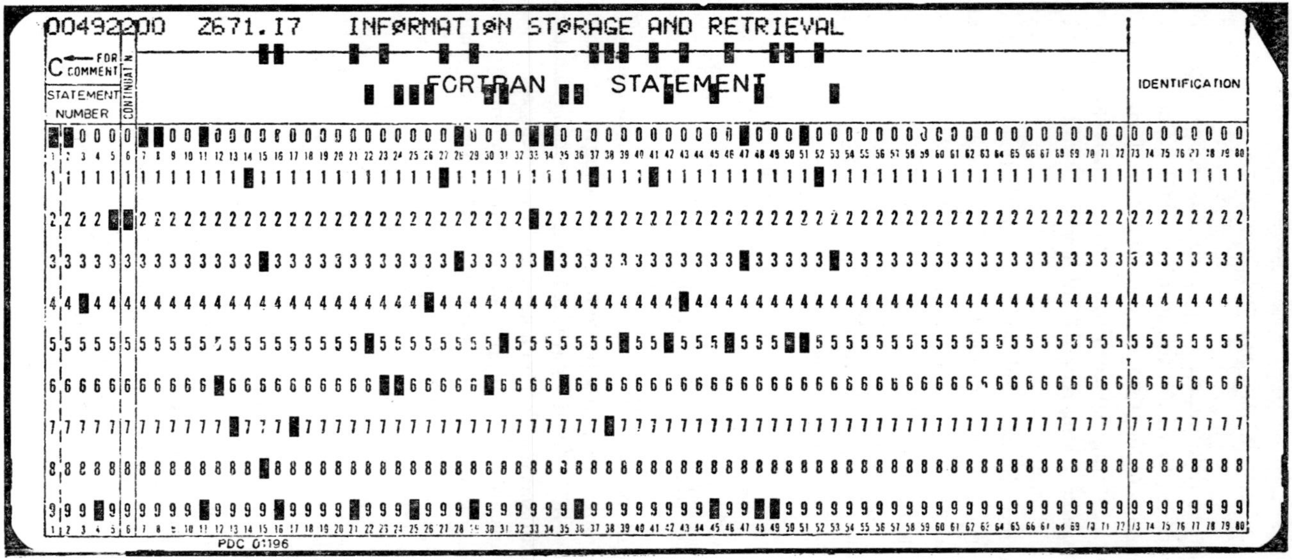

FIG. 5.2a.

FIG. 5.2. Input data on two punched cards, for one title in a serials holdings list system.

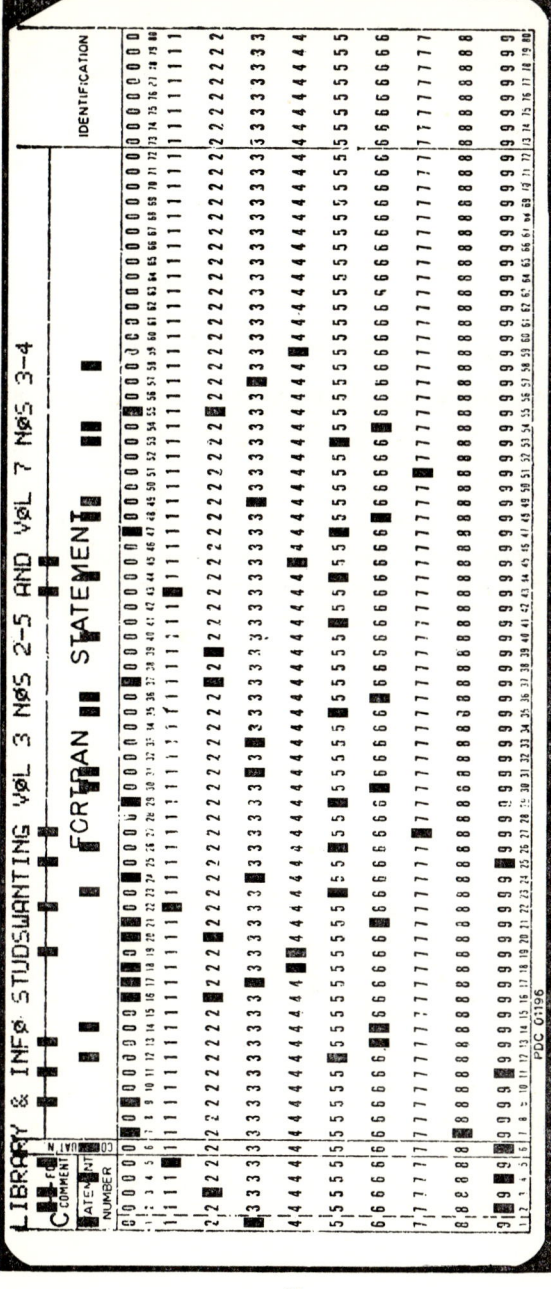

Fig. 5.2b.

that the full name of the location "Library and Information Studies" cannot be punched into the twenty-character location field, and a meaningful abbreviation has been punched instead. It will be convenient for users of the resulting list of serial holdings, and essential if a computer program is to perform any matching operations on the data in the location field, for this abbreviation to be used consistently whenever this particular library location is punched.

2. A BOOK-ORDERING SYSTEM

A system for ordering new books is more complex than a serials listing system. This is reflected in the more complex record structure needed for an ordering system. But since records in an order file have only a limited lifetime, and need not be of the same bibliographical quality as records for a library's catalogue, the structure of order records can be correspondingly simpler than that of catalogue records. However, since it is natural for a system designer to plan for order records to be converted eventually into catalogue records, in modern order systems a slightly more complex record structure may be adopted than that discussed below. In particular, order records may be in a MARC format, as described in the next section of this chapter.

The data fields which need to be identified in a typical ordering system for monographs are listed below:

>ISBN
>Order Number
>Author, Title, Edition
>Publisher, Date of Publication
>Price
>Fund to be charged to
>Number of Copies
>Bookseller or Supplier
>Date ordered

Some systems may identify more information than this, or may wish to treat separately such things as author and title which are here brought together in one field.

Some of the above data fields, such as the International Standard Book Number, are of known, fixed size, but others, such as the author, title and edition field, will vary greatly in length from record to record.

It is convenient, therefore, to specify a record structure for an order system, which makes it possible for the data fields to vary in length. To do this, the beginning and end of each field must be marked, and individual fields must be labelled. The beginning and end of each record must also be marked, either explicitly or implicitly.

Punched paper tape is a convenient medium for holding the initial machine-readable order record. Paper tape comes in large reels able to hold many thousands of characters (unlike punched cards, each of which may contain only eighty characters) and is more suitable for records whose fields may vary in length.

A simple numerical scheme will suffice to label each field in the record. A special character, e.g. "@", readily available on most typewriter keyboards, can serve to mark the end of each field. Two such end of field marks will mark the end of the complete record.

The record structure now becomes:

1. ISBN (End of field mark)
2. Order Number (End of field mark)
3. Author, Title, Edition (End of field mark)
4. Publisher, Date of Publication (End of field mark)
5. Price (End of field mark)
6. Fund to be charged to (End of field mark)
7. Number of copies (End of field mark)
8. Bookseller or Supplier (End of field mark)
9. Date ordered (End of field mark) (End of field mark)

When order data for a book is punched onto paper tape, using a tape typewriter, each character in the record is represented by a pattern of holes punched across the width of the tape. Figure 5.3 shows the characters that would be punched onto paper tape in this way, using the above order record structure for the book in Fig. 5.1. Note that the symbol ƀ is used to represent a blank space.

The example commences with the last twenty-one characters of the previous order record punched onto the tape. The end of this record is signalled by the end-of-record mark "@@". The first field of the new record, therefore, is that character string following upon the four characters "@@1". This is an unambiguous way of specifying the first field in the record because it is inconceivable that these four characters should occur elsewhere, as part of a title, for example. Each successive field in the record is signalled by a string of three characters,

68   Automation in Libraries

First character of the order record
↓
Book∤Shop.@9.051173@@1.0715343769@2.123456@3.Patterson,∤Edward∤

M.∤The∤County∤Donegal∤Railways.∤2nd∤Ed.@4.David∤&∤Charles,∤1969

.@5.£2.25.@6.XYZ.@7.1@8.Univ.∤Book∤Shop.@9.051173@@1.085157123X
                                                                ↑
                                                    Last character
                                                    of the order
                                                    record

FIG. 5.3. A string of characters punched onto paper tape, containing an order record.

thus; "@2.", "@3.", etc., and it is seen that the example finishes with the first field of the following order record. It is in this manner that the programmer is able to identify the various parts of the record for the computer.

3. CATALOGUING SYSTEM USING A SIMPLIFIED MARC-TYPE RECORD STRUCTURE

Consider the task of writing a computer program to find the price of the book in Fig. 5.3. The programmer is able to instruct the computer to look for specific named characters, and the program will have a structure as indicated by the flow chart in Fig. 5.4. Every character in the record must be examined in turn to find the sequence "@5.". With large and complex records, this sequential search, character by character, is slow and tedious, even for a computer. The MARC record structure enables specified fields in a complex record structure to be found much more easily by incorporating a map of the record into the record. This section describes a simplified MARC-type record structure with just such a map, or directory. The following section discusses the MARC record structure itself.

Data fields in MARC records are identified explicitly by a label or code—in MARC parlance, a tag. (The order record structure described above used single digit numerical labels to identify fields, whereas the serials holdings list record in the first section of this chapter identified fields by their position within a record of fixed size and structure.)

Bibliographic Record Structures 69

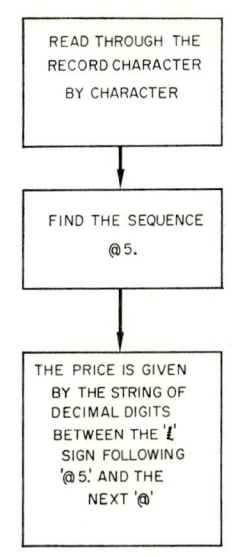

```
┌─────────────────────┐
│   READ THROUGH THE  │
│   RECORD CHARACTER  │
│     BY CHARACTER    │
└──────────┬──────────┘
           │
           ▼
┌─────────────────────┐
│  FIND THE SEQUENCE  │
│         @5.         │
└──────────┬──────────┘
           │
           ▼
┌─────────────────────┐
│   THE PRICE IS GIVEN│
│    BY THE STRING OF │
│    DECIMAL DIGITS   │
│    BETWEEN THE '£'  │
│    SIGN FOLLOWING   │
│    '@5.' AND THE    │
│       NEXT '@'      │
└─────────────────────┘
```

Fig. 5.4. To find the price field in the order record in Fig. 5.3.

Another important characteristic of MARC records is that every character in a record has an address, expressed as a distance in characters from some fixed point in the record. In particular the address of the first character of each labelled data field is known, and stated clearly in the map or directory. Figure 5.5 illustrates the general structure of a MARC record and shows a simple directory in action.

This simplified record contains four variable length data fields. For each data field there is one field in the directory. Each directory field is fixed in length and contains, among other things, the address of the first character of the corresponding data field. In this way the directory as a whole serves as a map of the data field section of the record, and in particular, individual directory fields serve as pointers to their corresponding data fields.

Consider this simplified example further, specifying the size and contents of each field, and using it to build up a complete bibliographic record as a string of characters.

We define the Descriptive Record Label as a fixed length field,

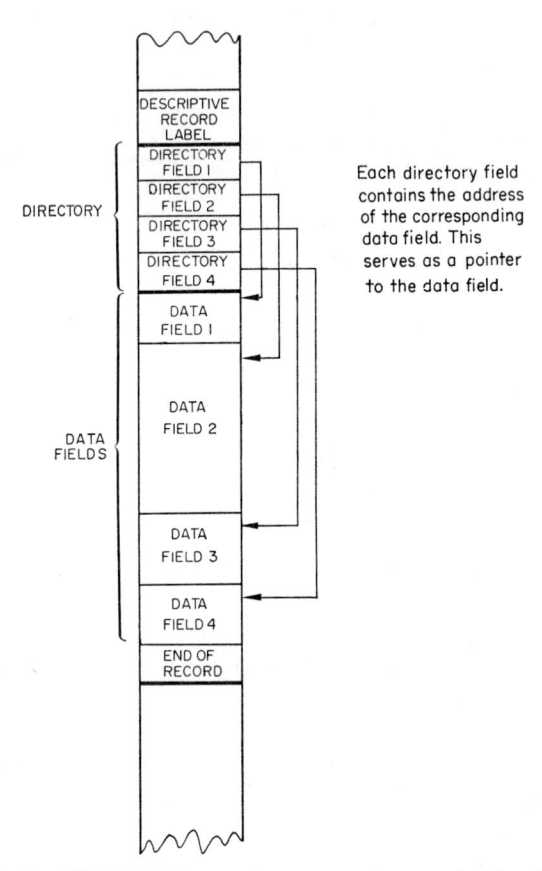

FIG. 5.5. Simplified MARC record on magnetic tape showing function of directory.

length four characters, which contains the overall length of the completed bibliographic record. Four numerical characters allow the maximum record length to be 9999 characters. For records that are shorter than this maximum possible length, the characters in the Descriptive Record Label are "right justified". That is, any unused character positions will be at the left-hand side of the field, and are filled with zeros.

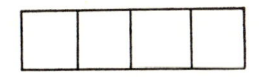

Descriptive record label; four characters

Each directory field is nine characters long in this simplified record structure. The first character contains the tag, or identifying label of the corresponding data field. Characters 2 to 5 inclusive contain the length of the data field. Characters 6 to 9 inclusive contain the address of the first character of the data field (the field's starting character position) with respect to the first character of the record.

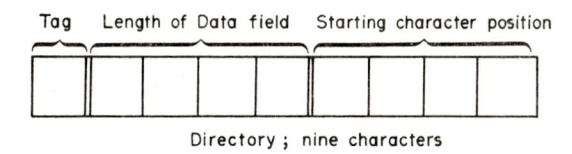

Tag   Length of Data field   Starting character position

Directory; nine characters

Data fields are not preceded by a tag, as they were in the example of the order record, but they are terminated by the same end of field mark "@". The end of record mark consists of a second "@" following after the one already there as the end of field mark of the last data field.

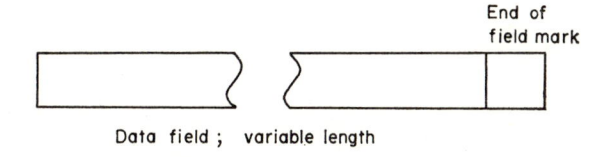

End of field mark

Data field; variable length

A very simple tagging scheme will suffice. Tag "1" identifies the author, tag "2" identifies the title, tag "3" identifies the publisher, tag "4" identifies the date of publication.

We start to build up this simple bibliographic record by writing down the four data fields, each with its end of field mark. Then count the

72   *Automation in Libraries*

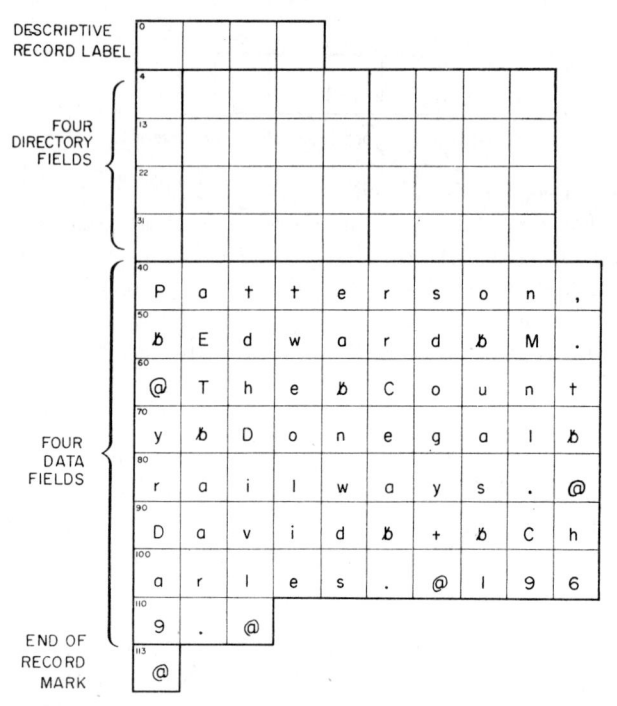

FIG. 5.6. Building up the complete MARC-type record—1.

number of characters in each, including all spaces and punctuation marks. Thus:

Author	Patterson,ƀEdwardƀM.@	(21 characters)
Title	TheƀCountyƀDonegalƀrailways.@	(29 characters)
Publisher	Davidƀ&ƀCharles.@	(17 characters)
Date	1969.@	(6 characters)

There is therefore a total of 21+29+17+6, i.e. 73 characters in the four data fields. For each data field, there will be a nine-character directory field, and in addition, the Descriptive Record Label is four characters long, and there is a one-character end-of-record mark. The total record has a length of

$$73 + 4 \times 9 + 4 + 1 = 114 \text{ characters.}$$

Figure 5.6 shows a matrix or grid laid out to help in building up

Bibliographic Record Structures 73

	0								
	0	1	1	4					

DESCRIPTIVE RECORD LABEL

4				
1	0	0	2	1

FOUR DIRECTORY FIELDS

13				
2	0	0	2	9

22				
3	0	0	1	7

31				
4	0	0	0	6

40								
P	a	t	t	e	r	s	o	n	,

50								
♭	E	d	w	a	r	d	♭	M	.

60								
@	T	h	e	♭	C	o	u	n	t

FOUR DATA FIELDS

70								
y	♭	D	o	n	e	g	a	l	♭

80								
r	a	i	l	w	a	y	s	.	@

90								
D	a	v	i	d	♭	+	♭	C	h

100								
a	r	l	e	s	.	@	1	9	6

END OF RECORD MARK

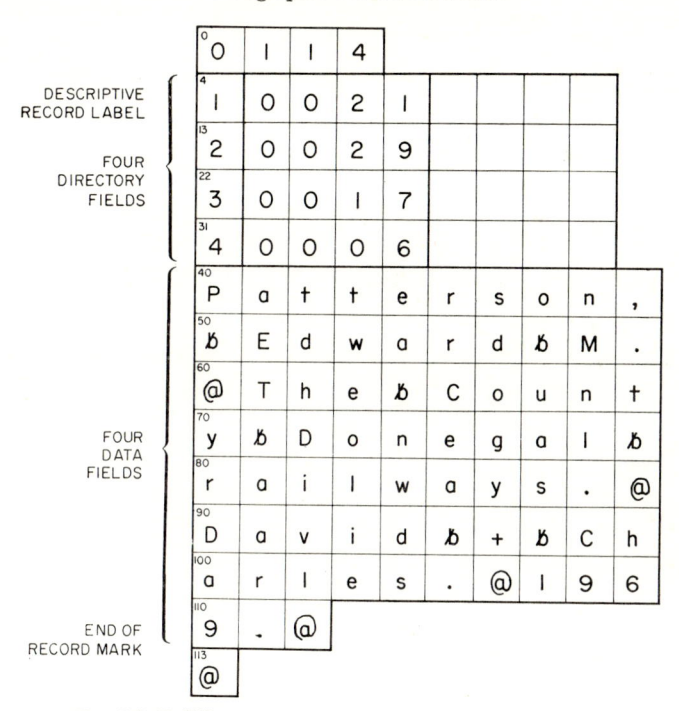

110		
9	.	@

113
@

FIG. 5.7. Building up the complete MARC-type record—2.

the four directory fields. Each square in the grid may contain one character. The address of the first character in each line is given in the box for that character, and the layout of the grid distinguishes clearly between the major parts of the record. In Fig. 5.6 the data fields are completed, and the end-of-record mark is inserted.

In Fig. 5.7 the Descriptive Record Label has been completed, by inserting the length of the whole record—already calculated to be 114 characters. Since the number 114 requires only three decimal digits, and the Descriptive Record Label field is four characters long, a zero is inserted in character position 0. The lengths of the four data fields have already been determined, so the first two sections of each directory field can now be completed. Thus the author field is identified by means of the tag "1", and it is twenty-one characters long. A figure 1

74 Automation in Libraries

	0	1	2	3	4	5	6	7
0	O	I	I	4				
4	I	O	O	2	I	O	O	4	0
13	2	O	O	2	9	O	O	6	I
22	3	O	O	I	7	O	O	9	O
31	4	O	O	O	6	O	I	O	7
40	P	a	t	t	e	r	s	o	n	,
50	♭	E	d	w	a	r	d	♭	M	.
60	@	T	h	e	♭	C	o	u	n	t
70	y	♭	D	o	n	e	g	a	l	♭
80	r	a	i	l	w	a	y	s	.	@
90	D	a	v	i	d	♭	+	♭	C	h
100	a	r	l	e	s	.	@	l	9	6
110	9	.	@
113	@

- Row 0: DESCRIPTIVE RECORD LABEL
- Rows 4–31: FOUR DIRECTORY FIELDS
- Rows 40–100: FOUR DATA FIELDS
- Rows 110–113: END OF RECORD MARK

FIG. 5.8. Building up the complete MARC-type record—3.

is therefore written in character position 4. The length of the author field is then written into character positions 5 to 8, filling up empty positions at the left with zeros. The same procedure is followed for the directory fields corresponding to the three other data fields.

Figure 5.8 completes the record by adding in the last four characters of each directory field, which give the address of the first character of the corresponding data field. The author field commences in box 40, so the last four characters of the first directory field are 0040. Similarly, the title field starts in box 61, the publisher field in box 90, and the date of publication field in box 107.

Written onto paper tape or magnetic tape, the structure which is visible in Figs. 5.6 to 5.8 disappears, as the record becomes a single string of characters, as shown in Fig. 5.9.

01141002100402002900613 0017
0090400060107Patterson,ƀEdward
ƀM.@TheƀCountyƀDonegalƀrailways.@
Davidƀ+ƀCharles.@1969.@@

Fig. 5.9. Unformatted MARC-type record as a string of characters.

THE MARC FORMAT

The MARC format (or, as it is sometimes called, the MARC II format, to distinguish it from an earlier MARC format used experimentally by the Library of Congress) is a communications format for bibliographic records. That is, a format designed for communicating records of books, periodicals, reports, etc., between libraries. It is not intended primarily to be suitable for use within individual library systems. So the format is comparatively complex from a systems viewpoint, and items of data within the record are labelled in a very detailed manner as far as the library cataloguer is concerned.

Strictly speaking it is incorrect to speak of "the MARC format" in the singular. A MARC communications format was introduced by the Library of Congress in March 1969, and slightly different versions have been used both by the British National Bibliography and by the Bibliothèque Nationale. But while the formats differ in detail, they adhere to the same basic structure.

MARC records of new books are currently being created by the Library of Congress in Washington and the British National Bibliography in London. A number of libraries subscribe to, or otherwise receive a magnetic tape each week, containing the records of newly catalogued books that have accumulated since the previous tape was "published". On receipt of the new tape, libraries use the records for SDI, for ordering new books, or for input to cataloguing systems.

In most cases the library will use a simpler record structure for internal processing purposes, in much the same way that most libraries' catalogue cards contain less bibliographical information than do national bibliographies. But if a library is engaged in a two-way communication of cataloguing records, and is both receiving and distributing MARC records, it will want to retain the full MARC

76   *Automation in Libraries*

record structure and the same level of cataloguing fullness within its own systems.

The remainder of this chapter is devoted to a description of the structure of the MARC format and a worked example. The Appendix to the chapter lists the data fields that have been identified for the format, with notes on some differences between the various national "versions" of the format. The references at the end of the chapter list the sources used.

Overall Structure

The MARC record structure consists of three main sections, identical in nature and purpose to the three sections in the simplified MARC structure already discussed.

The first is the Leader, corresponding to the Descriptive Record Label of the simplified record. It is of fixed length, and contains a statement of the overall length of the record, and other information.

The second section is the Directory, consisting, as before, of a series of fixed length fields, one for each data field.

Thirdly, the variable length data fields themselves.

Leader

This is a twenty-four character fixed-length field, and contains the following subfields:

	Character positions
Record length	0–4
Record status	5
Legend	
a. Type of record	6
b. Bibliographic level	7
c. Blank	8–9
Indicator count	10
Subfield code count	11
Base address of data	12–16
Encoding level	17
Blanks	18–19
Entry map	20–23

Record length (character positions 0–4) is the total number of characters in the bibliographic record, and is right justified, filling blank spaces to the left of the number with zeros. Since the record length

Bibliographic Record Structures

subfield is five characters long, the maximum possible length of the whole bibliographic record is 99,999 characters. This makes the MARC format capable of communicating textual data, such as abstracts or other document summaries, but not the full texts of documents.

Record status (character position 5). This one-character subfield enables new records to be distinguished from records which are corrected versions of records that have already been distributed to recipients of the MARC tapes. It also enables records that have been, or are to be deleted, to be reported.

A simple one-character alphabetical code is used:

- n   new record
- c   corrected or revised record
- d   deleted record

Legend (character positions 6–9). The purpose of the legend is to give a general statement about the nature of the item described in the MARC record. Two characters of this four-character subfield are used; the first specifies the kind of item, the second its "bibliographic level".

Twelve different kinds of library materials can be identified by the first of the two characters used in the legend, as follows:

- a   Printed text
- b   Manuscript text
- c   Printed music
- d   Manuscript music
- e   Printed maps and atlases
- f   Manuscript maps
- g   Motion pictures and filmstrips
- h   Microforms
- i   Sound recordings of the spoken word
- j   Sound recordings of music
- k   Pictures, designs and other two-dimensional representations
- l   Data in machine-readable form
- x   Authority data—names
- y   Authority data—subjects

Four different bibliographic levels are specified, and coded by the second character in the legend:

m   Monograph
a   Analytic
s   Serial
c   Collective

Indicator count (character position 10). In the simple MARC-type record structure discussed previously, there was only one way of identifying and describing a data field—by means of the tag located in the corresponding directory field. The full MARC record structure identifies data at three different levels and in three different places as follows:

three-character Tag, in the directory field;
two-character Indicator, as the first two characters of the data field;
two-character Subfield code, immediately preceding each subfield that is specified.

Tags, indicators and subfield codes are discussed in detail later. The indicator count in the leader specifies, in one character, how many characters, at the beginning of each data field, are occupied by the indicators. The indicator count is, at present, always set at "2" in MARC records.

Subfield code count (character position 11). In the same way, the subfield code count specifies the number of characters occupied by each subfield code. This is always two characters in MARC records.

Base address of data (character positions 12–16). This is simply the address of the first character of the first data field in the record. Since the first character in the record (the first character of the leader) is numbered zero, the base address of data is also equal to the number of characters in the leader plus the directory fields, and including also the single character end-of-field mark situated at the end of the directory section.

Bibliographic Record Structures

Encoding level (character position 17). This single character subfield shows whether the MARC record contains full or only incomplete cataloguing data, as follows:

ƀ(blank)   Full level. A full catalogue record derived from an inspection of the actual document.

1   Incomplete level. A catalogue record prepared without inspecting the actual document.

Entry map (character positions 20–23). Although this four-character subfield has not yet been implemented, it is proposed that it should describe characteristics of the directory fields, in the same way as other characteristics of the record and the document it represents are already described in the leader. The British Standards Institution and the American Standards Institute have recommended that the first of these four characters should record the length of the "Field length" section of the directory field (four characters at present), and that the second should record the length of the "Starting character position" section (five characters at present).

Directory

Each directory field in the MARC record is twelve characters long and subdivided as follows:

	Character positions
Tag	0–2
Field length	3–6
Starting character position	7—11

With the exception of the starting character position, the MARC directory functions in exactly the same way as the directory in the simplified MARC format already described. Starting character positions in MARC directory fields give the position of the first character of the data field in question relative to the first character of the first data field. The starting character position given in the directory field for the first data field, therefore, is 00000. Starting-character positions relative to the first character in the record can be calculated by adding the base address of data (characters 12–16 in the leader) to the starting-character position given in the directory field.

80   *Automation in Libraries*

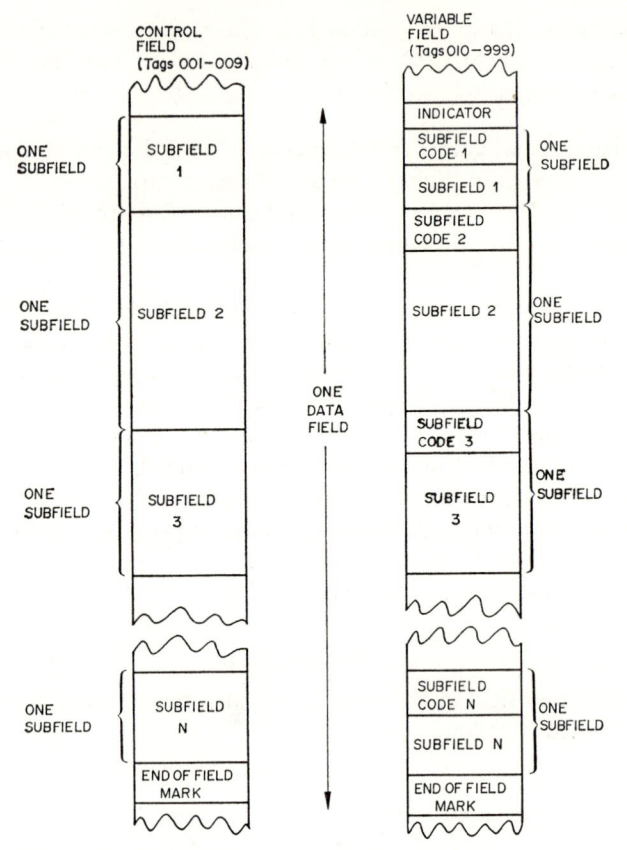

Fig. 5.10. Comparative structure of MARC control fields and variable fields.

The series of fixed-length twelve-character directory fields is followed by a one-character end-of-field mark, usually printed as the musical sharp sign "#".

Data fields

The data fields follow after the end-of-field mark at the end of the directory section. Some, e.g. the ISBN field, are always the same length, but the MARC format treats them in the same way as variable fields, in that each has a corresponding directory field. But a distinction is made between data fields which contain control numbers (called Control fields) and data fields which contain descriptive cataloguing data (called Variable fields). The control fields are those identified by tags 001 to 009 and are all fixed length fields.

Figure 5.10 illustrates the structure of control fields and variable fields. Both may consist of a number of separate subfields, and both are terminated with the end-of-field mark "#". But whereas the information in a control field is specified by means of the tag alone (situated in the corresponding directory field), information in a variable field is specified by tag, indicator, and subfield code.

WORKED EXAMPLE

The bibliographic record given in Fig. 5.1 is used for the worked example, to build up a complete MARC record. The Appendix to this chapter lists the tags that are used to identify data fields in MARC records, but for details of indicators and subfield codes, reference must be made to the published statements of full MARC formats listed at the end of the chapter, immediately preceding the Appendix. However, the indicators and subfield codes are explained fully for each data field that occurs in the worked example.

The procedure adopted is as follows:

1. Write down the contents of the twenty-four-character Leader.
2. Write down the contents of each control field and variable field, and determine the length of each.
3. Write down the contents of control and variable fields in a grid to enable starting character positions to be determined.
4. Build up the directory fields in a separate grid.
5. Write the completed record as a string of characters.

This is similar to that already used for the simple MARC-type record structure, except that now the data is more complete and the record structure is more complex.

Leader

Record length (character positions 0–4): this cannot be determined until the whole record is almost complete.

Record status (character position 5): this is a new record, coded "n".

Type of record (character position 6): this is printed text, coded "a".

Bibliographic level (character position 7): this is a monograph, coded "m".

Blank (character positions 8–9): coded "ƀƀ".

Indicator count (character position 10): coded "2".

Subfield code count (character position 11): coded "2".

Base address of data (character positions 12–16): this cannot be determined until the number of directory fields is known. Since the character positions are numbered from zero, the base address of the data is the number of characters in the leader and directory fields, plus one, and can be calculated as follows. The Leader is always twenty-four characters long. If there are N directory fields, then the directory will be 12N characters long. The directory is followed by a one-character end-of-field mark. So the base address of data is given by the expression

$$24 + 12N + 1.$$

Encoding level (character position 17): this bibliographic record was prepared with the book in hand, coded "ƀ".

Blank (character positions 18–19): coded "ƀƀ".

Entry map (character positions 20–23): coded "ƀƀƀƀ".

Leaving spaces for the record length and base address of data, the contents of the leader are now as illustrated in Fig. 5.11.

Bibliographic Record Structures 83

0	1	2	3	4	5	6	7	8	9	10	11
					n	a	m	♭	♭	2	2

12	13	14	15	16	17	18	19	20	21	22	23
					♭	♭	♭	♭	♭	♭	♭

FIG. 5.11. Leader of the MARC record (each character position is numbered in the top left-hand corner of its "box").

Control and Variable Fields

All data fields are considered in numerical order of their tag.

Field 001 International Standard Book Number. This is a control field (its tag lies within the range 001–009) and therefore has no indicators or subfield codes. It is followed by the end-of-field mark "#". Field 001 will therefore contain the following eleven characters:

0715343769#

Field 008 Fixed length data elements. This is a forty-one-character control field containing nineteen subfields as follows

1. Date entered on file (characters 0–5). This is the date on which the record was entered into the MARC system. It is a six-character subfield; two characters for the year, two for the month, and two for the day of the month. Thus, supposing that this record was entered into the MARC system on 6 November 1969, the following characters will be written into this subfield: "69 11 06."
2. Type of publication date (character 6).
3. Year 1 (characters 7–10).
4. Year 2 (characters 11–14).

These three subfields allow a variety of different imprint dates to be coded. Some simple examples will illustrate.

(a) Imprint date; 1970. Coded as
 "s 1970 ♭♭♭♭"
(b) Imprint date; 1970 (c1969). Coded as
 "c 1970 1969"
(c) Date of publication not known. Coded as
 "n ♭♭♭♭ ♭♭♭♭"

A.L.—D

In the case of this book, there is a single known publication date, coded as "s 1969 ҍҍҍҍ."

5. Country of publication code (characters 15–17). A two- or three-character alphabetical subfield, left justified. This book was published in England, coded as "enҍ."

6. Illustration codes (characters 18–21). Up to four alphabetical characters to indicate the presence of different kinds of illustrations. The book in hand is illustrated with maps, plates and facsimiles. Maps are coded "b", plates are coded "f", facsimiles are coded "h". One character remains blank. This subfield therefore, contains the four characters "bfhҍ".

7. Intellectual level code (character 22). At present, this single character subfield is used only to indicate a book for children, coded "j". This book is not for children, so this subfield is blank.

8. Form of reproduction code (character 23). Used to indicate micro-reproductions or large print versions of an original. Neither of these applies here, so the subfield is blank.

9. Form of content codes (characters 24–27). Up to four alphabetical characters, which enable bibliographies, catalogues, indexes, etc., to be identified specially. None of these apply, so this subfield remains blank.

10. Government publication indicator (character 28). This is not a government publication, so the character "0" is entered.

11. Conference or meeting indicator (character 29). This publication does not contain the proceedings of a conference or meeting, so the character "0" is entered.

12. Festschrift indicator (character 30). This is not a festschrift, so the character "0" is entered.

13. Index indicator (character 31). The book contains an index to its contents, so the character "1" is entered.

14. Main entry in body of entry indicator (character 32). Where the main entry is also found in the descriptive paragraph, or body of the entry, whether in the same form, or modified in some way, the character 1 is entered here. Otherwise this character position contains a zero. A "1" is therefore entered for this book.

15. Literary text and type of publication indicator (character 33). The Library of Congress distinguishes here between fiction and non-

Bibliographic Record Structures 85

fiction (coded 1 and 0 respectively). BNB use it to identify drama, essays, fiction, poetry, etc. None of the BNB categories relate to this work, which is therefore coded "ƀ".

16. Biography code (character 34). This is not a biography, so the character "ƀ" is entered in position 34.

17. Main language (characters 35–37). A three-character alphabetical field, which in this case contains the characters "eng" for the English language.

18. Modified record code (character 38). BNB signals the first issue of a periodical here. It is blank in this case.

19. Cataloguing source code (character 39). LC uses this character to identify the source of cataloguing data. It is blank in this case.

Figure 5.12 shows the full contents of field 008.

0	1	2	3	4	5	6	7	8	9
6	9	1	1	0	6	s	1	9	6
10	11	12	13	14	15	16	17	18	19
9	ƀ	ƀ	ƀ	ƀ	e	n	ƀ	b	f
20	21	22	23	24	25	26	27	28	29
h	ƀ	ƀ	ƀ	ƀ	ƀ	ƀ	ƀ	0	0
30	31	32	33	34	35	36	37	38	39
0	1	1	ƀ	ƀ	e	n	g	ƀ	ƀ
40									
#									

Fig. 5.12. Field 008 of the MARC record.

Field 015 National Bibliography number. This is the first variable field in the record, and contains indicators and subfield codes. The BNB number of the book (since it is a British book) is B69-10037. Both indicators are zero, and only one subfield is present. Subfield codes consist of two characters. The first is the "$" or "£" sign, the second a lower case alphabetical character, whose meaning is specified for the field in question. Subfield "£a" is used here, as the only subfield, to contain the BNB number. Field 015 therefore contains the following thirteen characters:

00£ab6910037#

Field 082 DC classification number. The class number given is 385.5094163. It is coextensive with the subject of the book, so the first indicator is 1. The second indicator is zero. Subfield £a contains the base number and £b contains extensions of the base number (LC uses subfield £a to contain the whole number). In our example, the digits 094163 relate to the geographical location of the railway (County Donegal) and are placed in subfield £b. Field 082 contains the following eighteen characters:

10£a385.5£b094163#

Field 100 Main entry—personal name. This is the first line of the printed record reproduced as Fig. 5.1. The first indicator is 1 to indicate that the author has a single surname. The second indicator is always zero. Subfield £a is the entry element (i.e. the surname). Subfield £h contains the two forenames. (LC include surname and forenames in subfield £a, and use the second indicator to show if the main entry is also the subject of the work.) Field 100 contains the following thirty characters:

10£aPatterson,£hEdwardʙMervyn#

Field 245 Title. The first indicator shows whether a title entry is required or not. A title entry is required in this case, so the first indicator is 1. The second indicator shows the number of characters that are to be ignored in filing the title, four in this case. Subfield £a contains the title proper, £b the subtitle, £d a simple single author statement. Field 245, therefore, contains the following fifty-eight characters:

14£aTheʙCountyʙDonegalʙrailways,£dbyʙ
EdwardʙM.ʙPatterson.#

Field 250 Edition statement. This is the second edition, and is the complete work. The second indicator is zero. The first is always zero. It is a simple edition statement, and is wholly contained within subfield £a. Field 250 contains the following twelve characters:

00£a2ndʙed.#

Field 260 Imprint. The first indicator is zero because the publisher is not the main entry author heading. The second indicator is zero because the imprint relates to the whole work rather than to part of it. Subfield £a contains the place of publication, subfield £b the publisher's name, and subfield £c the date of publication. Field 260 contains forty-three characters:

00£aNewtonƀAbbot,£bDavidƀ&ƀCharles,£c1969.#

Field 300 Collation. Both indicators are always zero. Subfield £a contains the pagination, subfield £b the illustration statement, and subfield £c the size. Field 300 contains sixty-eight characters:

00£a208p,£b22ƀplatesƀ(1ƀfold);ƀ(incl ƀ1ƀcol),ƀfacsims,ƀmaps.£c23ƀcm.#

Field 350 Price. Both indicators are zero. £a is the only subfield present. Field 350 contains ten characters:

00£a£2.50#

Field 440 Title series entry. The series statement relates to the whole work, so the first indicator is zero. Two characters at the beginning of the entry are to be ignored in filing, so the second indicator is 2. Subfield £a is the series title; subfield £v contains the number within the series. Field 440 contains seventy-four characters:

02£aAƀhistoryƀofƀtheƀnarrow-gaugeƀrailwaysƀ ofƀNorth-WestƀIreland,£vpartƀ1#

Field 503 Bibliographic history note. The first indicator is always zero. The second indicator is zero in this case because the note relates to the whole work. Subfield £a is the only subfield present. Field 503 contains thirty-three characters:

00£aPreviousƀed.ƀ(b6303939)ƀ1962#

Field 504 Bibliography note. The indicators are the same as for field 503, and £a is the only subfield present. Field 504 contains ten characters:

00£abibl.#

88   *Automation in Libraries*

000	001	002	003	004	005	006	007	008	009	010	011	012	013	014	015	016	017	018	019
0	7	1	5	3	4	3	7	6	9	#	6	9	1	1	0	6	s	1	9
020										030									
6	9	ƀ	ƀ	ƀ	ƀ	e	n	ƀ	b	f	h	ƀ	ƀ	ƀ	ƀ	ƀ	ƀ	ƀ	0
040										050									
0	0	1	1	ƀ	ƀ	e	n	g	ƀ	ƀ	#	0	0	ƒ	a	b	6	9	1
060										070									
0	0	3	7	#	1	0	ƒ	a	3	8	5	.	5	ƒ	b	0	9	4	1
080										090									
6	3	#	1	0	ƒ	a	P	a	t	t	e	r	s	o	n	,	ƒ	h	E
100										110									
d	w	a	r	d	ƀ	M	e	r	v	y	n	#	1	4	ƒ	a	T	h	e
120										130									
ƀ	C	o	u	n	t	y	ƀ	D	o	n	e	g	a	l	ƀ	r	a	i	l
140										150									
w	a	y	s	,	ƒ	d	b	y	ƀ	E	d	w	a	r	d	ƀ	M	.	ƀ
160										170									
P	a	t	t	e	r	s	o	n	.	#	0	0	ƒ	a	2	n	d	ƀ	e
180										190									
d	.	#	0	0	ƒ	a	N	e	w	t	o	n	ƀ	A	b	b	o	t	t
200										210									
,	ƒ	b	D	a	v	i	d	ƀ	+	ƀ	C	h	a	r	l	e	s	,	ƒ
220										230									
c	1	9	6	9	.	#	0	0	ƒ	a	2	0	8	p	,	ƒ	b	2	2
240										250									
ƀ	p	l	a	t	e	s	ƀ	(	1	ƀ	f	o	l	d	)	;	ƀ	(	i
260										270									
n	c	l	ƀ	l	ƀ	c	o	l	)	,	ƀ	f	a	c	s	i	m	s	,
280										290									
ƀ	m	a	p	s	.	ƒ	c	2	3	ƀ	c	m	.	#	0	0	ƒ	a	ƒ
300										310									
2	.	5	0	#	0	2	ƒ	a	A	ƀ	h	i	s	t	o	r	y	ƀ	o
320										330									
f	ƀ	t	h	e	ƀ	n	a	r	r	o	w	-	g	a	u	g	e	ƀ	r
340										350									
a	i	l	w	a	y	s	ƀ	o	f	ƀ	N	o	r	t	h	-	W	e	s
360										370									
t	ƀ	I	r	e	l	a	n	d	,	ƒ	v	p	a	r	t	ƀ	l	#	0
380										390									
0	ƒ	a	P	r	e	v	i	o	u	s	ƀ	e	d	.	ƀ	(	b	6	3
400										410									
0	3	9	3	9	)	ƀ	l	9	6	2	#	0	0	ƒ	a	b	i	b	l
420				422															
.	#	R																	

FIG. 5.13. Data fields of the MARC record, showing character positions numbered with respect to the first character of the first data field.

The contents of all data fields have now been written down separately. In Fig. 5.13 the same characters are written into a grid of numbered boxes, one character per box. The first character of the first data field is written in box 000, and so box numbers in this grid can be used as starting-character positions in the directory fields. For extra clarity the end of each field is marked with a double grid line after the end-of-field mark #. An end-of-record mark "R" has been added at the end of the record.

It is now possible to calculate the base address of data, to be inserted into character positions 12–16 of the leader. There are thirteen data fields, so $N=13$ in the expression given on page 82. The base address of data is

$$24 + 12 \times 13 + 1 = 181$$

Thus 181 characters in the record precede the data proper. There are 423 characters of data, so the record length (character positions 0–4 of the leader) is

$$181 + 423 = 604 \text{ characters}$$

In Fig. 5.14 the grid is twelve characters wide, corresponding to the length of each directory field. The first two rows of the grid contain the leader, now completed with the addition of the overall record length (character positions 0–4) and the base address of data (character positions 12–16). Each subsequent row of the grid contains one directory field. Heavy lines show the position in each directory field of the tag (characters 0–2), the length of the data field (characters 3–6) and the starting-character position of the field, with respect to the first character of the first data field.

The first directory field (row 3 in Fig. 5.14) is for field 001, the ISBN. The tag "001" is written into the first three character positions of the field. The field is eleven characters long, so "0011" is written into the following four character positions. Since this is the first data field, its starting character position is zero. So "00000" is entered into the last five character positions of the row.

The second directory field is row four in Fig. 5.14. It corresponds to field 008, the fixed length data elements. The tag "008" appears as the first three characters in the row. The field is forty-one characters long (i.e. forty characters plus an end-of-field mark) and commences at character position 011 in Fig. 5.13. Note that the starting-character position of the second field is also obtained by adding together the field length and the starting-character position of the previous field.

Similarly, field 015 is thirteen characters long, and starts at character position 052 in Fig. 5.13 (Check: $52=41+11$). Field 082 is eighteen

90 *Automation in Libraries*

000	001	002	003	004	005	006	007	008	009	010	011
0	0	6	0	4	n	a	m	♭	♭	2	2

012	013	014	015	016	017	018	019	020	021	022	023
0	0	1	8	1	♭	♭	♭	♭	♭	♭	♭

024											
0	0	1	0	0	1	1	0	0	0	0	0

036											
0	0	8	0	0	4	1	0	0	0	1	1

048											
0	1	5	0	0	1	3	0	0	0	5	2

060											
0	8	2	0	0	1	8	0	0	0	6	5

072											
1	0	0	0	0	3	0	0	0	0	8	3

084											
2	4	5	0	0	5	8	0	0	1	1	3

096											
2	5	0	0	0	1	2	0	0	1	7	1

108											
2	6	0	0	0	4	4	0	0	1	8	3.

120											
3	0	0	0	0	6	8	0	0	2	2	7

132											
3	5	0	0	0	1	0	0	0	2	9	5

144											
4	4	0	0	0	7	4	0	0	3	0	5

156											
5	0	3	0	0	3	3	0	0	3	7	9

168											
5	0	4	0	0	1	0	0	0	4	1	2

180
#

Fig. 5.14. Leader and directory fields for the MARC record.

characters long and starts at character position 65 (65=13+52). Field 100 is thirty characters long and starts at character position 083 (83=18+65). Field 245 is fifty-eight characters long and starts at character position 113 (113=30+83). Field 250 is twelve characters long and starts at character position 171 (171=58+113). Field 260 is forty-four characters long and starts at character position 183

(183=12+171). Field 300 is sixty-eight characters long and starts at character position 227 (227=44+183). Field 350 is ten characters long and starts at character position 295 (295=68+227). Field 440 is seventy-four characters long and starts at character position 305 (305=10+295). Field 503 is thirty-three characters long and starts at character position 379 (379=74+305). Field 504 is ten characters long and starts at character position 412 (412=33+379). The thirteen directory fields are followed by an end-of-field mark.

Finally, Fig. 5.15 shows the complete MARC record as a simple string of characters.

00604namƀƀ2200181ƀƀƀƀƀƀƀ001001100000008004 1
0001101500130005208200180006510000
3000083245005800113250001200171 26000
4400183300006800227350001000295 44000
740030550300330037950400100041 2 # 071 5 3 4 3 7 6 9 #
691106s1969ƀƀƀƀenƀƀfhƀƀƀƀƀƀƀ00011ƀƀengƀƀ # 00
£ab6910037 # 10£a385.5£b094163 # 10£aPatterson,
£hEdwardƀMervyn # 14£aTheƀCountyƀDonegalƀrail
ways,£dbyƀEdwardƀM.ƀPatterson. # 00£a2ndƀed. #
00£aNewtonƀAbbot,£bDavidƀ&ƀCharles,£c1969. #
00£a208p,£b22ƀplatesƀ(1ƀfold);ƀ(incl ƀ1ƀcol),ƀ
facsims,ƀmaps.£c23ƀcm. # 00£a£2.50 # 02£aAƀhistory
ƀofƀtheƀnarrow-gaugeƀrailwaysƀofƀNorth-Westƀ
Ireland,£vpartƀ1 # 00£aPreviousƀed.ƀ(ƀ6303939)ƀ
1962 # 00£abibl. # R

FIG. 5.15. The complete MARC record, built up in Figs. 5.13 and 5.14, now shown as a single string of characters.

REFERENCES

The following publications contain full statements of the various versions of the MARC II format.
1. USA standard for a format for bibliographic information interchange on magnetic tape. *Journal of Library Automation*, Vol. 2, No. 2, pp. 53–95 (June 1969).
2. U.S. LIBRARY OF CONGRESS, *Books: a MARC format*, 5th ed. 1972.
3. U.S. LIBRARY OF CONGRESS, *Films: a MARC format*, 1970.
4. U.S. LIBRARY OF CONGRESS, *Maps: a MARC format*, 1970.
5. U.S. LIBRARY OF CONGRESS, *Serials: a MARC format*, 1970.
6. U.S. LIBRARY OF CONGRESS, *Manuscripts: a MARC format*, 1973.
7. GORMAN, M. and LINFORD, J. E., *A description of the BNB/MARC record; a manual of practice*. BNB, 1971.

8. BLCMP MASS manual, input procedures for serials cataloguing. Birmingham Libraries Co-operative Mechanization Project, 1973. (MASS working paper No. 2.)
9. CHAUVEINC, MARC, *Monocle, projet de mise en ordinateur d'une notice catalographique de livre*, 2nd ed. Grenoble, 1972.
10. CHAUVEINC, MARC, Monocle. *Journal of Library Automation*, Vol. 4, No. 3, pp. 113–28 (Sept. 1971).

APPENDIX

Tags used in the LC and BNB MARC formats, the MASS serials format, and the French MONOCLE format.

Tag	Contents of field
001	Control number (LC places the LC card number here, BNB has the ISBN here. MASS puts the ISSN here, and it is not used in MONOCLE).
002	Subrecord directory (proposed by MONOCLE and LC; not used by BNB and MASS).
003	Relationship between main record and subrecords (MONOCLE only).
004	Related record directory (proposed by LC).
006	Linking field (LC only).
008	Fixed length data elements. (This is a forty-character field except in MONOCLE where it is sixty-nine characters in length.)
009	Physical description fixed field for archival collections.
010	Library of Congress card number (BNB and MONOCLE. LC uses field 001 for the LC card number).
011	Linking LC card number.
015	National bibliography number.
016	Link (proposed by MONOCLE).
017	US copyright number (allocated by LC but not used).
	Correction message (proposed by BNB but not used).
018	Amendment message (proposed by BNB but not used).
020	International Standard book number (ISBN), Standard film number.
021	Alternative international standard book numbers.
022	International standard serial number (ISSN).
025	Overseas acquisitions number (used only by LC in connection with its various overseas acquisitions programmes).
030	Coden.
035	Local system number.
036	Link (proposed by MONOCLE).
040	Cataloguing source (not used by BNB).
041	Languages (only if a translation is involved).
042	Search code (proposed by LC and MONOCLE).
043	Geographic area code.
044	Country of producer (LC only).
045	Chronological coverage code.
046	International source code.
050	Library of Congress call number (in BNB and MASS this field is shortened to become the Library of Congress classification number).

051	Copy, issue, offprint statement.
060	National Library of Medicine call number (not used by BNB and MASS).
061	National Library of Medicine copy statement (LC only).
070	National Agricultural Library call number (LC only).
071	National Agricultural Library copy statement (LC only).
080	UDC Classification number (given in MONOCLE; given in BNB and MASS if it is available; not given by LC).
081	BNB classification number.
082	DC classification number.
083	DC classification feature (not used by MONOCLE and LC).
086	US Superintendent of Documents number (LC and MONOCLE only).
090	Local library call number.
091	Microfilm shelf location.
100	Main entry—Personal name.
110	Main entry—Corporate name.
111	Main entry—Conference, congress, meeting, etc.
130	Main entry—Uniform title heading (MONOCLE and LC).
200	Title as it appears on the piece.
210	Abbreviated title.
222	Key title (MASS only).
240	Uniform title (LC, BNB and MASS). Collective filing title (MONOCLE).
241	Uniform title (Bible) (MONOCLE). Romanized title (LC) (not used by BNB and MASS).
242	Original title (MONOCLE only).
243	Translated title (MONOCLE). Used for filing Russian or Greek words according to the Roman alphabet. Collective title (BNB) (not used by LC).
244	Romanized title (MONOCLE only).
245	Title.
246	Varying forms of title.
247	Former titles or title variations.
249	Abbreviated periodical title (MONOCLE only).
250	Edition statement.
260	Imprint.
261	Production and release (films).
265	Subscription address.
270	Printer (MONOCLE only).
300	Collation, or physical description of a manuscript.
301	Physical description of visual materials.
302	Item count (number of items in a collection of manuscripts).
303	Unit count (number of containers in which a manuscript collection is housed).
304	Linear footage.
308	Physical description for archival collections.
310	Frequency (LC).
320	Current frequency of publication (MASS). Current frequency control (LC).
321	Former frequency (LC).

330	Publication pattern (LC).
331	Former publication pattern (LC).
350	Price, subscription price or value.
359	Rental price (LC only).
360	Price or value, in local currency (MONOCLE only).
362	Dates and volume designations.
400	Personal author series entry.
410	Corporate author series entry.
411	Conference name series entry.
440	Title series entry (BNB and LC).
	Collective filing title series entry (MONOCLE).
441	Uniform title series entry (MONOCLE only).
442	Original title series entry (MONOCLE only).
443	Translated title series entry (MONOCLE only).
444	Romanized title series entry (MONOCLE only).
445	Title series entry (MONOCLE only).
490	Series statement, untraced, or traced differently.
500	General note.
501	"Bound with" note.
502	Dissertation note.
503	Bibliographic history note.
504	Bibliography note.
505	Contents note.
506	Restrictions on use note.
508	Credits note.
510	Indexing and abstracting coverage note.
511	Alternative ISBN note.
	Cast (of motion picture) note.
512	Alternative ISSN note.
513	Subject note supplementary to the current edition DC classification (BNB only).
515	Explanatory note on dates, volumes, etc.
517	Categories of films for archival collections.
518	Change of control number note.
520	Abstract, annotation or summary.
521	"For children" note.
525	Supplement note.
527	Censorship note for archival collections.
530	Additional physical forms available.
535	Note explaining non-standard forms (MASS).
	Repository (of a manuscript collection) (LC).
541	Provenance.
543	Solicitation information.
545	Title of journal from which a single article, or supplement is taken (MONOCLE).
	Biographical tracings (LC).
546	Language note.
547	Variant title note.
550	Issuing body note.

Bibliographic Record Structures

555	Consolidated indexes (MASS, LC and MONOCLE).
	Finding aids (card indexes to a manuscript collection) (LC).
600	Personal name subject heading.
610	Corporate name subject heading.
611	Conference name subject heading.
630	Uniform title subject heading.
640	Uniform title subject heading (MASS and BNB).
	Collective filing title subject heading (MONOCLE).
641	Individual filing title subject heading (MONOCLE only).
642	Original title subject heading (MONOCLE only).
643	Translated title subject heading (MONOCLE only).
644	Romanized title subject heading (MONOCLE only).
645	Actual title subject heading (MONOCLE and BNB).
650	Topical subject heading.
651	Geographical name subject heading.
652	Political jurisdiction subject heading (specified but not used, by MONOCLE only).
653	Other proper names subject heading (MONOCLE only).
660–663	National Library of Medicine subject headings.
670–673	National Agricultural Library subject headings.
680–681	Local library subject headings.
690	PRECIS descriptors and manipulation codes (BNB and MONOCLE). Local subject headings (LC) (not used by MASS).
691	PRECIS Reference index numbers.
700	Personal name added entry.
710	Corporate name added entry.
711	Conference name added entry.
730	Uniform title added entry (LC only).
740	Uniform title added entry (BNB, MASS).
	Title traced differently (LC).
	Collective filing title added entry (MONOCLE).
741	Individual filing title added entry (MONOCLE only).
742	Original title added entry (MONOCLE only).
743	Translated title added entry (MONOCLE only).
744	Romanized title added entry (MONOCLE only).
745	Actual title added entry (MONOCLE only).
760	Main series entry.
762	Section or subseries entry.
765	Original title, if the periodical in hand is a translation.
767	Translations of a serial.
770	Supplement or special issue.
772	Parent record, when serial in hand is a supplement.
775	Other editions available.
776	Additional physical forms available.
777	"Published with".
780	Previous title of a serial.
785	Subsequent title of a serial.
787	Related title (MASS only).
790	Tracing data.

Automation in Libraries

800	Personal name series added entry.
810	Corporate name series added entry.
811	Conference name series added entry.
840	Series title added entry (BNB and LC).
	Collective series filing title added entry (MONOCLE).
841	Individual series filing title added entry (MONOCLE only).
842	Original series title added entry (MONOCLE only).
843	Translated series title added entry (MONOCLE only).
844	Romanized series title added entry (MONOCLE only).
845	Actual series title added entry (MONOCLE).
850	Holdings, national.
890	Holdings, local.
900–999	These tags are not used by LC.
900	Personal name cross references.
910	Corporate name cross references.
911	Conference name cross references.
940	Uniform title cross references (MASS).
	Collective filing title cross references (MONOCLE).
941	Conventional title cross references (MONOCLE).
942	Original title cross references (MONOCLE).
943	Translated title cross references (MONOCLE).
944	Romanized title cross references (MONOCLE).
945	Title cross references (MONOCLE and MASS).

CHAPTER 6

Listing and Accounting Systems

THE very simplest library housekeeping systems are based upon a series of records arranged in order to form one file. This must be kept up to date by the addition of new information and the deletion of old, and access to it must be possible either for library staff, the general public, or both. More complex systems involve the use of two or more files, or alternatively may require one file to be sorted differently for some stages of the operation of the system. But because simple one-file systems involve the most straightforward data-processing techniques, they are often the area in which libraries first gain experience of mechanized systems. Included in this category of "simple" systems are lists of serials, authority files, and subject indexes of various kinds, and, slightly more complex, accounting systems.

Figure 6.1 shows the basic operations of a very simple computer-based system. It will be seen later that more complex systems may be viewed as variations and elaborations on this simple fundamental theme.

Consider first a batch system working in the off-line mode. The file is updated when new information is added to the existing file by the program. This produces the new or updated file, which is usually also printed. The printed file, or "printout", may be produced either at the same time as the file is updated, or later. Library printouts are often large and take a long time to print. Computing laboratories therefore may arrange for such jobs to be done at an off-peak time, e.g. during a night shift.

The printout is then used in the library to give information about records in the file, until the passage of time and the accumulation of

98   *Automation in Libraries*

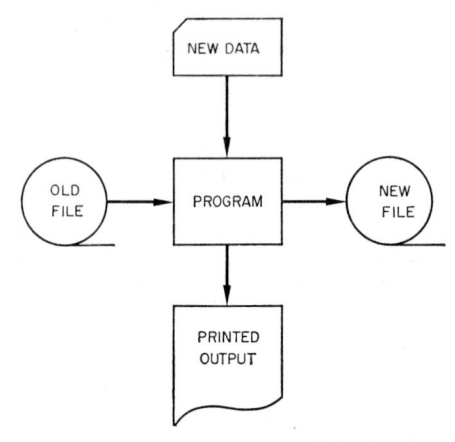

Fig. 6.1. Basic file updating process in an off-line batch mode system.

new records and amendments to existing ones make a re-run of the program necessary. During this time, of course, the printout is gradually getting out of date. This difficulty can be overcome by enabling users to have access to a growing manual file of amendments, or if the file is a large one, by producing one or more supplements to the printout.

Such procedures will be satisfactory only if the volume of updating activity is low, or if it is not always vital that users be supplied with absolutely current information. If current information is required, an on-line system may be needed. This can operate in "real-time", that is, when the state of the file corresponds exactly to the state of the part of the library that the file is describing. Another circumstance in which an on-line real-time system is indicated is when a number of users in different locations all require access to the one up-to-date file. This is the case with airline seat reservation systems, banking and stock exchange systems, and occasionally also with library circulation and cataloguing systems.

Figure 6.2 shows the overall structure of an on-line system. Unit costs are higher with on-line systems than with batch processing but they enable staff to be used more effectively, and, of course, they provide completely up-to-date information. So that if a monetary value can be placed on the improved system effectiveness obtained in this way, an

Listing and Accounting Systems 99

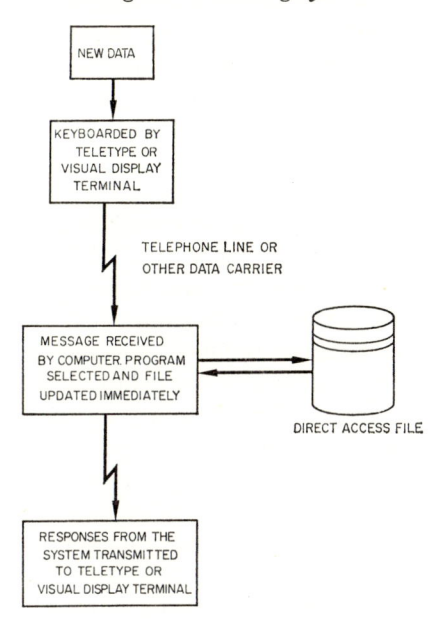

```
        ┌─────────────┐
        │  NEW DATA   │
        └──────┬──────┘
               ↓
        ┌─────────────┐
        │ KEYBOARDED BY│
        │  TELETYPE OR │
        │ VISUAL DISPLAY│
        │   TERMINAL   │
        └──────┬──────┘
               │ TELEPHONE LINE OR
               │ OTHER DATA CARRIER
               ↓
    ┌──────────────────┐         ┌─────────┐
    │ MESSAGE RECEIVED │         │         │
    │ BY COMPUTER PROGRAM│ ←──→  │         │
    │ SELECTED AND FILE │        │         │
    │ UPDATED IMMEDIATELY│       └─────────┘
    └────────┬─────────┘       DIRECT ACCESS FILE
             ↓
    ┌──────────────────┐
    │ RESPONSES FROM THE│
    │ SYSTEM TRANSMITTED│
    │  TO TELETYPE OR  │
    │VISUAL DISPLAY TERMINAL│
    └──────────────────┘
```

FIG. 6.2. Basic file updating process in an on-line real-time system.

on-line real-time system may be shown to be more cost-effective than an off-line system.

Listing and accounting systems seldom merit this expensive treatment, and the systems which are discussed in this chapter all operate in batch mode.

SERIALS LISTING SYSTEM

Libraries commonly include their serials holdings in their main catalogue which will probably be in card form. Entries are typically made under title and subject, with cross references from alternative and earlier titles. Holdings of each title are indicated, often by giving the starting date of the run and indicating any volumes or parts missing. It is not normally possible to include every part received, in particular the most recently received parts, in a conventional public serials catalogue. Locations for each title are indicated, either explicitly, or included as part of the library's call number or shelf mark.

The library Serials Department must, however, keep a full and accurate list of current titles to record individual serial parts as they are received. It must also include ordering and subscription details for each title, and should ideally enable the serials librarian to check for parts which have not arrived within a certain time of their due dates. A variety of visible index filing systems enable the clerical work involved with serials to be carried out quickly and efficiently.

In addition, many libraries make lists of serial titles currently received readily available to their users. This may take the form of a typed and duplicated list, or a photocopy of the visible index files. In some cases, these manually produced lists include the holdings of more than one library, and become union lists for a city or region.

It is possible to divide the data contained in manual serials records and files into two broad categories; that which changes or is liable to change or be superseded quickly—within a week or so—and that which changes or is liable to change only occasionally—perhaps with only a few changes from one year to the next. Examples in the first category are individual serial parts received in the library and the date when each was received, claims made for missing parts and replies received from suppliers. Examples of data in the second category are serial titles currently received, and subscription prices.

Data which changes seldom can conveniently be handled by an off-line system with infrequent updating runs, and may be included in a serials listing system of the type discussed below. Rapidly changing information requires a more complex computer system, discussed in Chapter 7, generally described as a serials accessioning system.

Overall System Description

Figure 6.3 gives an overall view of the operation of a serials listing system. Assuming that a manual file of serials holdings already exists, the first step is to check or edit these manual records. This is to check for and correct errors, to ensure consistency in the records and to mark them, where necessary, for subsequent keypunching. Secondly, the edited manual records are keypunched—that is, converted into a suitable machine-readable form. Punched cards are suitable for this, and in this chapter it is assumed that punched cards are used. But other

Listing and Accounting Systems 101

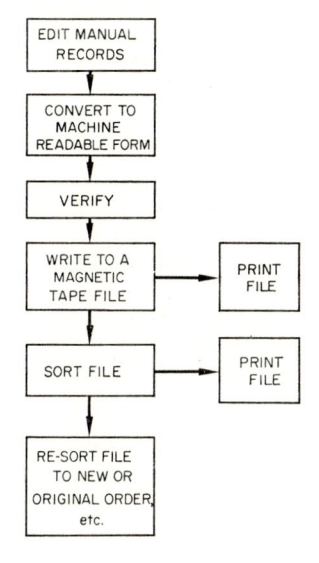

```
┌─────────────┐
│ EDIT MANUAL │
│   RECORDS   │
└──────┬──────┘
       ▼
┌─────────────┐
│ CONVERT TO  │
│   MACHINE   │
│READABLE FORM│
└──────┬──────┘
       ▼
┌─────────────┐
│   VERIFY    │
└──────┬──────┘
       ▼
┌─────────────┐     ┌─────────┐
│ WRITE TO A  │     │  PRINT  │
│  MAGNETIC   │────▶│  FILE   │
│  TAPE FILE  │     └─────────┘
└──────┬──────┘
       ▼
┌─────────────┐     ┌─────────┐
│  SORT FILE  │────▶│  PRINT  │
│             │     │  FILE   │
└──────┬──────┘     └─────────┘
       ▼
┌─────────────┐
│RE-SORT FILE │
│  TO NEW OR  │
│ORIGINAL ORDER│
│     etc.    │
└─────────────┘
```

FIG. 6.3. Generalized flow chart for serials listing system.

media such as punched paper tape or magnetic tape may be used, and are especially appropriate if variable length fields are used.

After the keypunched data has been checked or verified, it is ready for the computer. The holdings records are now contained in a file or "deck" of punched cards which will be read by the computer and written onto a magnetic tape. Essentially all that the computer does in this operation is to transfer a copy of the file onto another file-storage medium—for the data contained in the file of punched cards is not destroyed.

A computer program can now print the data in the magnetic tape file. A layout is chosen which is easy to read, and is as economical as possible with space on the paper. If a printout is needed in a different order, by subject for example, then the magnetic tape file is sorted and then printed again in the new order. It must, of course, be resorted back to its original order before any more new records are added.

Similar procedures hold when the magnetic-tape file is updated. This time the manual records consist only of information about additions,

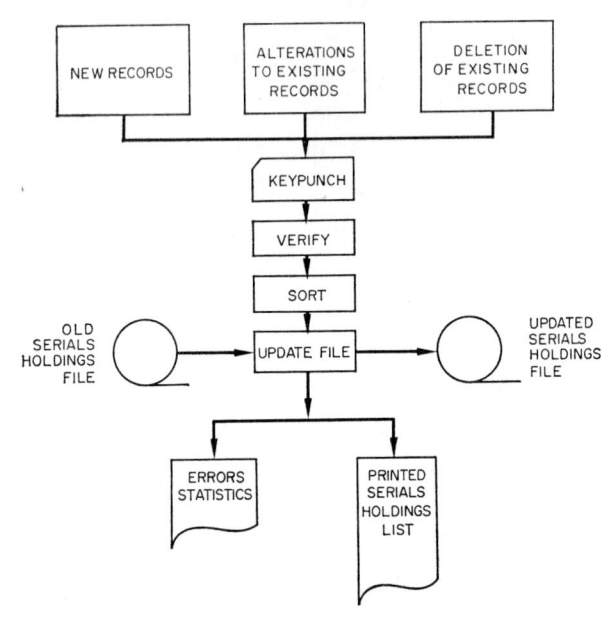

Fig. 6.4. Flow chart for serials listing system.

changes and deletions, rather than the entire file. They must be keypunched and verified as before. But this time the computer adds new records to the file and makes changes to and deletes existing records as instructed. This is, in fact, a straightforward serial file updating procedure as discussed in Chapter 4 on page 49. Figure 6.4 illustrates the system again, this time from the viewpoint of updating an existing file.

Figures 6.5, 6.6 and 6.7 are reproductions of pages from three computer-produced serials lists. Figure 6.5, a page from a holdings list produced by Exeter University Library, is reproduced full size to show the clarity that can be achieved with standard line printer output by means of good layout. The variety of cross references included on this one page shows that bibliographical fullness need not be sacrificed to the computer. The union list, a column from which is reproduced as Fig. 6.6, includes the holdings of a group of nineteen libraries in the Norwich area of England. It is of interest in showing

Temp

TEMPO.
26-28, 30, 32, 33, 36-38, 41,
43-45, 47, 53/54, 57+   780.5

TEMPS MODERNES.
16(177), 1960+   050

TENDANCES.
1, 1959+   054

TENSOR.
NEW SERIES: 18, 1967+   516.83

TEPLOENERGETIKA.
SEE THERMAL ENGINEERING

TERRE, AIR, MER.
56-70, 1931-1938   910.6

TERRESTRIAL MAGNETISM AND
ATMOSPHERIC ELECTRICITY.
53, 1948   530.5
FOR LATER VOLUMES SEE JOURNAL
OF GEOPHYSICAL RESEARCH

TETRAHEDRON.
1, 1957+   547.05

TETRAHEDRON LETTERS.
1959; 1962+   547.05

TEXTILE HISTORY.
1, 1968+   338.47677

THAILAND ILLUSTRATED.
CURRENT ISSUE ONLY

THEATER HEUTE.
1, 1967+   792.05

THEATRE.
1-4, 1878-1880   792.05

THEATRE ARTS MONTHLY.
21-31, 1937-1947   792.05
21(5); 27(1, 3); 30(2) MISSING

THEATRE DE FRANCE.
3-5, 1953-1955   792

THEATRE WORLD.
46-57, 1950-1961   792.05
FEB 1952 MISSING

THEOLOGY.
1, 1920+   205

THEORETICA CHIMICA ACTA.
3, 1965+   540.5

THEORETICAL CHEMICAL ENGINEERING
ABSTRACTS.
2, 1965+   660.5

THEORY OF PROBABILITY AND ITS
APPLICATIONS.
8, 1963+   519.1

THEOSOPHIST.
7, 9-13, 17-25, 31-33,
1885-1912   149.3

THERMAL ENGINEERING
(TEPLOENERGETIKA).
11, 1964+   621.4

THINK.
CURRENT ISSUE ONLY

THREE BANKS REVIEW.
1949+   332.05

TIJDSCHRIFT VOOR ECONOMISCHE EN
SOCIALE GEOGRAFIE.
37, 1946+   910.5
38-39; 41; 44; 47-49; 54-56
INCOMPLETE

TIME.
42-61, 1943-1953; 62(1-15),
1953   050
43(23); 45(21); 46(5); 52(3)
MISSING

TIMES.
1785+   * 072

TIMES, INDEXES.
1790+   072

TIMES, REPORTS OF COMMERCIAL
CASES.
1-46, 1895-1941   L 347.7

TIMES EDUCATIONAL SUPPLEMENT.
1935+   370.5

TIMES LAW REPORTS.
1-66(2), 1884-1950   L 346

TIMES LITERARY SUPPLEMENT.
1902+   805

FIG. 6.5. Sample page from the University of Exeter Library List of Periodicals Holdings.

JOUR

JOURNAL OF MATERIALS SCIENCE
   UEA   V.1, 1966-

JOURNAL OF MATHEMATICAL ANALYSIS AND APPLICATIONS
   UEA   V.1, 1960-

JOURNAL OF MATHEMATICAL PHYSICS
   UEA   V.1, 1960-

JOURNAL OF THE MATHEMATICAL SOCIETY OF JAPAN
   UEA   V.1, 1949/50-

JOURNAL OF MATHEMATICS AND MECHANICS
   UEA   V.6, 1957-

JOURNAL OF MATHEMATICS AND PHYSICS
   UEA   V.29-42, 1950-63 [INCOMPL.];   V.43, 1964-

JOURNAL DE MATHEMATIQUES PURES ET APPLIQUEES
   UEA   V.38, 1959-

JOURNAL OF MECHANICAL ENGINEERING SCIENCE
   NCC   5 YEARS

JOURNAL OF THE MECHANICS AND PHYSICS OF SOLIDS
   UEA   V.1, 1952-

JOURNAL OF MEDICINAL CHEMISTRY
   UEA   V.8, 1965-

JOURNAL OF MEDICAL MICROBIOLOGY
   VIC   V.1, 1968-

JOURNAL OF MEMBRANE BIOLOGY
   UEA   V.1, 1969-

JOURNAL OF METEOROLOGY
   UEA   V.11-18, 1954-61

JOURNAL DE MICROSCOPIE
   JII   V.8, 1969-

   JOURNAL OF MICROSCOPY ..SEE.. JOURNAL OF THE ROYAL MICROSCOPICA
      SOCIETY

   JOURNAL OF THE MINERALOGICAL SOCIETY OF AMERICA ..SEE.. AMERICA
      MINERALOGIST

   JOURNAL OF THE MINISTRY OF AGRICULTURE ..SEE.. AGRICULTURE

JOURNAL OF MOLECULAR BIOLOGY
   JII   V.1, 1959-
   UEA   V.1, 1959-

Fig. 6.6. Sample column from *Periodicals in Libraries of the Norwich area, a finding list*, produced by the University of East Anglia Library. Each page contains two such column.

MUSEUM
  1-, 1948-, BR.

MUSEUM AND ENGLISH JOURNAL OF EDUCATION
  May, July, Oct, 1867; Feb, Mar, Dec, 1868, LO.

MUSIC (SCHOOLS MUSIC ASSOCIATION)
  1-, Oct, 1966-, DR; KE; LC; LO; NO; RE; SO.

MUSIC EDUCATORS JOURNAL
  36 - 39, no. 4, 1949-1953; 41-, 1954-, (*Lacks*: 41, no. 3; 43, no. 4; 44, no. 1; 46, no. 1), RE.
  44, no. 3-, 1958-, (*Incomplete*), LO.
  53, no. 5-, 1967-, BH.

MUSIC IN EDUCATION, formerly MUSIC IN SCHOOLS
  2, no. 24-, Feb, 1939-, (*Lacks*: 6, nos. 60-63, 68-69; 7, nos. 70-73; 8, nos. 82-83, 9, nos. 96-97; 12, nos. 138-139; 13, nos. 142-143, 146-147, 150-151), RE.
  12-, 1948-, NO.
  15, no. 178-, Jan, 1952-, LD.
  17-, 1954-, LV.
  22-, 1958-, LO.
  23, no. 270-27, no. 302, 1959-63, MA.
  25, no. 290-, July 1961-, OX.
  26, no. 297-, Sept, 1962-, NW.
  26, no. 299-, 1963-, SH.
  26, 1963, SW.
  27, no. 301-, May, 1963-, SO.
  28, no. 309-, Sept/Oct, 1964-, DR.
  3 years only, LC.
  2 years only, CA.
  6 months only, HL.

MUSIC IN SCHOOLS. See MUSIC IN EDUCATION, formerly MUSIC IN SCHOOLS

MUSIC TEACHER
  25, no. 3 - 39, Mar, 1946 - 1960; 43-, 1964-, (*Incomplete*), NW.
  27, no. 10-, Oct, 1948-, NO.
  29-33, 1950-54; 35-, 1956-, RE.
  37-, 1958-, (*Lacks*: 37, no. 10, Oct, 1958; 43, nos. 9, 11, Sept, Nov, 1964), KE.
  39, no. 7-, July, 1960-, OX.
  41-, 1962-, LD.
  42, 1963, SW.
  42, no. 10-, Oct 1963-, DR.
  44-, 1965-, SO.
  3 years only, LC.   *(Continued on next page)*

FIG. 6.7. Sample page from *Union List of Periodicals held in Institute of Education Libraries as at 31st July 1968.*

how individual library locations may be handled; one per line underneath the title. Figure 6.7 shows how the use of a computer-controlled phototypesetter materially enhances the legibility of a union list. This particular list records the serial holdings of twenty-three libraries in Institutes of Education in Britain. The programs for compiling and updating the list, and preparing the file for typesetting by a Monophoto typesetter were written at the University of Newcastle upon Tyne as part of a general suite of programs for handling bibliographical records, the Newcastle File Handling System.[1,2,3]

Why Use a Computer?

More effort is involved in preparing the first edition of a computer-produced holdings list than the first edition of a manual list. In most cases the appearance of the computer-produced list will be inferior to that of a manually typed list. But from this point onwards, the computer system begins to show advantages over its manual counterpart.

Amendments to the list are made simply by keyboarding the amendments, whereas with a conventionally typed list, the entire list must be typed and proof-read again. It is possible to print lists (and catalogues of many kinds) by photographing "shingled" entries on cards or slips of paper, and then it is necessary to retype only the alterations, but of course, there remains the very considerable job of inserting the amendments in their correct places. The more frequently a list is updated, the greater the advantage a computer system has over a manual system. The cost of the systems and programming work is then spread over more editions of the list, so reducing the systems cost to be charged to each.

But a computer-produced listing system really comes into its own when something more must be done to the entries than just listing them in one order. If they are to be sorted and then printed in one or more different sequences, if sections of the file are to be printed out separately, if special purpose listings are needed with less information per entry, or with each entry laid out differently, then all this can be provided by the computer system for the cost of the extra programming and computer time needed.

Listing and Accounting Systems

A principle emerges from this, that if little is required of a computer-based system, it will yield little benefit. But if more is required, then the benefits are correspondingly greater.

Detailed System Description

RECORD FORMAT

A typical record format for a serials holdings list system has already been discussed (see page 62), and Fig. 6.8 shows the two punched cards used to input details of one new title in the Norwich Union list system. Changes to this format may be needed to cope with different system requirements, some of which are discussed here.

Three different kinds of input data have been mentioned already; Additions, Changes and Deletions. Input records can be coded to indicate their type. A simple one-character mnemonic code suffices for this, thus: A—addition record, C—change record, D—deletion record. Alternatively it is possible to write the update program without this specific identification of record type. For if a new title is being added to the file, then the same title will not already be on the file. However, if a change is being made to the record for an existing title, then that title must of necessity already be on the file, and will be found by the update program. On balance it is probably better to code input records explicitly, and so obtain greater power to detect errors in the file and in the program.

Filing serial titles in alphabetical order can present problems (filing rules for library catalogues are discussed in more detail later in Chapter 10). For serial titles, however, the main problem is to omit initial articles from consideration when filing, and perhaps also to pass over articles, prepositions and conjunctions that occur in the middle of titles. It causes users little inconvenience if initial articles are omitted entirely, so that, for example, the entry for
The Times
may be written simply as
Times
and filed as such. This can be seen in the Exeter University list in Fig. 6.5. Non-significant words in the middle of titles are not considered for filing purposes in the Norwich Union list, illustrated in Fig. 6.6.

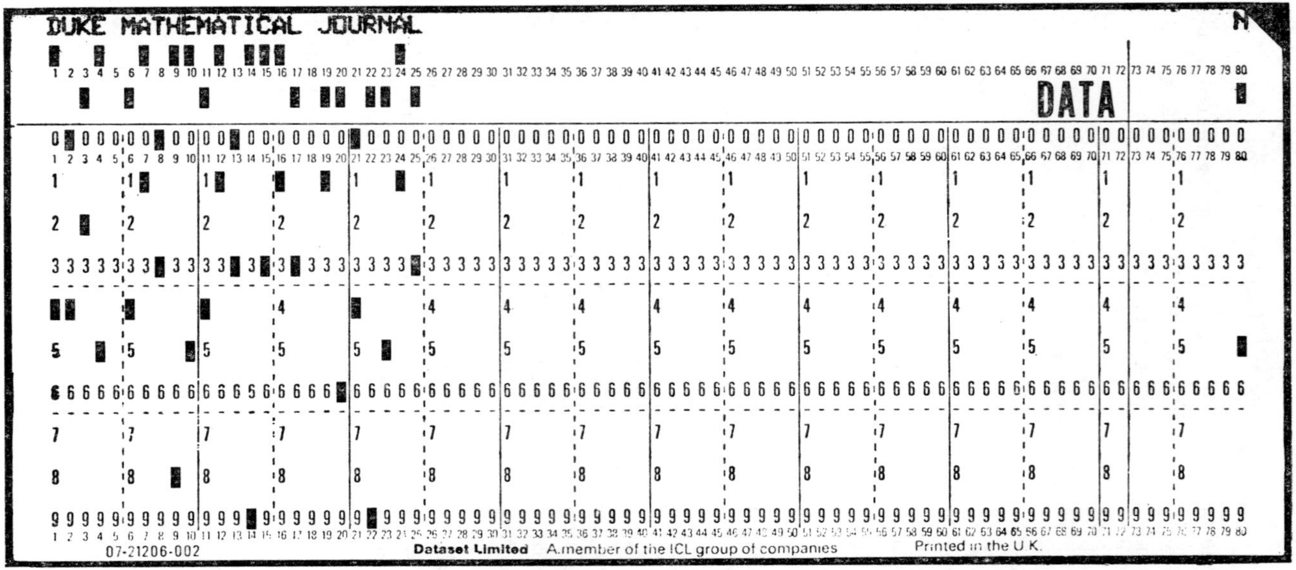

Fig. 6.8a.

Fig. 6.8. Punched cards to input data for one title in the Norwich Union List. The upper card contains the title of the journal, the lower contains the Holdings of one location.

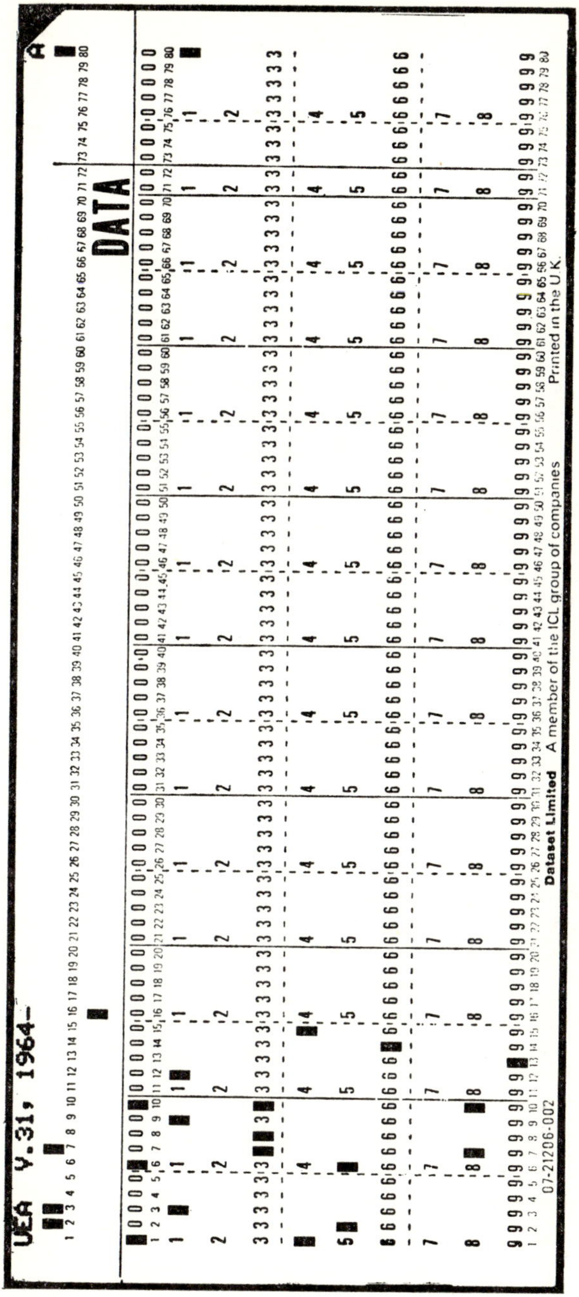

Fig. 6.8b.

Although the order of titles in the Norwich list is determined by manual filing of the input cards, this particular filing sophistication can be programmed by creating a special filing field in the record, which contains the title exactly as it is to be filed. Thus for

Journal of the mechanics and physics of solids

this filing field will contain

Journal mechanics physics solids

The full title is kept in a separate title field and the filing title in the filing title field. This enables the full title to be printed between *Journal of mechanical engineering science* and *Journal of medicinal chemistry*. The filing title field may be set up either manually, or by program. In the latter case, it is a fairly straightforward task of copying the full title into the filing title field, but eliminating all non-significant words contained in a special list.

Another simpler approach to filing titles is to by-pass the problem completely by assigning to each record a running serial or identification number. Filing then becomes a simple matter of arranging entries in identification number order. This method has been used by the libraries of the Atomic Energy Research Establishment at Harwell[4,5] and of the Woodstock Agricultural Research Centre, Shell Research Ltd., Sittingbourne, Kent.[6] Figure 6.9 shows a portion of the master tape printout from the Sittingbourne list, in which the identification number appears (it is not printed in the main holdings list). Note that gaps are left in the number sequence to allow new titles to be inserted into the correct position.

Some of the lists already mentioned include subscription information. This is appropriate for an infrequently updated file, data in which also changes infrequently. Accounting details are discussed in the next section of this chapter and subscription information can be included in the record structure simply by the addition of a few fixed length fields. The Harwell list includes the following fields for subscription details:

Period covered by multi-year subscriptions
Subscription rate per copy
Number of copies taken
Supplier

PAGE 3

	FREQUENCY	COST	SUPPLIER	NO.COPIES	DISCOUNT
A 52000 AGRICULTURAL INSTITUTE REVIEW. U15(1960)-	BM	0 17 6	DAWSON	1	5
A 53000 AGRICULTURAL METEOROLOGY. 001(1964)-003(1966)	BM	0 0 0	000000	0	0
A 57000 AGRICULTURAL RESEARCH (USDA). 005(1956)-	M	0 11 0	DAWSON	1	5
A 63000 AGRICULTURAL SITUATION (USDA). U40(1956)-	M	0 8 0	DAWSON	1	5
A 66000 AGRICULTURAL AND VETERINARY CHEMICALS. 001(1960)-	SM	3 0 0	DAWSON	1	5
A 67000 AGRICULTURE (MAFF). 056(1949)-	M	1 0 0	DAWSON	1	5
A 69000 AGRONOMIE TROPICALE. 014(1959)-021(1966)	M	0 0 0	000000	0	0
A 70000 AGRONOMY JOURNAL. 052(1960)-	BM	6 0 0	DAWSON	1	5
A 72000 AIR AND WATER POLLUTION. 004(1961)-009(1966)	M	0 0 0	000000	0	0
A 79000 AMERICAN DOCUMENTATION. U07(1956)-	Q	7 12 0	DAWSON	1	5

FIG. 6.9. A page from the master tape printout, Sittingbourne Laboratories' list of serials holdings.

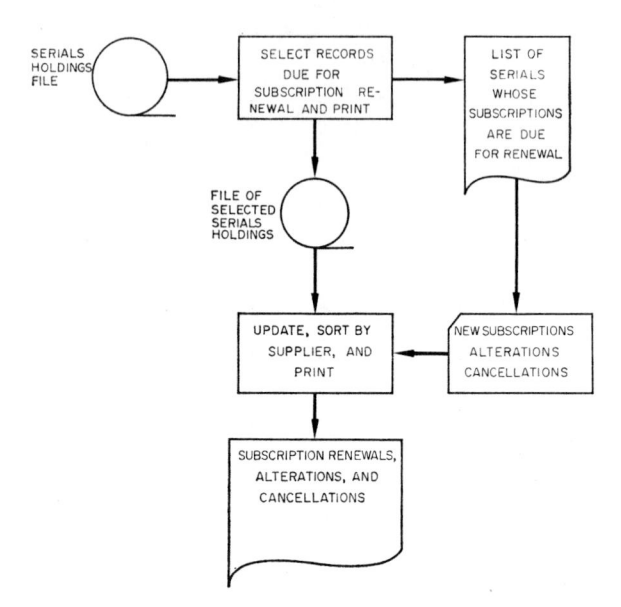

FIG. 6.10. Renewal of serials subscriptions.

Most subscriptions fall due at the end of each calendar year, although if subscriptions are taken out to last for 2 or 3 years, preferential rates may often be obtained. The main serials holdings list must therefore first be scanned to select those titles due for renewal (see Fig. 6.10). Records selected are printed for checking by library staff. This gives an occasion to review the library's current subscriptions, to cancel titles no longer required and to initiate new subscriptions. If multi-year subscriptions are not used, then this preliminary selection process is unnecessary, and the main holdings list can be used for reviewing subscriptions.

Any changes are keypunched and used to update the machine file of subscriptions due for renewal. This now includes three categories of record; subscriptions to be renewed, subscriptions to be terminated, and new subscriptions to be started. The file is sorted into supplier order and printed to provide renewals, cancellations, etc., of the library's serials subscriptions.

Listing and Accounting Systems 113

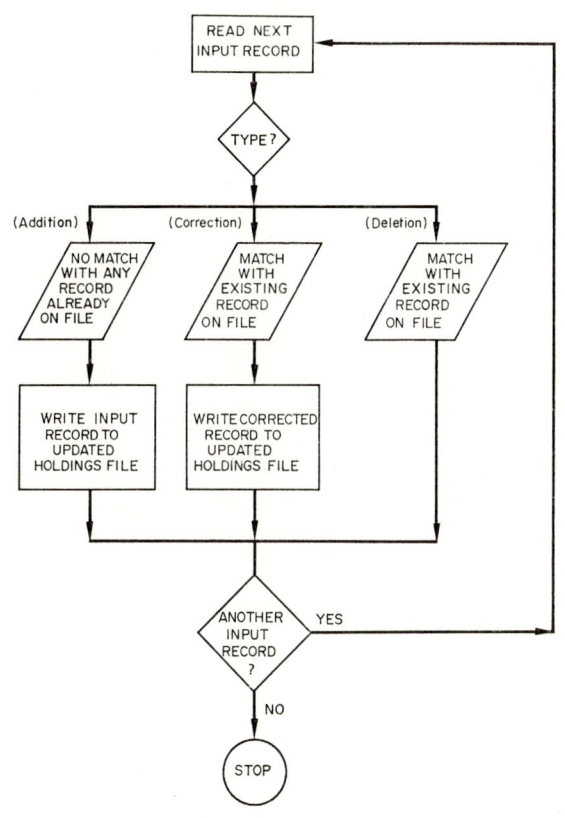

Fig. 6.11. Updating the serials holdings file.

Program logic

Figure 6.11 shows the general structure of the updating program. Figure 6.4 gives the complete system flowchart in which the new records, sorted into the same order as the main holdings file, are processed in sequence as illustrated in Fig. 4.5 on page 49. Input records and records on the main file are matched by identification number, otherwise by title.

Addition records should find no match on the file. The new record is written to the updated holdings file. Correction records should find a match on the file—a record with the same identification number or title. The correction is made, and the corrected record is written to the updated holdings file. Deletion records should also find a match on the file, but in this case, no record is written to the updated file. If there is another input record ready to be processed then the whole procedure is repeated; if not, the updating is finished and program stops.

AUTHORITY FILES AND SUBJECT INDEXES

Although very different from lists of serials holdings in content and use, computer-based systems which produce printed authority files (such as lists of subject headings) and subject indexes to classification schemes are very similar indeed to the former systems as far as structure and operation are concerned. In both cases the fundamental data-processing task is to create a machine-readable file, update it from time to time, perhaps sort it, and then print it in a specified format. As far as the logic of the system is concerned, it makes no difference whether the data consists of serial titles, subject headings, or class numbers.

Again, the same criteria for the suitability of a computer system apply. The contents of the file do not change rapidly, the file must be updated from time to time, and it is desirable to produce a number of printed copies of the file. In the case of an authority file, which is used daily in a cataloguing department, problems may arise in connection with the frequency of updating. Additions and changes are likely to be made daily, and it is desirable that every cataloguer who has a copy of the printed file should also be given information about all additions and changes.

This problem is the same as that encountered in connection with updating library catalogues. Additions and changes are made daily, and it is desirable that every copy of the catalogue should contain them. It is apparent that a card file is really a very efficient medium for storing this kind of data, except that it is difficult to maintain multiple copies of a card file. In a cataloguing department, additions and changes to a computer-based authority file can be notified to every holder of the printed list by distributing copies of the input punched cards, or manual input documents. Alterations can then be made by hand to each list. But for the catalogue of a large library, where the additions will be numerous and where the printed copies may be widely scattered, the task of updating assumes rather different proportions. Solutions to this updating problem are discussed in Chapter 10, but it should be mentioned here that the only really satisfactory solution is the very expensive one of having an on-line real-time system. This really is a matter of using the proverbial sledge hammer to crack the library nut.

Many libraries have produced authority files and subject indexes by computer, and because of their relative simplicity, the introduction of this kind of system now tends not to be reported in the literature. An early project undertaken at Loughborough University of Technology was a subject index to the DC classified catalogue,[7] followed shortly afterwards by a UDC subject index in the library of the City University, London.[8,9] A sample page from the latter is illustrated in Fig. 6.12.

More recently, a notable and valuable piece of work in this field has been the production of a classified index to the seventh edition of the Library of Congress list of subject headings.[10] The main subject heading list in its seventh edition was typeset from a magnetic tape by a computer-controlled phototypesetter. Records on this tape are in MARC format, and it was a fairly straightforward data-processing task to sort by LC class number those subject headings for which a class number is provided in the main subject heading list. A second volume produced as a result of this work is an alphabetical list of subject headings with their corresponding LC class numbers, a good example of the ease with which extra products can be obtained from a mechanised system with only very little extra effort. A sample page from the classified list is illustrated in Fig. 6.13.

ACCOUNTING SYSTEMS

Accounting was one of the first applications for data processing and computing machinery. Manual and semi-mechanized accounting procedures for any but the smallest units remain cumbersome, error-prone, and slow, and most computer manufacturers now sell package programs for standard procedures. Most libraries are part of a larger

A.L.—E

```
                                                              PAGE   35
      371.212.233          SOCIAL CLASS: SELECTION PRINCIPLES: EDUCATION
      371.212.72           FAILURE: GRAMMAR SCHOOL EDUCATION
      371.212.73           EARLY LEAVING: SCHOOL EDUCATION
      371.212.73           LEAVING SCHOOL EARLY
      371.212.8            SCHOOL LEAVING: EDUCATION
    P 371.214.431: 372     CURRICULUM, SIXTH-FORM
      371.255              SIXTH FORMS: CLASSES: EDUCATION
      371.255: 372         SIXTH FORM CURRICULUM
      371.26               EDUCATIONAL MEASUREMENT
    P 371.262.7'           CERTIFICATE OF SECONDARY EDUCATION
      371.262.7            CERTIFICATE OF SECONDARY EDUCATION
    P 371.27               COMMON ENTRANCE EXAMINATION
      371.27               EXAMINATIONS: EDUCATION
    P 371.27               EXAMINATIONS, SCHOOL
      371.27*5             SCIENCE: COMMON ENTRANCE EXAMINATION
    P 371.27*71            LATIN, COMMON ENTRANCE: EDUCATION
      371.274/.276         A-LEVELS: EXAMINATIONS: EDUCATION
      371.274/.276         EXAMINATIONS, SCHOOL CERTIFICATES
      371.279.6            EXAMINATION QUESTIONS: EXAMINATIONS: SCHOOL ORGANIZATION: EDUCATION
      371.279.6            EXAMINATION QUESTIONS: EXAMINATIONS: SCHOOL ORGANIZATION: EDUCATION
    B 371.279.7            EXAMINATION MARKS: EDUCATION
      371.3                TEACHING METHODS: EDUCATION
    B 371.3                TEACHING METHODS: EDUCATION
      371.3                TEACHING METHODS: EDUCATION SYSTEM: EDUCATION
      371.3                TEACHING METHODS: EDUCATION SYSTEM: EDUCATION
      371.3                TEAM TEACHING: TEACHING METHODS
      371.315: 510         MATHEMATICS, TEACHING METHODS
      371.315: 510         MATHEMATICS, TEACHING METHODS
      371.315: 510         TEACHING METHODS, MATHEMATICS
      371.315: 530         PHYSICS, TEACHING METHODS
      371.315: 530         PHYSICS, TEACHING METHODS
    P 371.315.7            GROUP LEARNING: EDUCATION
    P 371.315.7            LANGUAGE LABORATORIES: EDUCATION
    B 371.315.7'           PROGRAMMED INSTRUCTION: TEACHING METHODS: EDUCATION
    P 371.315.7'           PROGRAMMED LEARNING: EDUCATION
      371.315.7            PROGRAMMED LEARNING: TEACHING METHODS
    B 371.315.7'           PROGRAMMED LEARNING: TEACHING METHODS: EDUCATION
    B 371.315.7            PROGRAMMED TEXTS: TEACHING METHODS: EDUCATION
      371.315.71 600       PROGRAMMED INSTRUCTION, INDUSTRY
      371.322.6            STUDY, SYSTEMATIC: WORK OF THE STUDENT:
                             ORGANIZATION OF EDUCATIONAL SYSTEM
      371.322.6            STUDY GUIDANCE: WORK OF THE STUDENT: ORGANIZATION OF EDUCATIONAL SYSTEM
      371.33               RADIO: TEACHING METHODS
      371.335              EDUCATIONAL TELEVISION: TEACHING METHODS
      371.335              TELEVISION, EDUCATIONAL: TEACHING METHODS
      371.335              VISUAL AIDS: TEACHING
      371.34               MACHINES, IN TEACHING
      371.4                EDUCATIONAL SYSTEMS: EDUCATION
      371.48               EDUCATION, SPECIAL METHODS: EDUCATIONAL SYSTEMS: EDUCATION
    B 371.67               TEACHING EQUIPMENT: EDUCATION
    B 371.67               TRAINING EQUIPMENT: EDUCATION
      371.68               AUDIO-VISUAL AIDS: EDUCATIONAL AIDS: ORGANISATION OF EDUCATION
      371.68               LANGUAGE LABORATORIES: AUDIO-VISUAL AIDS: TEACHING AIDS
      371.684/.687         BROADCASTING: EDUCATIONAL AIDS: EDUCATION
      371.684              RADIO: AUDIOVISUAL AIDS: EDUCATIONAL AIDS: EDUCATION
    P 371.686              FILM AS TEACHING AID
      371.686              FILMS: AUDIO-VISUAL AIDS: EDUCATIONAL AIDS
      371.686              PROJECTORS, OVERHEAD: AUDIO-VISUAL AIDS: TEACHING AIDS
      371.686: 778.2       OVERHEAD PROJECTORS, TEACHING AIDS
      371.686.778          PROJECTORS, OVERHEAD, TEACHING AIDS
```

FIG. 6.12. Sample page from the classified sequence of the UDC subject index produced at The City University, London.

organization which will quite probably employ a computer-based accounting system. So that in many instances, the librarian need not be concerned with the minutiae of accounting. This is right and proper. Some libraries, however, have felt the need for their own separate accounts, as an aid in distributing the library book fund evenly among many competing claims.

When a library automates its ordering functions (discussed in detail in Chapter 9) accounting procedures are usually also included. But it

QC463 — QC761

QC463	KERR CELL SHUTTERS	QC605	STORAGE BATTERIES — ADDITIVES
QC463	KERR EFFECT	QC607	OHM'S LAW
QC463.H9	HYDROCARBONS — SPECTRA	QC607-611	ELECTRIC CONDUCTIVITY
QC465	SPECTROSCOPE / physics	QC611	CORBINO EFFECT
QC465	SPECTROGRAPH / general spectroscopy	QC611	ELECTRIC INSULATORS AND INSULATION / physics
QC467	MONOCHROMATOR	QC611	ELECTRIC RESISTANCE
QC467	SPECTROPHOTOMETER	QC611	ELECTRIC CONDUCTORS / physics
QC467	STARK EFFECT	QC611	HALL EFFECT
QC475	RADIATION	QC611	PHOTOELECTRICITY / electric conductivity
QC476	GEIGER-MZLLER COUNTERS	QC611	SUPERCONDUCTIVITY
QC476	PHOSPHORS	QC615	VOLTAMETER / physics
QC476	VACUUM-TUBES / radiation	QC618	ELECTROMOTIVE FORCE
QC477	FLUORESCENCE	QC618	POLARIZATION (ELECTRICITY) / physics
QC478	PHOSPHORESCENCE / optics	QC621	BENEDICKS EFFECT
QC481	X-RAYS	QC621	THERMOELECTRICITY
QC481	X-RAYS — APPARATUS AND SUPPLIES / physics	QC621	THOMSON EFFECT
QC482	X-RAYS — SCATTERING	QC623	ELECTRIC CURRENTS — HEATING EFFECTS
QC482	X-RAYS — DIFFRACTION	QC631-645	ELECTRODYNAMICS
QC483	ELECTRIC RADIATION	QC631-8	INDUCTION (ELECTRICITY) / electromagnetic
QC484	BLACKBODY RADIATION	QC638	INDUCTANCE
QC485	COSMIC RAYS	QC638	MUTUAL INDUCTANCE
QC485	LE BON'S RAYS	QC638	RESISTANCE-COILS
QC485	N-RAYS	QC638	SELF-INDUCTANCE
QC490	CHERENKOV RADIATION	QC641	ELECTRIC CURRENTS, ALTERNATING / theory
QC490	GAMMA RAYS	QC643	CORONA (ELECTRICITY)
QC495	COLORS — ANALYSIS	QC645	INDUCTION COILS
QC495	COLORIMETRY	QC655	ELECTRIC RESONATORS / electric waves
QC495	COLOR / physics	QC661	ELECTRIC FILTERS
QC495	COLORS / physics	QC661	OSCILLATIONS / electric waves
QC495.Y	YELLOW / color	QC661	WAVE GUIDES
QC501-721	ELECTRICITY	QC661-5	ELECTRIC WAVES
QC514-515	ELECTRICIANS / physics	QC661-675	ELECTROMAGNETIC THEORY
QC516-517	ELECTRICITY — EARLY WORKS TO 1850	QC665	COHERER / physics
QC523	ELECTRICITY — JUVENILE LITERATURE	QC665	ELECTRIC WAVES — DAMPING
QC527	ELECTRICITY — EXPERIMENTS / popular works	QC671	ABERRATION / physics
QC529	ELECTRICITY — TABLES, ETC.	QC675	MAGNETO-OPTICS
QC532	ELECTRICITY — PROBLEMS, EXERCISES, ETC.	QC680	QUANTUM ELECTRODYNAMICS
QC533-4	ELECTRICITY — EXPERIMENTS / study and teaching	QC701-3	ELECTRIC ACTION OF POINTS
QC534	ELECTRICITY — LABORATORY MANUALS	QC701-715	ELECTRIC DISCHARGES
QC535	ELECTRIC MEASUREMENTS / physics	QC702	ELECTRIC LEAKAGE
QC535	ELECTRONIC MEASUREMENTS / physics	QC702	IONIZATION
QC536	AMPERES	QC702-721	IONIZATION OF GASES
QC536	ELECTRIC UNITS	QC702-721	IONS / physics
QC537	ELECTRIC STANDARDS	QC703	ELECTRIC SPARK
QC541	ELECTRIC LABORATORIES / physics	QC703	EXPLODING WIRE PHENOMENA
QC543-4	ELECTRIC APPARATUS AND APPLIANCES / scientific apparatus	QC705	ELECTRIC ARC
		QC711	CANAL RAYS
QC543-4	ELECTRIC APPARATUS AND APPLIANCES — CATALOGS / scientific apparatus	QC711	CATHODE RAYS
		QC711	ELECTRIC DISCHARGES THROUGH GASES
QC544	CYCLOTRON	QC711	PLASMA (IONIZED GASES)
QC544.A5	AMMETER	QC711	PROTONS / electric discharges
QC544.C3	CATHODE RAY TUBES	QC715	PHOTOELECTRIC CELLS
QC544.C7	ELECTRIC COILS / physics	QC715	PHOTOELECTRICITY / electric discharges
QC544.E3	ELECTRODYNAMOMETER	QC717	ION FLOW DYNAMICS
QC544.E4	ELECTROMETER	QC721	ALPHA RAYS
QC544.E6	ELECTROPHORUS	QC721	ATOMS / disintegration
QC544.G2	GALVANOMETER	QC721	AUGER EFFECT
QC544.P5	PHONIC WHEEL	QC721	BECQUEREL RAYS
QC544.P8	POTENTIOMETER	QC721	DELTA RAYS
QC544.V3	AMPLIFIERS, VACUUM-TUBE	QC721	DEUTERONS — SCATTERING
QC544.V3	VACUUM-TUBES / electric apparatus	QC721	ELECTRONS — DIFFRACTION
QC571-595	ELECTROSTATICS	QC721	ELECTRONS
QC573	ELECTRIC MACHINES	QC721	ELECTRONS — SCATTERING
QC577	ELECTROCAPILLARY PHENOMENA	QC721	NEUTRONS — DIFFRACTION
QC581	ELECTRIC CHARGE AND DISTRIBUTION	QC721	POLONIUM / radioactivity
QC581	INDUCTION (ELECTRICITY) / electrostatic	QC721	RADIUM / physical properties
QC581	VOLTA EFFECT	QC721	RADIOTHORIUM
QC585	DIELECTRICS	QC721	THORIUM / radioactivity
QC587	CONDENSERS (ELECTRICITY)	QC751	MAGNETISM — EARLY WORKS TO 1800
QC589	ELECTRIC CAPACITY	QC751-761	MAGNETISM — EXPERIMENTS
QC595	FERROELECTRICITY	QC751-771	MAGNETISM
QC595	PYRO- AND PIEZO-ELECTRICITY	QC757	MAGNETS
QC601	ELECTRIC CIRCUITS	QC760	ELECTROMAGNETS
QC601-641	ELECTRIC CURRENTS	QC760	ELECTROMAGNETISM
QC603	CONCENTRATION CELLS / physics	QC761	ALLOYS / magnetic induction
QC603	POLARIZATION (ELECTRICITY) / physics	QC761	HYSTERESIS
QC603	SELENIUM CELLS	QC761	MAGNETIC TESTING
QC603	STANDARD CELLS	QC761	MAGNETIC INDUCTION
QC603-5	ELECTRIC BATTERIES	QC761	MAGNETIC MATERIALS / physics
QC605	STORAGE BATTERIES	QC761	MAGNETOSTRICTION

FIG. 6.13. Sample page from *Classified Library of Congress Subject Headings.* Edited by J. G. Williams *et al.*, Marcel Dekker Inc., 1972.

is possible to develop a computer-based accounting system without including the considerably more complex bibliographic data required to place an order for a book. Such an accounting system has been operational in the City University library since 1968[11] and in Queen's University, Belfast, since 1971.

Overall System Description

A library receives a sum of money each year, with which it must purchase books, journals and other library materials, divided fairly among the various subjects or departments in the library. Some money will be reserved also for such special purposes as binding, purchasing duplicate copies, adding to special collections, etc. Salaries, equipment and capital expenditure are usually treated separately.

This money (termed the "book fund" or sometimes the "book grant") is therefore divided for accounting purposes into a number of sections, funds or accounts, each of which is identified with a name and convenient code. Each purchase made by the library must be charged to one fund, and it is the purpose of the accounting system to keep a record of all expenditure from each fund, and from time to time to provide summaries of the state of each fund to assist the acquisitions librarian in his task of controlling the library's expenditure.

Some simple arithmetical computations are, of course, required in this work. They are not difficult for human beings, but rather tedious by reason of their number. And human arithmetic (even when assisted by desk calculators) is notorious for its inaccuracy when dealing with accounts.

A computer system has the great advantage of reducing error by requiring, in most instances, just one keyboarding of financial data. Once this has been input correctly to the system, it stays there correctly. This aspect of computer systems, the once-and-for-all keyboarding of input data, features again and again in library applications. Once the data has been input correctly, no more proof-reading is required. The computer's speed is also relevant here, for it enables financial statements to be prepared much more frequently than with a manual system, thereby making possible closer and better financial control.

Listing and Accounting Systems 119

		10/07/72		SUMMARY OF UNIVERSITY ACCOUNT BALANCES		
	DEPARTMENT		ACCOUNT	FREE BALANCE	ACTUAL BALANCE	OUTSTANDING ORDERS
LIBRARY	(EDUCATION	)	D/-PE-LY-	0.00	0.00	0.00
LIBRARY	(ENGLISH	)	D/-PF-LB-	464.78CR	464.78CR	0.00
LIBRARY	(ENGLISH	)	D/-PF-LP-	3.90DB	3.90DB	0.00
LIBRARY	(ENGLISH	)	D/-PF-LY-	0.00	0.00	0.00
LIBRARY	(FRENCH	)	D/-PG-LB-	561.29CR	582.64CR	21.35
LIBRARY	(FRENCH	)	D/-PG-LP-	16.50DB	16.50DB	0.00
LIBRARY	(FRENCH	)	D/-PG-LY-	0.00	0.00	0.00
LIBRARY	(GERMAN	)	D/-PH-LB-	228.29CR	231.14CR	2.85
LIBRARY	(GERMAN	)	D/-PH-LP-	23.23DB	23.23DB	0.00
LIBRARY	(GERMAN	)	D/-PH-LY-	1.75DB	1.75DB	0.00
LIBRARY	(GREEK	)	D/-PJ-LB-	266.75CR	287.14CR	20.39
LIBRARY	(GREEK	)	D/-PJ-LP-	0.00	0.00	0.00
LIBRARY	(GREEK	)	D/-PJ-LY-	0.00	0.00	0.00
LIBRARY	(HISTORY	)	D/-PK-LB-	298.43CR	298.73CR	0.30
LIBRARY	(HISTORY	)	D/-PK-LP-	0.60DB	0.60DB	0.00
LIBRARY	(HISTORY	)	D/-PK-LY-	0.00	0.00	0.00
LIBRARY	(HIST & PHIL OF SCIENCE	)	D/-PL-LB-	56.24DB	27.61DB	28.63
LIBRARY	(HIST & PHIL OF SCIENCE	)	D/-PL-LP-	59.35DB	59.35DB	0.00
LIBRARY	(HIST & PHIL SCIENCE	)	D/-PL-LY-	0.00	0.00	0.00
LIBRARY	(LATIN	)	D/-PN-LB-	112.84CR	112.84CR	0.00
LIBRARY	(LATIN	)	D/-PN-LP-	3.46DB	3.46DB	0.00
LIBRARY	(LATIN	)	D/-PN-LY-	0.00	0.00	0.00
LIBRARY	(LIBRARY STUDIES	)	D/-PP-LB-	51.27CR	52.12CR	0.85
LIBRARY	(LIBRARY STUDIES	)	D/-PP-LP-	5.20DB	5.20DB	0.00
LIBRARY	(LIBRARY SCHOOL	)	D/-PP-LY-	0.00	0.00	0.00
LIBRARY	(MEDIAEVAL FRENCH	)	D/-PQ-LB-	0.00	0.00	0.00
LIBRARY	(MEDIAEVAL FRENCH	)	D/-PQ-LP-	0.00	0.00	0.00
LIBRARY	(MEDIAEVAL FRENCH	)	D/-PQ-LY-	0.00	0.00	0.00
LIBRARY	(MUSIC	)	D/-PR-LB-	326.45DB	326.45DB	0.00
LIBRARY	(MUSIC	)	D/-PR-LP-	15.97DB	15.97DB	0.00
LIBRARY	(MUSIC	)	D/-PR-LY-	2.03DB	2.03DB	0.00
LIBRARY	(PHILOSOPHY	)	D/-PS-LB-	360.14CR	370.92CR	10.78
LIBRARY	(PHILOSOPHY	)	D/-PS-LP-	0.00	0.00	0.00
LIBRARY	(PHILOSOPHY	)	D/-PS-LY-	0.00	0.00	0.00
LIBRARY	(SCHOLASTIC PHILOSOPHY	)	D/-PT-LB-	152.96DB	133.56DB	19.40
LIBRARY	(SCHOLASTIC PHILOSOPHY	)	D/-PT-LP-	0.00	0.00	0.00
LIBRARY	(SCHOLASTIC PHILOSOPHY	)	D/-PT-LY-	0.00	0.00	0.00
LIBRARY	(SOCIAL ANTHROPOLOGY	)	D/-PU-LB-	97.12DB	82.55DB	14.57
LIBRARY	(SOCIAL ANTHROPOLOGY	)	D/-PU-LP-	2.93DB	2.93DB	0.00
LIBRARY	(SOCIAL ANTHROPOLOGY	)	D/-PU-LY-	0.00	0.00	0.00
LIBRARY	(SPANISH	)	D/-PV-LB-	113.55CR	118.95CR	5.40
LIBRARY	(SPANISH	)	D/-PV-LP-	4.00DB	4.00DB	0.00
LIBRARY	(SPANISH	)	D/-PV-LY-	0.00	0.00	0.00
LIBRARY	(SLAVONIC STUDIES	)	D/-PW-LB-	250.51CR	268.79CR	18.28
LIBRARY	(SLAVONIC STUDIES	)	D/-PW-LP-	0.00	0.00	0.00
LIBRARY	(SLAVONIC STUDIES	)	D/-PW-LY-	0.00	0.00	0.00
LIBRARY	(SEMITIC STUDIES	)	D/-PX-LB-	514.03CR	523.53CR	9.50
LIBRARY	(SEMITIC STUDIES	)	D/-PX-LP-	0.00	0.00	0.00
LIBRARY	(SEMITIC STUDIES	)	D/-PX-LY-	0.00	0.00	0.00
LIBRARY	(PALAEOGRAPHY	)	D/-PY-LB-	201.24CR	201.24CR	0.00
LIBRARY	(PALAEOGRAPHY	)	D/-PY-LP-	0.00	0.00	0.00
LIBRARY	(PALAEOGRAPHY	)	D/-PY-LY-	0.00	0.00	0.00
BURSAR'S OFFICE	(TEMPORARY HEADER	)	D/-QD-LB-	0.00	0.00	0.00
LIBRARY	(AERO ENGINEERING	)	D/-RC-LB-	19.04CR	32.29CR	13.25
LIBRARY	(AERO ENGINEERING	)	D/-RC-LP-	55.83DB	55.83DB	0.00
LIBRARY	(AERO ENGINEERING	)	D/-RC-LY-	0.00	0.00	0.00
LIBRARY	(ARCHITECTURE	)	D/-RD-LB-	35.08CR	35.41CR	0.33

Fig. 6.14. Summary statement of accounts, Queen's University Library, Belfast.

An accounting system will typically provide two kinds of financial statement; transactions grouped by book fund and transactions grouped by supplier. In each case, summary statements and detailed listings of individual purchases may be provided. Summary statements will be produced as frequently as possible, for the great advantage of a computer system over a manual system lies in its ability to give frequent and up-to-date statements of this kind. Individual transactions will be listed from time to time, and may be cumulated to facilitate reference back to old orders. A variety of statistical analyses of trends is, of course, also possible.

In a summary statement of accounts, three figures are given for each fund; the actual balance, the amount of any outstanding orders not yet paid for, and the free balance. The free balance is the actual balance that will be left in the account, after the outstanding orders have been paid for. This is illustrated in Fig. 6.14, which shows part of the fortnightly summary statement produced in Queen's University Library.

Figure 6.15 is a detailed statement of account for one of the Queen's University Library funds. It lists the date, invoice number, supplier, amount and in some cases the library order number also, for each purchase from that account during a period of one month. A summary statement is included at the bottom.

Detailed System Description

Figure 6.16 shows the operation of an accounting system of the kind just described. Its similarity to Fig. 6.4 should be noted: both are basic and straightforward data processing operations.

The magnetic tape accounts file lies at the heart of the system. This file is in book fund order, arranged either by fund code or by fund name. For each fund, an historical list of transactions is retained, probably extending back to the start of the current financial year. In addition, the three figures required for the summary statements of account are also held.

New orders must be input to the system, along with details of cancellations, alterations and invoices now paid or ready to be paid. Manual records of these transactions must be keyboarded, most conveniently using a fixed field record structure on punched cards. After verification, the input cards must be sorted into book fund order; the same order as the main magnetic-tape file. This is done manually for small input volumes, but for large numbers of input cards, a punched-card sorting machine is used. Alternatively (and this is becoming increasingly more common nowadays as card sorters become rarer and magnetic disc stores more widespread), this pre-sort can be done by the computer using a disc memory store. For small files, disc sorts can be performed very rapidly.

The task of updating is quite straightforward. Cancellations and

Listing and Accounting Systems 121

Q.U.B.	DEPARTMENTAL EXPENDITURE.		Statement of University Account	
	ACCOUNT NUMBER S/-SE-LB		LIBRARY	
	GRANT £7200.00 CR		13/05/71 1	
Date	University Ref.		Order Number	Amount
18/02/71	INV 70515 WE MAYNE			6.50
18/02/71	INV 70511 WE MAYNE			8.40
18/02/71	INV 70513 WE MAYNE			8.50
19/02/71	INV 70498 WE MAYNE			2.20
19/02/71	INV 70500 WE MAYNE			3.15
03/03/71	INV 70508 WE MAYNE			1.75
03/03/71	INV 70511 WE MAYNE			6.75
03/03/71	INV 70501 WE MAYNE			1.40
26/03/71	INV 70510 WE MAYNE		70510	4.80
26/03/71	INV 70516 WE MAYNE		70516	15.00
26/03/71	INV 70517 WE MAYNE		70517	3.30
01/04/71	INV 70512 WE MAYNE		70512	3.50
27/04/71	INV 58541 WE MAYNE		58541	5.75
27/04/71	INV 52037 WE MAYNE		52037	4.50
28/04/71	INV 51933 AMERICAN DATA PROC INC		51933	6.71
21/01/71	INV 00009 EXPENDITURE TO DATE			4015.84
	ACTUAL BALANCE			702.96CR
	TOTAL OUTSTANDING ORDERS			59.91
	FREE BALANCE			643.05CR

FIG. 6.15. Detailed listing of transactions on one library fund, Queen's University Library, Belfast.

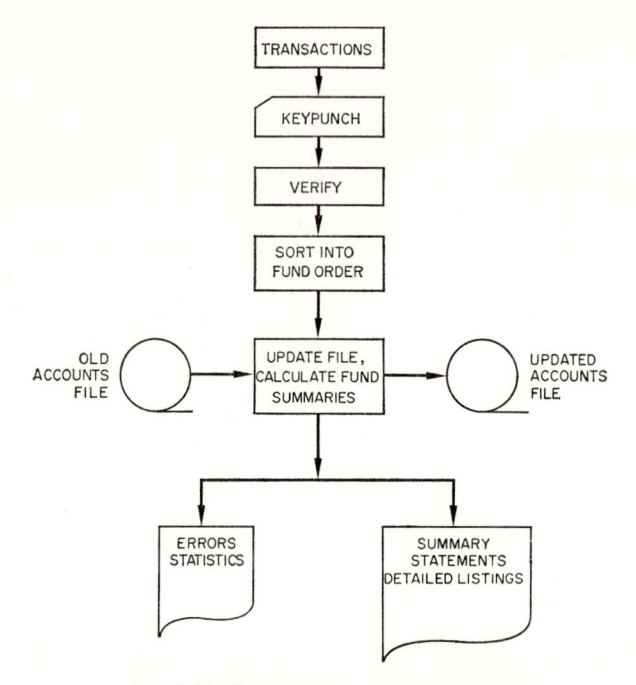

FIG. 6.16. Flow chart for accounting system.

alterations to existing transactions are made as instructed. New transactions are added to the growing list of transactions, and fund summaries and detailed listings are printed as required.

If the system provides details of transactions grouped by supplier as well as by book fund, it is possible to sort the main accounts file into supplier order, calculate summary statements for each supplier and print as required. But it is simpler to duplicate the data in the main file, arranging transactions by supplier in the second part of the file.

Figure 6.17 shows how the batch of input cards is first sorted into book-fund order to update the book-fund section of the main accounts file (which is presumed to come first on the tape). It is then sorted into supplier order and used in exactly the same way to update the supplier section of the file.

Listing and Accounting Systems 123

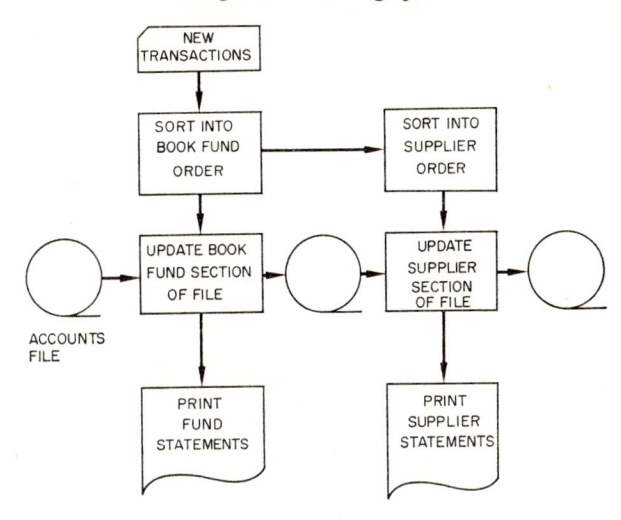

FIG. 6.17. Flow chart for accounting system to produce statement by book fund and by supplier.

REFERENCES

1. DEWS, J. D. and SMETHURST, J. M. *The Institutes of Education Union List of Periodicals processing system.* Newcastle upon Tyne, Oriel Press, 1968. (Symplegades, No. 1.)
2. Cox, N. S. M. and DEWS, J. D. The Newcastle File Handling System. In Cox, N. S. M. and GROSE, M. W. (Eds.) *Organization and handling of bibliographic records by computer.* Newcastle upon Tyne, Oriel Press, 1967, pp. 1–21.
3. COOKE, M. and GRAY, W. A. A redesigned record structure for the Newcastle File Handling System. *Program*, Vol. 7, No. 1, pp. 1–23 (Jan. 1973).
4. BISHOP, S. M. Periodical records on punched cards at AERE Library, Harwell. *Program*, Vol. 3, No. 1, pp. 11–18 (April 1969).
5. GREENHALGH, K. R. and BISHOP, S. M. Revision of the periodical records system at AERE Library, Harwell. *Program*, Vol. 6, No. 3, pp. 248–57 (July 1972).
6. GRIFFIN, J. Computer handling of periodical subscriptions and holdings at Shell Research Limited, Sittingbourne. *Program*, Vol. 3, No. 3, pp. 120–6 (Nov. 1969).
7. EVANS, A. J. and WALL, R. A. Library mechanisation projects at Loughborough University of Technology. *Program*, Vol. 1, No. 6, pp. 1–4 (July 1967).
8. COWBURN, L. M. and ENRIGHT, B. J. Computerized UDC subject index in the City University Library. *Program*, Vol. 1, No. 8, pp. 1–5 (Jan. 1968).
9. HANSON, D. G. A computer program to maintain a subject index file on magnetic tape in alphabetical and classified order. *Program*, Vol. 1, No. 8, pp. 6–12 (Jan. 1968).
10. WILLIAMS, J. G., MANHEIMER, M. L. and DAILY, J. E. Classified Library of Congress subject headings; Vol. 1, *Classified List.* Vol. 2, *Alphabetic List.* New York, Dekker, 1972.
11. STEVENSON, C. L. and COOPER, J. A. A computerized accounts system at the City University. *Program*, Vol. 2, No. 1, pp. 15–29 (Apr. 1968).

CHAPTER 7

Serials Accessioning Systems

THE type of system discussed in the previous chapter under the heading Serials Listing System yields as its end product one or more printed listings of the serial holdings of a library or a group of libraries. Updated from time to time by machine-readable records of recent additions, such lists perform a valuable reader service function in an important area of library activity. Although they are comparatively straightforward to design and implement, and although they contribute substantially to a library's reader services, listing systems make no contribution to the main work of a serials department—accessioning periodical parts, initiating new orders, and claiming issues which fail to arrive when expected.

A number of libraries have successfully developed and implemented computer-based serials accessioning systems which include the above activities. Although the number of functions they perform varies, all include as a central and key aspect of their design, the "mechanization" of the job of accessioning new parts of serials as they arrive in the library.

Figure 7.1 illustrates very simply the essential parts of a typical serials accessioning system. Referring to Fig. 6.4 (the flow chart for the listing system) the serials-holdings file there is essentially the same file as the serials-holdings file in Fig. 7.1 although the latter naturally contains more detail in the record for each serial. In Fig. 6.4 new records and alterations to this file had first to be keypunched and verified before the file was updated and a printed list obtained. In Fig. 7.1 the computer itself produces the documents (which are in machine-readable form) which are subsequently used to update the file. The updated file is then printed in whole or in part in both systems.

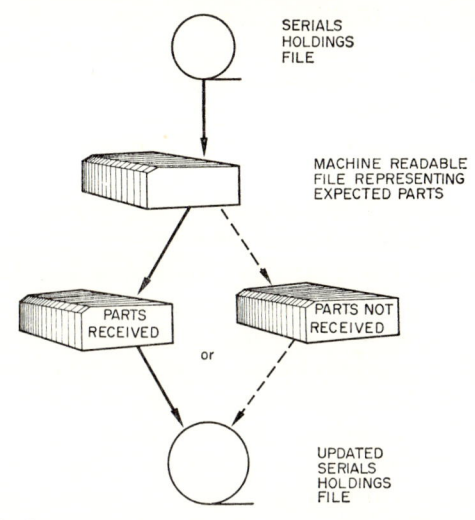

Fig. 7.1. Generalized flow chart for serials accessioning system.

It must be emphasized, however, in making this comparison, that the two updating tasks are not exactly similar. The serials listing system is updated by adding new titles, and deleting and altering existing ones as necessary. The file of the accessioning system is updated by the addition of data about newly arrived parts of existing serials. But new subscriptions, as before, require the new data to be keypunched and then written to the file.

OVERALL SYSTEM DESCRIPTION

The fundamental task of any serials accessioning system, manual or mechanized, is to record the arrival of each serial part in the library. Additional tasks are to place subscriptions for new titles, cancel subscriptions, follow up delayed and missing parts, prepare lists of newly arrived parts and serials holdings for consultation by library users, answer users' queries about the library's holdings, etc.

Manual accessioning systems work very simply and reliably. In one very widely used system, each card in a visible index file contains the holdings information for one serial title, including subscription details, location, shelf mark, binding treatment, detailed holdings and wants, etc., together with the arrival date of each part. The accessioning task then simply requires the librarian to scan the file for the correct card, and write details of the part in hand onto it. The periodical is then stamped with the library's mark of ownership and processed as necessary before shelving.

No computer-based serials accessioning system can substantially improve upon this aspect of an efficient manual system. Computer systems are complex and expensive to develop, and if they were able to do no more than the above accessioning tasks, very few libraries would have changed from their manual systems. Once again, therefore, one must look for the justification of such computer-based systems to the "extras" that they can provide, over and above the basic accessioning that manual systems perform so effectively.

Figure 7.1 shows that the key to the operation of a computer-based accessioning system lies in the machine-readable file representing expected parts. This is produced by the computer from the main serials-holdings file, and in the figure is shown as a card file. The earliest accessioning systems employed a single punched-card file; alternatively nowadays, the file may be duplicated, one part consisting of a printed list, the other being a file of numbered cards, one card for each expected part included in the list. On the other hand, the file may be retained in direct-access storage for interrogation on-line by a suitable communications terminal. Whatever form of file is used, the librarian's task is to separate in some way the records for those parts that arrive from the records for those parts which do not arrive. Both sets of records may then be used by the system for further action as required.

The advantage of having the computer prepare the machine-readable records which will subsequently update the holdings file is that a higher degree of accuracy is obtainable than with a manual system or manual keypunching for input to a computer system. The work of the librarian may also be simplified, at least in so far as regular items are concerned. But in order to produce a file of records, one for each serial part expected, it becomes necessary to predict the arrival of parts. Herein lie the major difficulties associated with computer-based serials accessioning systems.

Serials Accessioning Systems

Problems of prediction are considered in detail later in the chapter. It is sufficient to mention here that prediction can never be completely reliable because of the many perturbations superimposed upon the underlying regularity of serials publication. For example, individual parts may be unexpectedly delayed either in publication or in distribution; unannounced supplements may be published; a periodical's pattern of publication may change, e.g. from four to six parts per volume; titles may cease publication, merge with others or split into two or more sections. Because of such irregularities, and because of a small number of serials with a permanently irregular publication pattern, it has been found that prediction can never be more than approximately 80 per cent successful.

To enable the remaining 20 per cent of new serial parts to be handled by the system, semi-manual procedures are required. These may involve writing down the details of unexpected parts on work sheets from which punched cards are later keypunched. Alternatively, it may be preferable for a card to be punched and verified on the spot. Manual input is, of course, also necessary for additions and alterations to the main serials-holdings file to reflect new and cancelled subscriptions, changed publication patterns, etc.

Libraries vary quite widely in the outputs they require from a serials accessioning system. All systems provide output which enables the basic accessioning function to be carried out: many others give daily or weekly lists of parts received, which are valuable where, for some reason, library users are unable themselves to inspect the newly arrived parts. Lists of completed volumes now ready for binding are often produced as a by-product which is of especial value to the library staff. Such lists may even be so scheduled to try to provide a regular work load for the library bindery, for the majority of serials complete volumes at the end of each calendar year. And, of course, a full and comprehensive list of the library's serials holdings, with detailed specification of wants and bound and unbound volumes, is also commonly printed from time to time. Subsets of the main list, e.g. the serial holdings of one branch or divisional library, and rearrangements of the main list, e.g. in subject, keyword or supplier order, etc., are also produced, just as with the simpler serials-listing systems.

Subscription and accounting information is also often included in the record for each title, and this can enable the computer system to expedite the process of renewing subscriptions. Where serials are purchased on the specific recommendations of individual persons, who may be librarians or library users, they may be asked periodically to authorize the renewal of subscriptions. It is a straightforward matter to print letters addressed to such individuals requesting their authorization in good time before the subscriptions become due.

DETAILED SYSTEM DESCRIPTION

Figure 7.2 shows in some detail the main operations, files and listings involved in a typical computer-based serials accessioning system. Although no two systems are identical, the majority conform in large measure to this pattern. There are many variations from the pattern, some small, some large (for example, an on-line system is very different indeed). The more important variations are discussed below.

Two valuable surveys should be mentioned at this point. A brief survey by Massil was published in 1970,[1] and a more comprehensive survey including numerous illustrations of output documents was published the following year as part of the IBM series on library automation.[2]

Main Serials-Holdings File

This is the master file in the serials-accessioning system, corresponding to the file of visible index cards in a manual system, and to the holdings file in a serials-listing system. It contains more data than both of these, however; in particular, explicit information on the publication pattern of each serial, and detailed records of individual parts received, at least for current volumes.

There is one record in the file for each title, whether it is a currently received serial, one no longer currently received, or a cross reference rom an alternative title. The following information must be included n each record:

        Identification number
        Coden or ISSN
        Full title

Serials Accessioning Systems

(Abbreviated title)
Call number and location
Publication pattern
Next issue expected
Detailed holdings and wants
Volumes bound and unbound
Supplier and subscription price

It is seen that some of these data fields are identical to those in the listing system record discussed on page 62, and serve the same

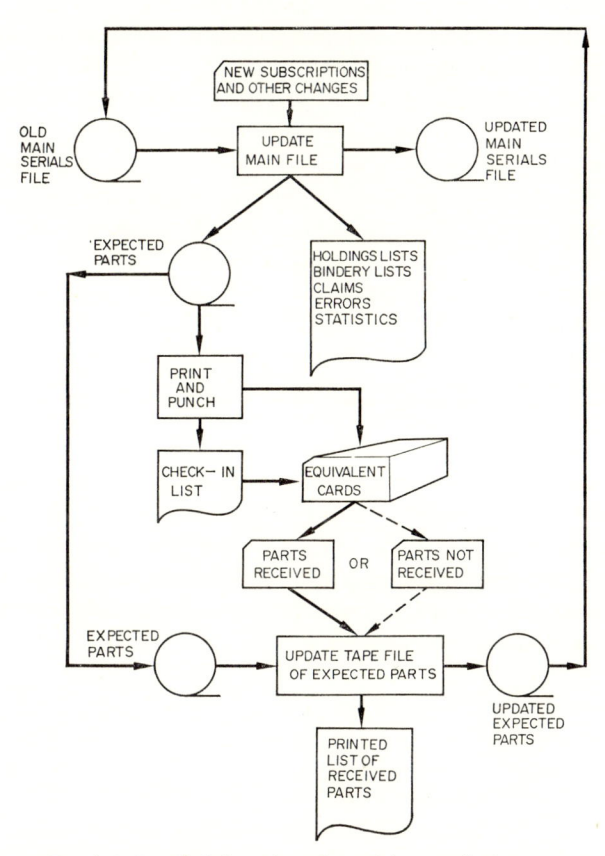

Fig. 7.2. Detailed flow chart for serials accessioning system.

purpose. For example, an identification number commonly serves both as a unique identifier for the record and as a simple device for sorting the file into alphabetical order by title. It is unusual not to find a full title held somewhere in the record for a serials accessioning system. If the title is not held in a variable field, then a fixed field of sufficient length must be used. Fayollat studied the distribution of the lengths of serial titles in the Biomedical Library of the University of California, Los Angeles, where an on-line serials accessioning system is operational.[3] He found that only 8 per cent of titles were over eighty characters in length, the longest being 215 characters. An abbreviated title will be required if the system punches cards for the expected parts but does not produce a printed list.

In order to predict the arrival of periodical parts, each record must contain information about the publication pattern of the serial. This relates to the number of volumes in each calendar year, the number of parts per volume, the presence of any regular supplements, the pattern of numbering parts, and the frequency of publication. Given a knowledge of the "real" calendar, algorithms can be written which use the above information to predict when each issue will arrive. Some systems, such as that at the University of California, San Diego,[4] have refined the prediction process to take account of regular delays in publishing whereby each issue appears later (or earlier) than the date printed on the cover, and further delays arising from the distribution of the journal from the printer to the receiving library.

Details about the supplier and the price per volume are required if the system is to handle subscription renewals and accounting functions. The same information and the same procedures are involved as when subscriptions are renewed as part of a serials listing system, and when a simple accounting system is used for new monographs. Both have already been discussed in Chapter 6.

Prediction

Computer-based serials accessioning systems may be predictive or non-predictive. Predictive systems predict the arrival of individual parts. They are the more common type and it is this kind that is represented in Fig. 7.2. Predictive systems may have positive or negative input. Positive input is illustrated in Figs. 7.1 and 7.2, in which it is the arrival cards for those parts which have arrived in the library which are used to update the files. In systems with negative input, it is the arrival cards for the parts which have not arrived which update the files.

Non-predictive systems do not predict the arrival of individual parts, so that they require positive input, i.e. details of the parts that arrive must be given to the system. Manual systems and on-line computer systems are non-predictive with positive input. The experimental off-line serials accessioning system using a light pen and machine-readable labels, which is being developed at the library of Loughborough University of Technology, is also of this kind.[5]

Prediction essentially means the ability to state that a named issue of a named serial will arrive in the library within a stated time interval. This definition may be interpreted loosely. For example, if one issue of a journal has just been received, it is possible to "expect" another issue immediately, without regard to the frequency of publication of the journal and the frequency of the computer run which makes the prediction. Provided that a sufficient number of issues are predicted for those journals which are published more frequently than the computer run is carried out, this kind of "loose prediction" has the twin advantages of being simple and safe. It is better to predict the arrival of an issue well before it is likely to arrive than to have it arrive before it is expected, because of too "tight" prediction. The one disadvantage of such loose prediction is that the file of expected parts is larger than it would be with tighter prediction, and correspondingly more difficult to search. This method was used at the UCLA Biomedical Library for the batch system which preceded the present on-line one.[6]

It is more usual, however, to employ more stringent procedures than this in selecting parts for prediction within a given time period. Selection is typically done on a monthly basis, and the selection algorithm normally determines which issues of the serials received by the library will be published during the next month. Assuming that an individual title is published regularly, its frequency of publication is specified to the system. Common publication frequencies are weekly, monthly, quarterly and annually. More complex frequencies such as bi-weekly (26 issues a year), semi-monthly (24 issues a year), semi-annual (2 issues a year), etc., may also be specified, as multiples of days or weeks or as fractions of a year.

In addition to this frequency data, one or more publication dates must be specified. Thus a weekly journal may be published each Friday, a quarterly is published in January, April, July and October, etc. Frequency and date information must be combined, typically into a single code, before one can specify how many parts will be published within a stated time interval, e.g. 1 March to 31 March.

Yet more is required. If, say, the publication pattern code is interpreted by the selection algorithm and the system expects an issue of a stated title during the month of March, it is necessary to know just which issue it will be. This is not difficult if the last issue received is known and its date of publication. If, for example, the last issue received was Volume 15 Number 4 of a quarterly journal, published with four parts per bibliographic volume and parts being published in March, June, September and December, then one part, namely Volume 16 Number 1, should be published during the month of March.

Predicting issues more "tightly" or more "accurately" in this way reduces the size of the file of cards or the printed list for the expected parts. It still allows a good margin of error, however, because, especially with scientific and foreign journals, the date of receipt in a library is normally some time after the publication date. A simple and very effective way of improving on the above method of prediction has been developed at the University of California, San Diego, and described by Bosseau.[4]

This method uses two "calendars", a publication calendar and a receipt calendar. Because the selection algorithm is run monthly, and because prediction is done on a monthly basis, each calendar consists simply of twelve monthly divisions. In each monthly division of the publication calendar is noted the number of parts that should be published. In each monthly division of the receipt calendar are written the number of parts as they arrive. Thus, over a period of time, a picture is built up in the machine-readable record of the actual pattern of arrival of each serial. And this, rather than the stated publication pattern, can be used for making predictions of arrival.

Serials Accessioning Systems 133

Because the actual arrival times in the library are used as the basis of prediction, this method includes delays arising from parts not being published at the same time as stated on their covers, and delays occurring in the post from printer or distributor to the library. The arrival data can be cumulated over a period of time, so that prediction can be made increasingly more reliable. Thus a minimum delay can be established between publication and receipt (AB in Fig. 7.3) so that the system may be ready to receive each part before this minimum delay period has elapsed. Similarly, although there will not be a corresponding maximum possible delay (the maximum possible will be infinite, for a part that, for example, has been irretrievably lost in transit), some time period can be established (AE in Fig. 7.3), within which a part really ought to arrive and after which a claim will be sent to the publisher or the supplier.

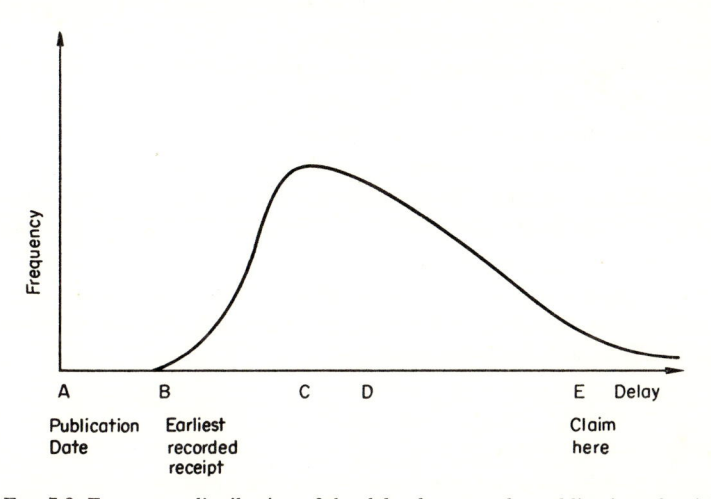

Fig. 7.3. Frequency distribution of the delay between the publication of serial parts and their receipt in a library. AC is the most common delay (the mode), AD is the mean delay. There is a very high probability that parts will have arrived by the time point E has been reached: claims may then be made.

Check-in

Two main types of check-in procedures are found with the off-line predictive systems that are operational at the present time. One involves the use of a file of punched cards, the other uses a printed list of expected parts, which may also have a card file associated with it.

PUNCHED-CARD SYSTEMS

One card is punched for each part that is expected to arrive in the library during the next prediction period. All these "check-in cards" are kept in a file in the library serials department, normally in alphabetical order of title. As each periodical arrives, the corresponding punched check-in card is pulled from the file and set on one side, to be used later to update the serials-holdings file. Figure 7.4 shows a check-in card used in the Biomedical Library of the University of California, Los Angeles, up to 1971. This shows the unique identification number used to identify and sort the serials records (columns 74–80), and the title, volume, issue and date of the part.

Because of the limitation to eighty characters of data on each check-in card, most titles must be abbreviated on the cards if necessary extra information such as location, call number, and issue designation, etc., are all to be included within the eighty characters available. More space can be obtained by punching only a sequential transaction number on the card, and printing full bibliographical information by line printer using prepunched continuous roll card stock. Figure 7.5 shows a check-in card of this type, used in San Francisco Public Library. In either case, cards must be punched manually for any serial parts which arrive without being predicted.

PRINTED LIST SYSTEMS

It was this need to overcome the eighty-character limitation of punched check-in cards coupled with fears about the unreliability of the printed punched card type of system that led to the introduction of printed lists of expected parts. This has been widely accepted as superior to punched check-in cards.

A printed list is much easier to scan than a file of cards. Instead of pulling a check-in card from the file, the appropriate place on the check-in list is marked by hand to indicate the receipt of the part. This,

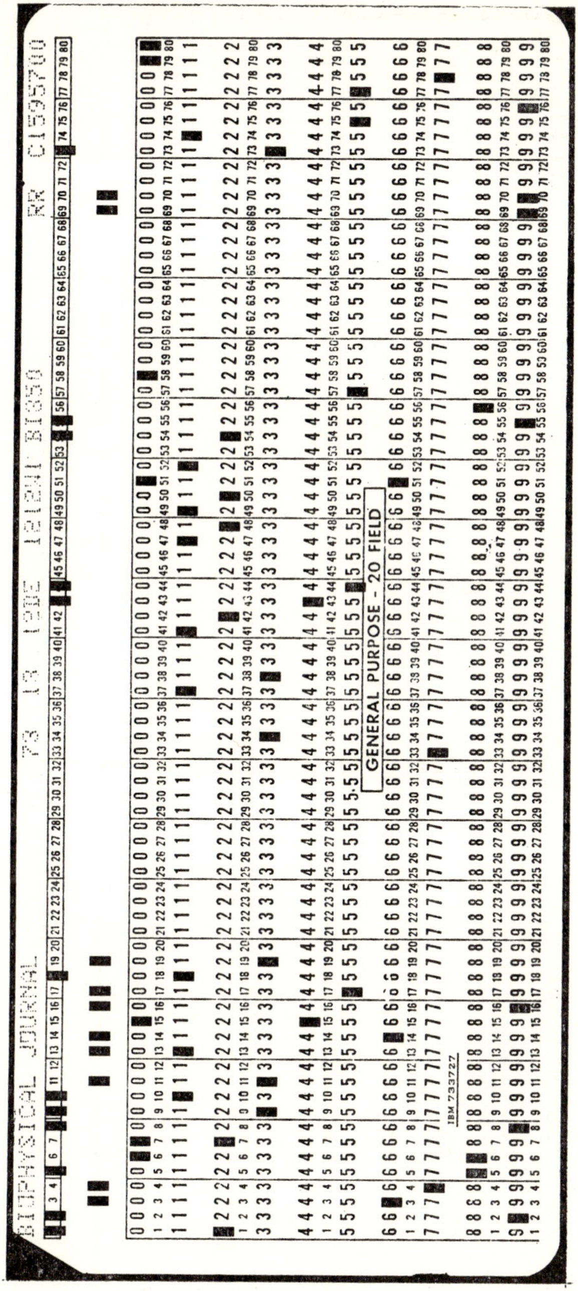

FIG. 7.4. Check-in card used in the serials accessioning system at the Biomedical Library of the University of California, Los Angeles, up to 1971.

135

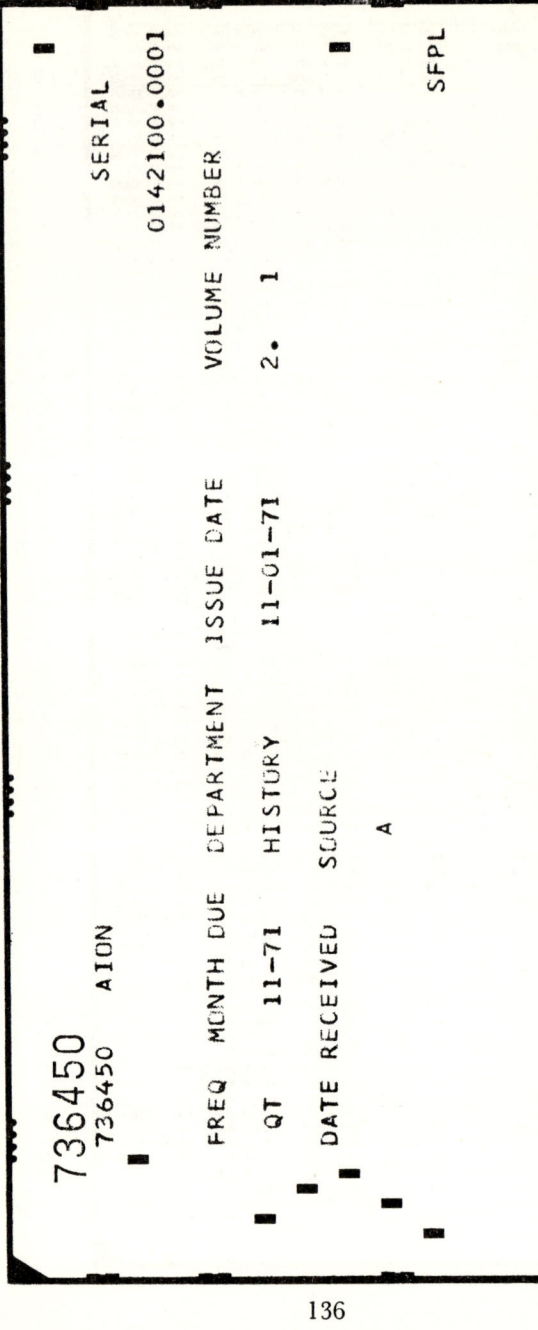

Fig. 7.5. Check-in card used by San Francisco Public Library.

however, does not create a machine-readable record for updating the files. A simple way of doing so was found in the use of a file of sequentially numbered (and punched) eighty-column transaction cards with each check-in list that is printed. Such card files are purchased as standard stock items.

Periodically (as often as a listing is required of received parts), the transaction cards are pulled for those parts that have been marked off on the list as having arrived. This is a very easy task, and Bosseau has reported that the two-stage process of marking off received parts on the check-in list, and pulling the corresponding transaction cards takes about half the time as the single-stage process of pulling a punched check-in card. Figure 7.6 shows a sample page from the University of California, San Diego, check-in list.

The Loughborough Experiment

Wall[5] argues with some justification that none of these predictive computer-based systems is as satisfactory as a good manual system from the point of view of quick and efficient procedures in the library's serials department. When prediction fails, then these computer-based systems must revert to manual keyboarding and verification of check-in cards for parts that arrive unexpectedly. The idea at Loughborough University of Technology is to design a non-predictive off-line serials accessioning system embodying very efficient semi-mechanized data-capture procedures. Because the system is non-predictive no parts can arrive "unexpectedly" and slow down the serials assistant's rate of working. All parts which arrive are treated in the same way.

The central idea behind the experiment is to use a mobile Plessey light pen unit, in conjunction with a conventional manual visible index filing system. A machine-readable (bar coded) label on each index card will contain the coded title of the journal. The remainder of the card is devoted to a chart with bar coded strips for each month, week and day of the week. To accession a newly arrived periodical part the light pen is "stroked" along the title code and the appropriate publication day, week or month. A fairly complex algorithm would be required to convert such calendar-type data into bibliographic designators, and to check for possible missed parts.

```
     *                         SERIALS EXPECTED ARRIVALS LIST       AUGUST 1973 (8.1)              PAGE 15Δ9

19338   UGESKRIFT FOR LAEGER                                          W1                 544544544544
   MA S                                                               UG375              776678ABB123 AC
          NOTE- ROUTE ALL SUPPS.FOR STIC                                                     0152  1

                                      919379  U135N17,30APR1973                 071973
                                      919380  U135N18,07MAY1973                 071973
                                      919381  U135N22,04JUN1973                 071973
                                      919382  U135N21,28MAY1973                 081973
                                      919383  U135N23,11JUN1973                 081973
                                      919384  U135N24,18JUN1973                 081973
                                      919385  U135N25,25JUN1973                 081973
                                      919386  U135N26,02JUL1973                 081973

26191   UKRAINIAN MATHEMATICAL JOURNAL                                QA1                -1-1-1-1-1-1
   EA S                                                               U531               -----3-5-7-A Z9
                                                                                             0606  1
                                      919387  U24N3,JUN1972                     071973
                                              U24N4, AUG 1972
                                              U24N5, OCT 1972
23888   UKRAINIAN PHYSICS JOURNAL                                     QC1                111111111111
   EB S                                                               U348               ------------ AA
                                                                                             1212  1
                                      919388  U14N1,JUL1969                     101969

32061   UKRAINIAN QUARTERLY,NEW YORK                                  DK508              --1--1--1--1
   GA S                                                               A2U66              --5--8--1--4 Z9
                                                                                             0404  1
                                      919389  U29N1,MAR1973                     051973

31839   UKRAINIAN REVIEW,LONDON,1954-                                 DK508              --1--1--1--1
   GA S                                                               A2U664             --4--6--2--3 Z9
                                                                                             0404  1
                                      919390  U20N3,SEP1973                     081973

35467   UKRAINS KYI BIOKHIMICHNY ZHURNAL                              W1                 ------------
   MA S                                                               UK650              ---6-------- AC
                                                                                             0606  2
                                      919391  U45N2,   1973                     071973

29392   UKRAINS KYI BOTANICHNYI ZHURNAL,KIEV,1940-                    QK1                ------------
   IA S                                                               U35                ---66-8-A-B1 AL
                                                                                             0606  2
                                      919392  U30N3,   1972                     081973

35468   UKRAINS KYI FIZYCHNYI ZHURNAL                                 QC1                111111111111
   EA E                                                               U351               456------244
                                                                                             1212  1
                                      919393  U17N9,AUG1972                     021973
                                      919394  U18N4,APR1973                     071973
```

FIG. 7.6. Sample page, University of California, San Diego, Library, Serials check-in list.

ON-LINE ACCESSIONING

On-line serials accessioning systems are operational at Laval University Library in Quebec[7] and the Biomedical Library of the University of California, Los Angeles.[3] Both are non-predictive positive input systems, and are very similar in their overall procedures to manual systems. The computer becomes, in effect, a device for helping the serials assistant to find the correct place in the serials-holdings file, and of course it also provides the extra outputs not possible with a manual system, such as holdings lists, bindery lists and claims for missing parts. As with manual records, the on-line records are always completely up to date, which can be an important consideration where library users do not have access to the serials themselves.

In the Laval system, serial records are retrieved from direct-access storage by means of a seven-digit identification number. At the UCLA Biomedical Library any combination of significant title words may be used to retrieve the record. Fayollat has shown that the on-line UCLA system is a better financial proposition than the older batch system.[8]

Claims

If prediction can be carried out successfully, then serial parts which are predicted to arrive within a specific time span yet fail to do so, can be assumed to have failed to reach the library through the normal pattern of distribution, and claims may be made for replacement copies. Most operational prediction systems of the kinds already discussed can be said to be successful in this sense, and the computer-based systems' ability to alert librarians' attention quickly to delayed or missed issues is one of their major benefits.

Very simply, punched check-in cards remaining in the file at the end of the prediction period, and periodical parts not marked off on a printed check-in list represent those parts for which claims procedures should be considered. It is normally prudent for a librarian to examine such remaining parts before claims are made: he may know, in a way that the computer can never know, of reasons why some serial parts have not arrived, and for which it would be foolish to claim replacement parts. He may know, for example, that certain journals are

```
WAITING FOR THIS AND SUBSEQUENT ISSUES        8/1/73
PURCHASE ORDER NO. 34X20352
    COMMENTS ON ATOMIC AND MOLECULAR PHYSICS

VOL.      4      NO.      1      1972


GORDON & BREACH SCIENCE
PUBLISHERS LTD
41 & 42 WILLIAMS IV ST
LONDON WC2 ENGLAND

REMARKS-




*  *  *  *  *  *  *  *  *  *  *  *  *  *  *  *  *  *  *  *  *  *  *  *

VENDOR RESPONSE - PLEASE CHECK APPLICABLE STATEMENTS
    OUT OF PRINT
    CLAIM SENT TO PUBLISHER
    NOT YET PUBLISHED
    NOT PUBLISHED AT ALL
    WILL SUPPLY LATER
    CAN NOT SUPPLY


REMARKS-






    REFOLD AND RETURN TO

    ORNL LIBRARY
    ATTN - ORDER DEPT.
    BLDG. 4500, P.O. BOX X
    OAK RIDGE, TENN.   37830
```

FIG. 7.7. Claims letter prepared by the Oak Ridge National Laboratory Library serials system.

currently having publication or distribution difficulties, or that a postal or dock strike may be the cause of delay for other journals.

Figure 7.7 reproduces a claim notice from the Oak Ridge National

```
CENTRAL RESEARCH LIBRARY BINDERY INFORMATION          07-12-73

A3500000  AMERICAN INDUSTRIAL HYGIENE ASSOCIATION. JOURNAL. DETROIT

VOLUME       33              1972     LETTERING ON SPINE
PUBLISHED    12 ISSUES                      HORIZONTAL
TITLE PAGE   NO                             GOLD
CONTENTS     NO                       FIRST COVER ONLY IN
INDEX        YES                            ADS              CUT
SUPPLEMENTS  NO                             COLOR  8857
BINDERY HAS PATTERN                         INDEX BACK
BIND AS IS   NO

SPECIAL HANDLING NO
```

FIG. 7.8. Bindery notice prepared by the Oak Ridge National Laboratory Library serials system.

Laboratory serials accessioning system showing a typical "letter format" for a claim, providing space for reply from the supplier.

A wide range of policies exists with regard to when claims are made. It is general practice to subject claims to human vetting, but in the Washington University Library system skipped issues are claimed automatically, while in the Oak Ridge National Laboratory system, regular domestic (i.e. US) serials are claimed automatically if issues are not received within the expected time period.

Binding

A further valuable feature of computer-based serials accessioning systems is their ability to inform the librarian of volumes that have been completed and are now ready for binding, and to spread the binding load to give an even distribution of work in the bindery throughout the year. This avoids the manual checking of shelves to ascertain which volumes are complete, but as Wall emphasizes, it is the presence of all parts in a volume on the library shelf, together with title-page and index, that finally determines whether a volume is ready to be bound or not. A computer listing of volumes ready for binding can be a helpful reminder and can assist in work scheduling but cannot entirely eliminate the need to check library shelves.

But the computer list can save the librarian a considerable amount of clerical work. Binding lists can include complete instructions to the binder regarding colour of binding, treatment of advertisements, issue covers, title-page and index, etc. In addition, a punched card may be produced which, when the bound volume is returned to the library, can be used to update the main holdings file record of bound volumes for the title in question. Figure 7.8 shows a binding notice produced by the Oak Ridge National Laboratory System.

REFERENCES

1. Massil, S. W. Mechanisation of serials records: a literature review. *Program*, Vol. 4, No. 4, pp. 156–68 (Oct. 1970).
2. *Library automation—computerised serials control*. IBM Corporation, May 1971, 106 pp. (GE 20 0352 0).

3. FAYOLLAT, J. On-line serials control system in a large biomedical library. Part II. Evaluation of retrieval features. *Journal of the American Society for Information Science*, Vol. 23, No. 6, pp. 353–8 (Nov.–Dec. 1972).
4. BOSSEAU, D. L. The University of California at San Diego serials system—revisited. *Program*, Vol. 4, No. 1, pp. 1–29 (Jan. 1970).
5. WALL, R. A. A proposed experiment in automated serials accessioning. *Program*, Vol. 5, No. 3, pp. 141–51 (July 1971).
6. ROPER, F. W. A computer-based serials control system for a large biomedical library. *American Documentation*, Vol. 19, pp. 151–7 (1968).
7. DE VARENNES, R. On-line serials system at Laval University Library. *Journal of Library Automation*, Vol. 3, No. 2, pp. 128–41 (June 1970).
8. FAYOLLAT, J. On-line serials control system in a large biomedical library. Part III. Comparison of on-line and batch operations and cost analysis. *Journal of the American Society for Information Science*, Vol. 24, No. 2, pp. 80–86 (Mar.–Apr. 1973).

CHAPTER 8

Circulation Control

MOST libraries lend books, periodicals and other materials to be read elsewhere by users. This is convenient for the users, increases the use made of the libraries' collections and reduces demands for reading space within library buildings themselves. And having lent, almost all libraries feel the need for some kind of records of what has been lent. There are two good reasons for keeping such records; they reduce the loss of library materials (whether they do so on a cost effective basis is another question) and also help library staff to answer users' queries about the location of items not on the shelves. Out of such records of loans have arisen a rich variety of systems of record keeping—"loans" or "circulation" systems.

It is important to be aware of the wide range of types of circulation systems, characterized by speed of operation, capital investment required, amount of labour needed, controls and other outputs provided. Some, such as manual slip or book card systems, are suitable for small libraries where speed of operation is not critical; others such as photocharging are of particular value where rapid charging is essential, but where few other controls are needed other than the fact that a record of each loan does exist somewhere. Public libraries have found photocharging economical to operate and well suited to their needs. Computer-based loans systems require high capital investment, and are therefore restricted to situations where a large volume of loans will ensure that the capital cost per loan is small. And of course computer systems are characterized by their ability to handle complex situations and to provide a wide variety of outputs. This means that computerized circulation systems are most appropriate to the needs of large libraries, and those with special requirements such as efficient and prompt control of reservations, overdues, etc.

Typically, the costs of computer circulation systems are higher than those of manual systems. Published cost figures vary quite widely, and, of course, the computer systems do much more than manual systems, so that it is seldom possible really to compare like with like. But in large libraries, the cost per loan transaction of a simple, efficient, batch-processing circulation system need be very little higher than a single slip or book card system, and may be less. This, despite the fact that the computer system provides greater control and gives more useful by-products than the manual system. Photocharging appears to remain the cheapest system which retains any measure of control over loans. On-line real-time systems incur costs of up to two or three times those of batch systems, because of high direct-access file-storage costs and charges for data transmission between the library and the computer. But it is only such real-time systems which are able to provide the absolutely up-to-date information that is often needed in circulation control. Circulation is the area of library housekeeping where such current information is most needed, and it is fortunate that real-time systems are probably simplest to design and implement in this area. A number of such systems are operational in the US and UK, and their number is growing steadily.

BASIC CONCEPTS OF CIRCULATION SYSTEMS

A computer-based circulation system is very simple in its basic concept, and is essentially similar to the serials listing system discussed in Chapter 6. In both cases a machine-readable file of records is updated periodically with new records, and the new file is printed. It may subsequently be sorted into a different arrangement and printed again, or a subset of the main file may be selected and printed or processed in some other way.

In a circulation system, the machine-readable file consists of records for all items on loan from the library, normally arranged by a unique accession number, call number, or a number assigned specially for the purpose. The file is updated with records of new loans, items returned from loan, and such extra information as reservations, cancelled reservations, etc. The updated file, when printed, is used by the circulation staff to answer borrowers' queries about books that are on loan. The file is sorted and printed from time to time to provide loans listings arranged by borrower, by author and title, or by date due for return. Simple selection procedures enable letters to borrowers (or instructions to library staff) to be printed in respect of overdue books, books required for other borrowers, books now available for loan, etc.

It is clear that such a system is very simple in nature, and that it can yield many varied and valuable by-products for borrowers and library staff alike.

Figure 8.1 shows these basic concepts of a computer-based circulation system. There are, however, some characteristics of circulation control which result in important differences that are not immediately apparent from a simple diagram, between computer-based loan systems and other computerized library systems.

Firstly, the need for rapid charging requires that the machine-readable records of new loans should be created mechanically, rather than by manual keyboarding. Several operational systems work quite satisfactorily with manual data collection, but this imposes considerable strain on the operators if loans traffic is heavy, and will result in more inaccurate loans records. This need for mechanical data capture fits in quite well with the distribution of loans over the collection of a typical library. Although many books will be borrowed only seldom, there will be a core collection of popular and valuable books which are borrowed many times during their useful life. It makes sense, especially in the case of such heavily used books, to prepare some kind of machine-readable book card for each loanable item. This speeds up data capture and conversion when items are borrowed, increases the accuracy of the loans data, frees library staff from repetitive keyboarding work, and, especially in the case of frequently used items, means that the same data is not keyboarded over and over again, each time the book is borrowed.

So most computer-based loans systems employ machine-readable book cards punched with a unique identification number and perhaps also with brief author, title and subject information. Borrowers are similarly supplied with a machine-readable identification card (ID card). Loan data, therefore, is converted into machine-readable form handling reservations. As soon as a held book is returned to the library, the fact that a hold exists for it is reported at the discharge terminal. The librarian then knows immediately to keep it for the borrower who reserved it, and to prevent it from being borrowed again by any other library user.

Effectively the same ability to trap reserved books immediately on their return to the library is also provided by a number of off-line systems operational in the UK which have a small core store associated with the machines used to read punched book and reader cards. Functioning exactly like a tiny computer, the core store, or "trapping store", can hold the identification numbers of held books, and is in effect a computerized visible index of reservations operating in real-time. As soon as a reserved book is returned to the library, the loans assistant is informed of the fact by a warning panel lighting up in the trapping store control panel. In the same way, individual borrowers may be recognized when they borrow an item and perhaps told of a reserved book now available for loan. Recalcitrant borrowers may similarly be identified and debarred from their normal borrowing privileges until such a time as they again comply with the library's loans regulations.

DETAILED SYSTEM DESCRIPTION

Circulation control has been one of the most popular areas of library housekeeping to mechanize. Generally speaking, systems have been very successful so that it is possible nowadays for a library to install a computer-based circulation system, purchased (or otherwise obtained) "off the shelf". Not every new system is written up in the literature, nor need it be, since there are large areas of practice common to many systems. And new systems especially, learning lessons from existing operational systems, building upon past experience, often contain little that is new. The purpose of this section is to discuss such modern standardized systems systematically and in detail, to mention novel and alternative techniques, and to indicate the main trends in the design and function of loans systems.

In the United States, where IBM have a very large share of the computer market, circulation systems using IBM equipment predominate. Since file processing is quite straightforward in batch loans systems, interest tends to focus on hardware, particularly that used for data capture in the library. Here, US librarians are well served by IBM with their 357 and 1030 data-collection units. Such a system has been well described in Library Technology Reports.[1]

In the UK, where IBM equipment is much less widespread, a greater variety of systems and of data-collection equipment is found. In 1969 Wilson published a detailed comparison of the four computer-based loans systems that were then operational.[2] Subsequently, similar comparisons, using a schedule of headings developed by the Circulation Working Party of the Aslib Computer Applications Group, have appeared, covering systems in the Federal Republic of Germany[3] and the United States.[4] The latter tabulation was based partly on an earlier survey by McGee of on-line circulation systems in the United States.[5] A good account of a modern British system using Automated Library Systems (ALS) equipment has been given by Young and others.[6] The best known German system, at the University of Bochum, has been described in the published report of a 1967 colloquium.[7]

Identification Numbers

The simplest method of identifying to the computer system each item that is on loan is by means of a numerical identification number. The main loans file can be conveniently arranged in order by this number, and it is simplest if this sort key can consist entirely of decimal digits. If the number also includes a check digit, this can be used to test for errors whenever identification numbers have to be handled manually.

The most obvious candidate for such an identification number is the ten-digit international standard book number (ISBN). It possesses both the above properties and has the additional advantage of being linked to complete bibliographical descriptions, by means of MARC files, for example. To the best of the author's knowledge, no library has yet used ISBNs as identification numbers in a computerized loans system. The facts that ISBNs are still by no means to be found on every book acquired by a university library, that many loans systems were designed and became operational well before ISBNs became a reality (e.g. that at the University of Southampton Library[8]), and that an identification number, to be really useful, must relate in some way to other existing library records, such as the catalogue or accessions register, account for libraries' use of other numbering schemes.

Three alternative numbers are available; call numbers, accession numbers and specially assigned identification numbers.

United States practice tends to favour the use of call numbers. These have the slight disadvantage of including alphabetical characters, but enjoy the twin advantages of already existing on catalogue cards (thus saving time and effort when a computerized loans system is being introduced) and of being easily extended to include identification of multiple copies of a title.

Many libraries have already assigned unique identification numbers to their stock in the form of accession numbers. These numbers already appear in the books and on catalogue cards or in a special accessions register to provide the necessary linkage between the number and the conventional bibliographic description. Since accession numbers in manual systems have not needed check digits, these may be added upon the introduction of a computer system. The opportunity may also be taken to add a two-digit year prefix to existing numbers, for possible future analysis of loans by publication dates.

A long-standing problem with the use of accession numbers for identification of items on loan has been the handling of reservations for titles of which multiple copies are held. The one reservation should ideally relate to all copies, any one of which may satisfy and cancel the reservation, thus leaving other copies free. A loans system's ability to do this depends on the structure of the identification numbers used for multiple copies. Conventional call numbers as used in US loans systems are often of the following form for multiple copies:

Z699.K4C1

Z699.K4C2

where "C1" signifies the first copy and "C2" the second copy. A reservation would be placed for "Z699.K4", and since this character string is found in the call numbers for both of the above copies, either will be caught by the reservation request.

Similar techniques using numerical accession numbers have been described by Ford[9] and Beale.[10]

Borrower identification has presented few problems. Many libraries have been in the habit of issuing their readers with library tickets which, if they are not an essential feature of the loans system, at least provide a simple check on borrowers' rights to use the library. To change to cards which include a numerical borrower identification number in machine-readable form has not been difficult, and two such cards are illustrated in Fig. 8.2. Numbers may either be specially assigned by the library, or existing identification numbers may be used, such as social security numbers in the United States, or student and staff identification numbers in many universities. Such university numbers normally contain an explicit indication of a student's year of study, so that, for example, before a student finally completes a course of study, the library can make sure that he has no outstanding loans.

In principle, it is possible to code into identification numbers details of each borrower's educational background, place of residence, occupation, marital status, etc. Some librarians have suggested the value of computer analyses of library use based on parameters such as the above, and there is no denying their interest, and potential value in improving library services. No such analyses have been reported in the literature, and given present-day attitudes towards individual privacy and computerized records, it is perhaps best that librarians have not made studies of this kind.

Data Capture

In Fig. 8.1 the processes of data capture are represented very simply as the conversion of records of new loans, returns, etc., into machine-readable form such as punched cards or paper tape. Figure 8.3 enlarges upon this, showing the main variations that are currently found in operational systems.

Input data to a circulation system can conveniently be divided into three categories; information about the book or other item being borrowed, information about the person who is borrowing the item, and thirdly a variety of other data such as reservations made and cancelled, loans and returns made in the absence of the normal machine-readable book and reader cards, registration of new borrowers, requests for special listings, and alterations to incorrect existing loan records. The first two categories naturally make use of machine-

FIG. 8.2. Borrower identification cards; above, University of Sussex Library; below, University of Bochum Library.

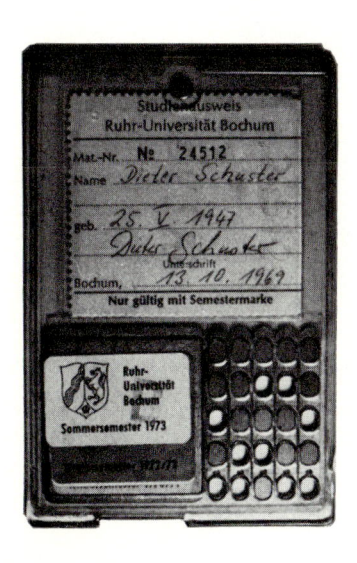

Fig. 8.4a.

Fig. 8.4. Four views of a typical Automated Library Systems installation; (a) the loans desk showing the sloping desk top on which patrons place their books;

Fig. 8.4b.

(b) close-up view of book card and borrower card readers, let into the surface of the desk;

Fig. 8.4c.
(c) book card being inserted into the reader:

Fig. 8.4d.
(d) trapping store control panel.

Fig. 8.5. The Plessey Library Pen, showing bar-coded labels in the book and on the borrower's card.

Circulation Control

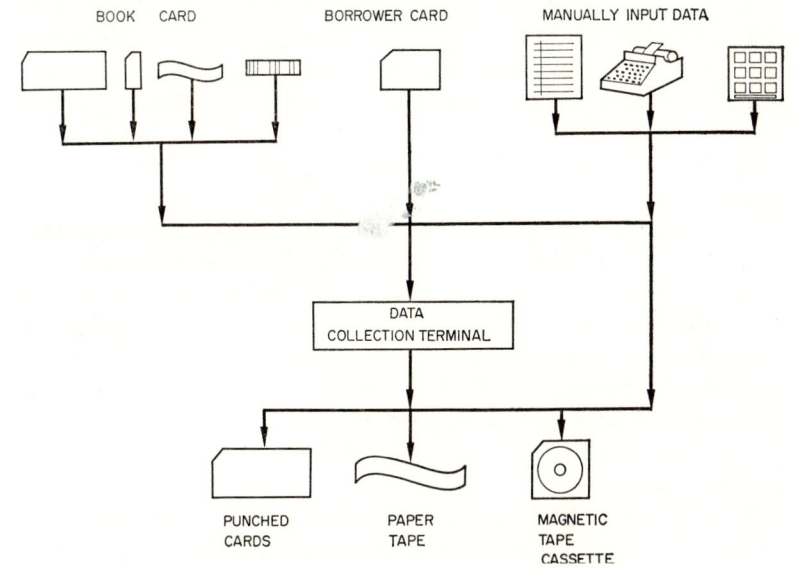

FIG. 8.3. Data capture for circulation control.

readable book and borrower cards for rapid, accurate data collection. For the third category of data, where machine-readable cards do not exist or are not available, then manual keyboarding of some kind is required.

The function of the data-collection machine or terminal is to convert all data which is to be input to the loans system into one machine-readable form and in a format which can subsequently be interpreted by the programs which update the main loans file.

The data-collection terminal, then, must be able to read a borrower card and a book card, and write the data contained in them onto a punched card, paper tape, or magnetic tape cassette. If the terminal can be operated on-line, then this data is transmitted directly to the computer, where it may update the loans file immediately (in the case of real-time systems) or alternatively be kept in a direct-access file for updating in batch mode. In addition, a facility is needed for writing the same or other data to the machine-readable file of new transactions, by some manual process.

It is convenient if there can be a keyboard as an integral part of the data collection unit, so that data input through the keyboard can be written to the transactions file in correct chronological sequence. Alternatively a separate keyboard may be used to punch cards or tape. Manual work sheets, filled up in the library, may be used for the initial recording of this data, which is subsequently keyboarded elsewhere.

An alternative to punched book and reader cards has recently been provided by the "library pen" data collection system developed by Plessey Telecommunications. This is a light-sensitive pen which reads bar-coded labels, one affixed to the book itself, the other carried on the borrower card. Book and borrower data is written to a magnetic-tape cassette, the contents of which can be transmitted automatically by telephone line to a remotely located computer.

Figure 8.4 illustrates an ALS data collection station; Fig. 8.5 shows a Plessey library pen in use.

The use of an ALS trapping store, which is used in the loans system at the University of Sussex Library, has been described by Young.[11] A control panel for the trapping store (illustrated in Fig. 8.6) is located convenient to the charge and discharge positions at the circulation desk. The panel enables a book number and/or a reader number to be set up on two sets of wheel switches. One or both of these numbers may be written to the trapping core store or erased from it, and may also be punched onto the transaction paper tape which is the normal output from the ALS data-collection terminal. A set of switches and instruction panels show the operator what combination of book and reader numbers is required for each possible transaction input through the control panel.

Possible transactions include: make and cancel a reservation, input and cancel a borrower number, check for the presence of a book or borrower number in the trapping store already, punch book or borrower number to the transaction tape without entering it into the trapping store (to request special book or borrower searches), and normal charge and discharge transactions in the absence of book and borrower cards.

Circulation Control 155

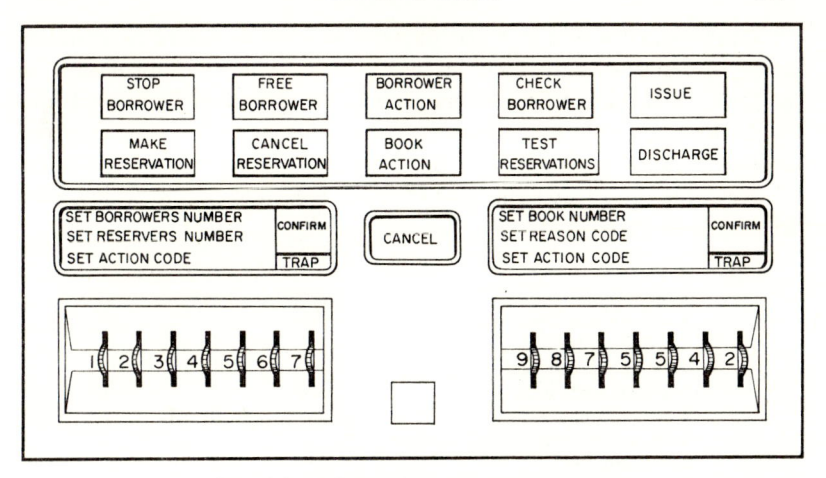

Fig. 8.6. ALS trapping store control panel.

Record Structure

A simple fixed field record structure will normally suffice for computer-based loans systems. Each record must contain information about the book and the borrower, together with data regarding date of loan, or date due, or alternatively the number of days remaining until the expiry of the loan. In addition, provision must be made for holding a short list of identification numbers of borrowers who have placed a reservation for the item. It is usually possible to specify a maximum number of reservations which will be accepted for any item, thus enabling a fixed-field fixed-size record structure to be retained.

Assuming that book and borrower identification is by number only, the following gives an idea of the kind of fixed field record structure that can be used:

Data field	Size
Record status	1 character
Reserves present	1 character
Book number	8 characters
Borrower number	8 characters
Return date	6 characters
First reserver (Borrower no.)	8 characters
Second reserver	8 characters
Third reserver	8 characters
Fourth reserver	8 characters

Many libraries find it unsatisfactory to identify books by number only, and accordingly include brief bibliographical information in addition to the identification number in the punched book card and in the loans record. The following record format which is used in the on-line system operational in the Booth Library of Eastern Illinois University[12] illustrates the type of fuller record structure which may be required.

Data field	Character positions
Control	1
Call number (first ten characters for sorting)	2–11
Accession number	12–17
Rest of call number	18–27
Edition, year, series	28–30
Volume number	31–34
Part, index, supplement number	35–37
Copy number	38–39
Location code	40–41
Author	42–51
Title	52–78
Control character	79
Cumulative no. of loans for this item	80–82
Status of item	83
Borrower number	84–92
Borrower status	93
Due date	94–99
Format code	100
Reserver number	101–109
Reserver status	110
Reservation present	111
Unused characters	112–124

A variable length record structure used in an experimental on-line system has been described by Boyd.[13] The complete loan record for any item consisted of a series of unit records chained together, each consisting of a book number, borrower number, transaction type, date and control information. Complete flexibility was afforded thereby in respect of the number of reservations that could be accepted for any item while still retaining a basically simple record structure.

File Processing

Full details of programs and files for a typical batch-processing circulation system are given in the published report of the University

Circulation Control 157

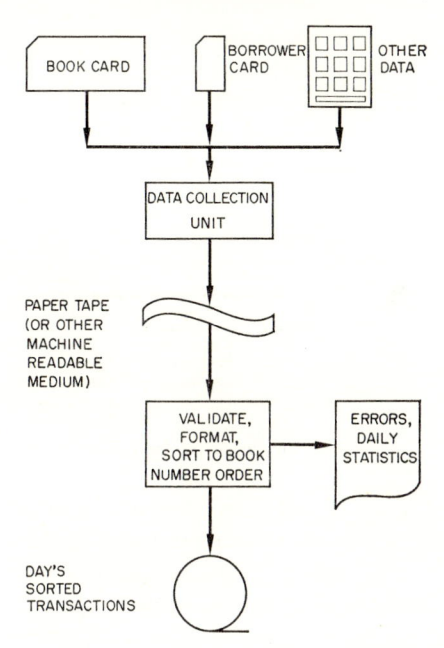

FIG. 8.7. Production of magnetic tape of records of day's transactions.

of Southampton Library system,[8] and the present section is an adaptation and simplification of the data given in that report.

The output from a data-collection unit will consist of a series of book and borrower numbers together with associated transaction category codes and author and title information, etc., if this is given in each book card, arranged in chronological order of transactions. Because the main loans file is arranged in book identification number order, new transactions must be sorted into book number order before the main file is updated. New records are checked for accuracy (such computer checks can be made on the format of the data in each data field, and tests made on numbers supplied with check digits), and formatted into the record structure used in the main loans file. Figure 8.7 shows this process schematically.

Figure 8.8 shows the next stage in the process, in which the main loans file is updated with the new sorted transactions, and a variety of

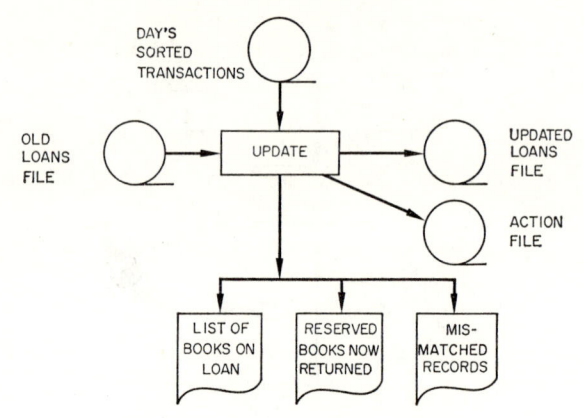

FIG. 8.8. Updating the loans file.

outputs produced. Each record in the new transactions file is matched with a corresponding record in the main loans file, or else inserted in the correct position in that file. Discharge, or return, transactions, reservation and cancel reservation transactions should all match with existing loan records. New loans should not. Exceptions to these rules are printed in a list of mismatched records. The main loans file is also printed in book number order.

Returned books for which reservations have been recorded in the main loans file are listed to enable library staff to prevent them from being reshelved, and may also be written to the magnetic-tape action file which will be used to print letters to the reservers to tell them that the books are now available. This action file also contains records of books now overdue and for which overdue letters must be printed, and records of books to be recalled from their present borrowers (because reservations have been placed). Also included in this file are books on loan to individual borrowers for whom personal on-loan lists have been requested.

Figure 8.9 shows the subsequent processing of this action file. It is first sorted into borrower number order. This serves the purpose of bringing together all book records which are to be communicated to each borrower, and enabling the sorted file to be passed against the borrowers' register. The program which prints the letters reads the

Circulation Control

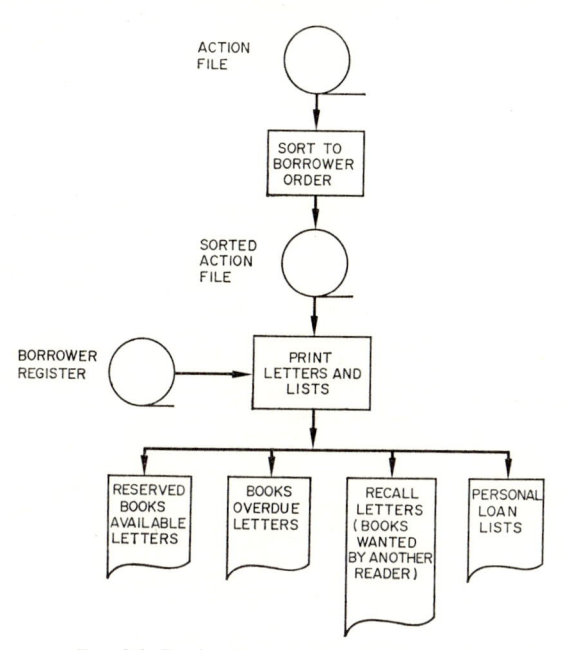

FIG. 8.9. Production of letters to borrowers.

borrower number from the sorted action file, picks up the corresponding full name and address from the borrowers' register and includes these in the printed letters.

From time to time, the main loans file is sorted into borrower order and printed to give a listing by borrower (Fig. 8.10). This list groups together the books on loan to each borrower, and if the library's loan regulations specify a maximum number of items which may be on loan to any individual at one time, this list shows clearly those individuals with more than the permitted maximum number of items on loan. The sorted loans file may be searched by program to find such offending borrowers, and warning letters can be printed.

It is a straightforward, though not necessarily quick, task to sort the main loans file in a variety of different ways and print it to produce listings for use by library staff in answering users' queries. Author/title and subject lists are sometimes prepared in this way, provided, of

Automation in Libraries

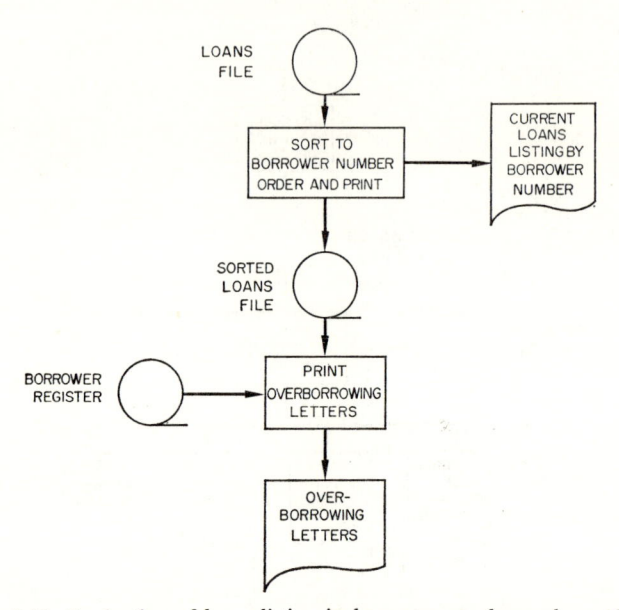

FIG. 8.10. Production of loans listing in borrower number order and over-borrowing letters.

course, that this information has been included in the original loan record, or alternatively, if the library's shelf list or catalogue is in machine-readable form.

Figures 8.11 to 8.16 show samples of printed lists and letters produced by the University of Southampton circulation system. They may be regarded as typical examples of what is possible with a quite "standard" system. There are many other layouts, and texts for letters; for example, Fig. 8.17 shows a letter printed by the Bochum University Library system. Laid out more formally than the Southampton letters, this letter is to let Frl. Kroll know that the book, call number GA 28990, has been available for her at the circulation desk for the past 8 days, and should be collected as soon as possible.

Circulation Control

```
SOUTHAMPTON UNIVERSITY LIBRARY          LIBRARY CIRCULATION CONTROL                            ISSUES AT:- 06/09/73        PAGE 283

BOOK NO.          AUTHOR AND TITLE                                                  CLASS MK   LOAN DATE   BORROWER

72-54310 7    EICHRODT,W.,/THEOLOGY OF THE OLD TESTAMENT V.1 61                     BS11V2     04/09/73    7089279
72-54311 6    EICHRODT,W.,/THEOLOGY OF THE OLD TESTAMENT V.2 67                     BS11V2     29/05/73    7125046
72-54313 4    SJOQUIST,J.A.,/SEARCHING FOR STRUCTURE 71                             QA76       22/06/73    1258788
72-54371 0    GELLING,M.,/PLACE-NAMES OF BERKSHIRE,V.1 73                           DA600      04/09/73    2002264
72-54372 8    RAMSAY,A.,/WORKS V.5 72                                               PR4635     09/02/73    7100469
72-54377 9    WAGNER,M.H.,/INTRO TO THEORY OF MAGNETISM 72                          QC753      29/06/73    1102801
72-54377 3    TRILLING,L./SINCERITY & AUTHENTICITY 72                               PN56       08/02/73    1043986
72-54309 6    OTNES,R.K.,/DIGITAL TIME SERIES ANALYSIS 72                           QA76       06/08/73    7089724
72-54301 5    INT.INST.LAND RECLAM,& IMPROV./PUBL.16:DRAIN.PRINC. 72                TC801      06/08/73    7201737
72-54407 9    FORSTER,F.M.,/LIFE TO COME 72                                         PR6011     16/07/73    1235311

72-54428 4    WINNICOTT,D.W.,/CHILD & THE FAMILY 57                                 HQ772      02/02/73    S.L.C.
72-54429 3    WINNICOTT,D.W.,/CHILD & THE OUTSIDE WORLD 57                          HQ781      08/02/73    S.L.C.
72-54430 5    LAING,R.D.,/POLITICS OF THE FAMILY 71                                 HQ734      08/02/73    S.L.C.
72-54435 7    HADFIELD,/PSYCHOSOCIAL INTERIOR OF THE FAMILY 68                      HQ734      02/02/73    S.L.C.
72-54437 4    GOLDBERG,F.M.,/HELPING THE AGED 70                                    HV1481     29/03/73    S.L.C.
72-54445 5    DICKS,H.V.,/MARITAL TENSIONS 67                                       HQ728      08/02/73    S.L.C.
72-54445 5    RUDDOCK,R.,/ROLES & RELATIONSHIPS 69                                  HM131      29/05/73    S.L.C.
72-54445 0    GRIDLEY,J.M.,/PRINCIPLES ELECTRIC TRANSMISSION LINES 67               TK5221     15/05/73    7242018      R1
72-54455 0    G.B. CENTRAL OFF. OF INF./ENGLISH LEGAL SYST.,4TH ED. 72              KD703      31/01/73    1025805
72-54471 0    QUINTON,A.,/NATURE OF THINGS 73                                       BD351      09/07/73    1234684

72-54473 4    ALCOCK,L.,/BY SOUTH CADBURY IS THAT CAMELOT 72                        CC330      01/05/73    7202776
72-54410 0    DORR,M.H.,/SOVIET ECONOMIC DEVELOPMENT SINCE 1917 66                  HC335      04/06/73    7017928
72-54435 0    CAMBRIDGE ECONOMIC HISTORY OF EUROPE,V.6 PT.1 66                      HC240      29/05/73    6911153
72-54424 5    DINGLE,F.H.,/SCIENCE AT THE CROSSROADS 72                             QC        05/07/73    6911811
72-54524 5    KONINGSTEIN,J.A.,/INTRO.THEORY OF RAMAN EFFECT 72                     QC461      09/05/73    1231227
72-54534 8    BLUMER,H.,/SYMBOLIC INTERACTIONISM 69                                 HM24       02/07/73    1265542
72-54536 4    MCCANN,J.J.,/SKINBURNE AN EXPERIMENT IN CRITICISM 72                  PR4554     22/05/73    7120974
72-54557 7    SKELOV,J.J.,/GROWING UP ABSURD 72                                     HM25       07/05/73    7121759
72-54557 7    SALLOW,J.,/MAPS FOR THE LOCAL HISTORIAN 72                            DA29       29/05/73    1025805
72-54500 7    MCLAFFERTY,F.W.,/INTERPRETATION OF MASS SPECTRA 66                    QC470      18/05/73    1045836

72-54568 0    KIRK,R.,/STATISTICAL ISSUES 72                                        HA29       10/05/73    1066897
73-00001 0    FORSTER,E.M.,/MAURICE                                                 PR6011     16/08/73    1242296
73-00003 1    INT.AFRICAN SEMINAR,8TH/IDEAS AFRICAN CUSTOMARY LAW 69                KOS        21/06/73    7135696
73-00029 8    PUDLE,C.P.,/THEORY OF MAGNETIC RESONANCE 72                           QC765      13/06/73    2008334
73-00057 7    WOLF,E.,/SEMICONDUCTORS 71                                            QC612      02/05/73    7208049
73-00080 6    PATEL,V.J.,/GRAPHS & NETWORKS                                         QA166      29/05/73    7108410
73-00082 5    HAIR,G.G.,/APPLIED GROUP THEORY 67                                    QA171      31/05/73    7100469
73-00089 7    SOMORJAI,G.A.,/PRINCIPLES OF SURFACE CHEMISTRY 72                     QD550      07/05/73    6912974
73-00110 4    NOVE,A.,/ECONOMIC HISTORY OF U.S.S.R. 69                              HC335      01/05/73    7125151
73-00122 9    INTERNAT.INST.OF PHILOSOPHY/ENTRETIENS,1970 72                        BD161      22/03/73    1234684

73-00125 2    CLARK,M.,/SOLID STATE PHYSICS 68                                      QC176      09/07/73    1254782
73-00145 8    CODING PROCESSES IN HUMAN MEMORY 72                                   BF507      13/07/73    1025964
73-00147 6    SCHWARTZ,A./NEW POLITICAL ECONOMY 72                                  BS507      16/03/73    1032299
73-00157 5    ARSWORTH,L./BANKS & MONETARY SYSTEM IN U.K. 73                        HG2988     05/02/73    1031317
73-00161 0    ISAACS,V.,/MASSES,ED.H.STAEHELIN 70                                   M321       06/02/73    1045962
73-00164 5    HARRIS,V.,/UNEMPLOYMENT & POLITICS 72                                 HD5767     29/03/73    S.L.C.
73-00170 0    MARGFAVES,D.H./INTERPERSONAL RELATIONS 72                             HM132      16/08/73    3500748
73-00176 0    WAPP,W.B./RELIGION & SOCIETY IN ENGLAND,1790-1850 72                  BR759      12/07/73    7129394
73-00177 5    YEATS,W.B.,/MEMOIRS,ED.D.DONOGHUE 72                                  PR5907     06/08/73    1035789
73-00182 3    BEYNON,H.,/PERCEPTIONS OF YORK 72                                     HD4904     04/06/73    4294971
```

Fig. 8.11. University of Southampton Library, print of the main loans file in book number order.

BORROWER NO	MUBR	CAT	BLOK NO	AUTHOR/TITLE	CLASSMARK	LOAN DATE
				LIBRARY RESEARCH GROUP – BORROWER PRINT		
6908861	4		65-040265	I.E.E./CONVENTION ON H.F.COMMUNICATIONS	TK6561	23/06/72
	4		65-068362	CHAMPION,F.A./COMMON TESTING PROCEDURES	TA462	25/06/72
	2		65-042938	COTTON,H./ELECTRICAL TECHNOLOGY	TK146	26/06/72
	2		65-011189	CASSELL,W.L./LINEAR ELECTRIC CIRCUITS	TK3000	07/07/72
	2		66-081667	REDFORD,A.H./MECHANICAL ENGINEERING DESIGN	TJ230	07/07/72
	2		67-035598	MILLMAN,J./PULSE DIGITAL & SWITCHING WAVEFORMS	TK7816	07/07/72
	2		69-015618	LOW,B.R./THEORY OF MACHINES	TJ170	07/08/72
	2		70-047675	GRAY,P.F./ELECTRONIC PRINCIPLES 69	TK7815	07/07/72
6908896	4		70-060155	DUGGAN,T.V./APPLIED ENGINEERING DESIGN & ANALYSIS 70	TJ230	20/07/72
	2		71-059259	TRYLINSKI,W./FINE MECHANISMS & PRECISION INSTRUMENTS71	TA165	07/08/72
	2		71-044474	SHEPHERD,J./HIGHER ELECTRICAL ENGINEERING 70	TK145	11/05/72
	2		71-112529	GRAEME,J.G./OPERATIONAL AMPLIFIERS 71	TK7872	14/06/72
	2		50-214777	SOLID STATE PHYSICS V12 1961	QC753	16/05/72
	2		67-086650	PARRATT,L.G./MOD.MAGNETISM	QC753	16/05/72
	2		66-104486	MORRISH,A.H./PHYSICAL PRINCIPLES OF MAGNETISM	QC753	16/05/72
	2		67-108628	CARFV,R./MAGNETIC DOMAINS	TA13	16/05/72
	2		68-083056	POTMA,T./STRAIN GAUGES	QC451	08/05/72
6908920	4		69-067505	SHURE,R.W.X./PRINCIPLES OF ATOMIC SPECTRA 68	QC753	03/07/72
	2		59-458050	KRUPICKA,S./ELEMENTS OF THEORETICAL MAGNETISM 68	QD181	10/07/72
	2		60-031702	WILLIAMS,H.E./CYANOGEN COMPOUNDS	QC753	13/07/72
	2		66-045641	LEVER,R.B.P./INORGANIC ELECTRONIC SPECTROSCOPY 68	QA251	13/07/72
6908934	2		59-293092	MONTGOMERY,D K/10 POLOGICAL TRANSFORMATION GROUPS	QA611	13/07/72
	2		62-053572	WEINBERG,L./NETWORK ANALYSIS	TK3001	31/07/72
	2		64-067144	BALABANIAN,N./NETWORK SYNTHESIS	TK5000	31/07/72
	2		64-079419	STORER,J.E./PASSIVE NETWORK SYNTHESIS	TK5000	10/07/72
	2		66-030713	TUTTLE,D.F./ELECTRICAL NETWORKS	TK5000	24/03/72
	2		66-062750	VAN VALKENBURG,M.E./INTRO.TO MODERN NETWORK SYNTH.	TK5000	31/07/72
	2		68-143163	LEPAGE,W.R./LINEAR SYSTEMS OF SYNTHESIS 66	TK3000	23/07/72
	2		68-127949	MACOMBER,W./LIE GROUPS & LIE ALGEBRAS 66	QA385	13/07/72
	2		69-041738	HAUSNER,M./LIE GROUPS & LIE ALGEBRAS 66	TK7835	31/08/72
6908970	2		70-082009	NICHOLS,K.G./TRANSISTOR PHYSICS 66	TK5000	31/08/72
	4		71-075174	ZEPLER,E.E./TRANSIENTS IN ELECTRONIC ENGINEERING 71	QC174	21/08/72
	4		68-022767	FLINT,H.T./WAVE MECHANICS	QC416	24/08/72
6908993	2		71-069276	TROUP,G.J.F./OPTICAL COHERENCE THEORY 67	QC355	26/05/72
6909027	4		71-066163	SMITH,F./OPTICS 71	QB301	24/08/72
	2		52-158586	RASPAJIAN,J.V./MUSCLES ALIVE:ELECTROMYOGRAPHY 67	QB320	11/02/72
	2		65-108654	HOOPER,A./A HISTORY OF THE FORESHORE	Q310	19/07/71
	2		65-040025	ASHBY,W.R./INTROD.TO CYBERNETICS	KD320	15/07/71
	2		65-122741	COULSON/THE LAW OF WATERS	HD82	06/07/72
	2		67-006665	BAUDOL,W.J. WELFARE ECONOMICS & THEORY OF STATE	HC257	21/06/72
	2		67-035539	YORKSHIRE AND HUMBERSIDE ECON PLANNING COUNCIL REVIEW*	TA710	15/05/72
	4		68-109408	WU,T.H./SOIL MECHANICS	TA710	19/07/71
	2		69-025275	ROSENAK,S./SOIL MECHANICS 65	HC257	06/07/72
	2		69-049277	BUCHANAN,J.M./DEMAND & SUPPLY OF PUBLIC GOODS	HJ141	06/07/72
	2		69-115406	CENTRAL UNIT FOR ENVIRONMENTAL PLANNING/HUMBERSIDE 69*	HT391	13/05/72
	2		70-082175	MCLOUGHLIN,J.B./URBAN & REGIONAL PLANNING 69	TA180	08/05/72
	2		71-047975	MARKS,R.J./ASPECTS CIVIL ENG.CONTRACT PROCEDURE 65	TC205	14/02/72
				AM.SOC CIVIL ENGINEERS/12TH COASTAL ENGINEERING CONF		

FIG. 8.12. University of Southampton Library, print of the main loans file in borrower number order.

LIBRARY RESEARCH GROUP - ALPHABETIC PRINT 30/08/73

BOOK NO.	AUTHOR/TITLE	BOOK NO.	AUTHOR/TITLE
52-082694	PHILP,R./HOW A PENNY BECAME A THOUSAND POUNDS	66-034177	PHINES,F.N./PHASE DIAGRAMS IN METALLURGY
50-234396	PHLA VOL 57 1942	50-933890	PHOENIX 26 72
50-985894	PHONETICA 26 73	50-987487	PHOTOCHEMISTRY & PHOTOBIOLOGY 17 73
71-112725	PHY.TECH.IN BIOL.RES./PHYSICAL TECH.IN BIOL.RES	68-117711	PHY.TECH.IN BIOL.RES./PHYSICAL TECH.IN BIOL.RES
71-098463	PHY.TECH.IN BIOL.RES./PHYSICAL TECH.IN BIOL.RES	59-725374	PHYS SOC/MET FACTORS IN RADIO-WAVE PROPAGATION
50-984141	PHYSICA FENNICA 7 72	50-984477	PHYSICA SCRIPTA 7 73
50-979950	PHYSICA STATUS SOLIDI B 57 73	50-936707	PHYSICA STATUS SOLIDI 16 A 73
50-986695	PHYSICA STATUS SOLIDI B 56 73	59-489126	PHYSICAL SOC./STRENGTH OF SOLIDS
50-983395	PHYSICS & CHEMISTRY GLASSES 13 72	50-982857	PHYSICS ABS INDEX 75 SUBJECT A JUL-DEC 72
50-979923	PHYSICS ABS AUTHOR INDEX 76 73 JAN-JUN	50-983742	PHYSICS LETTERS B 44 73
72-027899	PIAGET,J./CHILD'S CONCEPTION OF NUMBER 52	72-028131	PIAGET,J./CHILD'S CONCEPTION OF GEOMETRY 60
72-045035	PIAGET,J./CONSTRUCTION OF REALITY IN THE CHILD	52-228504	PIAGET,J./INTELLECTURAL OPERATIONS & THEIR DEVE
72-027741	PIAGET,J./MENTAL IMAGERY IN THE CHILD 71	71-070777	PIAGET,J./MECHANISMS OF PERCEPTION 69
72-027961	PIAGET,J./ORIGIN OF INTELLIGENCE IN THE CHILD 5	72-082085	PIAGET,J./PLAY,DREAMS & IMITATION IN CHILDHOOD
71-070683	PIAGET,J./PSYCHOLOGY OF THE CHILD 69	71-090841	PIAGET,J./SIX PSYCHOLOGICAL STUDIES 68
52-228522	PIAGET,J./THEORY OF STAGES IN COGNITIVE DEVELOP	59-112787	PIAGET,J./THE LANGUAGE & THOUGHT OF A CHILD
59-068592	PIAGGIO,H.T.H./ELEM.TREAT.ON DIFFEREN.EQUATIONS	59-068754	PIAGGIO,H.T.H./DIFFERENTIAL EQUATIONS
73-063287	PIANKO,M./MOD.METHS TESTING ROTATING COMPS TURB	59-780654	PICKERT,G./PROJEKTIVE EBENEN
72-073216	PICKFORD,R.W./PSYCHOLOGY AND VISUAL AESTHETICS	67-073244	PICKLES,D./THE UNEASY ENTENTE
71-061681	PICKLES,D.M./DEMOCRACY 70	72-536328	PICKLES,D.M./UNEASY ENTENTE 66
64-051442	PICKLES,W./ACCOUNTANCY	59-974668	PICKLES,W./FRENCH CONST.OF OCT.4TH 1958
72-010903	PICOZZI,R./HISTORY OF TRISTAN SCHOLARSHIP 71	71-073512	PIEPER,J./FOUR CARDINAL VIRTUES 65
70-066063	PIERCE,A./FUNDAMENTALS OF NONPARAMETRIC STATIST	68-010652	PIERCE,J.F./SEMICONDUCTOR JUNCTION DEVICES
65-148769	PIERCE,J.R./THEORY AND DESIGN OF ELECTRON BEAMS	59-641755	PIERCE,J.R./THEORY & DESIGN OF ELECTRON BEAMS
65-057094	PIERCE,J.R./SYMBOLS SIGNALS & NOISE	67-117059	PIERCE,W.H./FAILURE-TOLERANT COMPUTER DESIGN
67-016394	PIGGOTT,/THE PREHISTORIC PEOPLES OF SCOTLAND	65-026849	PIGGOTT,S./GUIDE CATALOGUE OF NEOLITHIC & BRONZ
70-079616	PIGGOTT,S./NEOLITHIC CULTURES OF THE BRITISH IS	72-519040	PIKE,E.R./HUMAN DOCUMENTS OF LLOYD GEORGE ERA 7
59-963886	PIKE,M./TOWNSMAN'S FOOD	72-516094	PIKE,R./ARISTOCRATS & TRADERS:SEVILLIAN SOCIETY
73-061434	PIL'NYAK,B./BOR.PIL'NYAK:STAT'I I MATERIALY 73	68-088606	PILAR,F.L./ELEMENTARY QUANTUM CHEMISTRY 68
63-020677	PILGRIM TRUST/MEN WITHOUT WORK	69-073435	PINCHBECK,I./WOMEN WORKERS AND THE IND.REVOL.17
71-090814	PINCHERLE,L./ELECTRONIC ENERGY BANDS IN SOLIDS	59-262299	PINCHES,T.G./RELIGION OF BABYLONIA & ASSYRIA
52-939109	PINCUS,L./MARRIAGE 60	52-939118	PINCUS,L./MARRIAGE 60
70-010628	PINDER,J./EUROPE AFTER DE GAULLE 69	73-036418	PINDYCK,R.S./OPTIMAL PLANNING FOR ECON.STABILIZ
73-076175	PINEAUX,J./POLEMIQUE PROTESTANTE CONTRE RONSARD	73-076184	PINEAUX,J./POLEMIQUE PROTESTANTE CONTRE RONSARD
72-055128	PINES,D./ELEMENTARY EXCITATIONS IN SOLIDS 64	72-058567	PINKER,R./SOCIAL THEORY & SOCIAL POLICY 71
72-067541	PINKNEY,R./GHANA UNDER MILITARY RULE 1966-1969	62-029858	PINKUS,O./THEORY OF HYDRODYNAMICS LUBRICATION
59-906388	PINNEY,/ORDINARY DIFFERENCE DIFFERENTIAL EQUATI	66-064099	PINNEY,E./FEDERALISM BUREACRACY & PARTY POL IN
68-126423	PINNEY,R./VANISHING TRIBES	69-011665	PINTNER,W.M./RUSSIAN ECONOMIC POLICY UNDER NICH
66-111724	PINTO,V.DES./WILLIAM BLAKE	71-002796	PIPER,D./PAINTING IN ENGLAND,1500-1880 65
66-065560	PIPER,H.D./F.SCOTT FIZGERALD	70-078392	PIPES,L.A./APPLIED MATHS FOR ENGINEERS & PHYSIC
63-069966	PIPES,L.A./MATRIX METHODS FOR ENGINEERING	70-028360	PIPES,R./SOC.DEMOCRACY & ST.PETERSBURG LABOR MO
69-015711	PIRANI,M.S./PRINCIPLES OF VACUUM ENGINEERING 61	63-001945	PIRRE,A./BACH,J.S.
52-929249	PISTON,W./ORCHESTRATION 55	52-226751	PITCHER,D.R./XYY SYNDROME
72-078350	PITKIN,H.F./WITTGENSTEIN & JUSTICE 72	72-056938	PIVEN,F.F./REGULATING THE POOR 72
72-056956	PLACE,F./AUTOBIOGRAPHY OF FRANCIS PLACE,1771-18	72-023695	PLAGER,S.J./NEW APPROACHES IN THE LAW OF PROPER
67-003518	PLAMENATZ,J./MAN AND SOCIETY VOL I	66-039181	PLAMENATZ,/READINGS FROM LIBERAL WRITERS
67-079069	PLANK,R./HANDBUCH DER KALTE TECHNIK V.4.	59-703251	PLANK,R./HANDBUCH DER KALTETECHNIK 2
67-079036	PLANK,R./HANDBUCH DER KALTE TECHNIK V.8.	72-079665	PLANNING & MARKET RELATIONS 71
50-980330	PLANNING & TRANSPORTATION ABS 70/2	50-980349	PLANNING & TRANSPORTATION ABS 72/3

FIG. 8.13. University of Southampton Library, print of the main loans file in author/title order.

```
1021893      1

NR A.I.          SOUTHAMPTON UNIVERSITY LIBRARY.                    OVERDUE NOTICE            25/07/73
   HISTORY
                 PLEASE RETURN THE FOLLOWING BOOK(S), WHICH IS/ARE OVERDUE:-
                 DRECHSLER,H./SOZIALISTISCHE ARBEITERPARTEI 65    DD253    12/04/73   72-518155


       RESERVED BOOKS (MARKED R) ARE REQUIRED IMMEDIATELY.    OTHER BOOKS MAY BE RENEWED IF BROUGHT TO LIBRARY.
                                       PLEASE RETURN THIS SLIP IN CASE OF QUERY.
```

FIG. 8.14. University of Southampton Library, overdue note to borrower.

Circulation Control

```
7090099          2                SOUTHAMPTON UNIVERSITY LIBRARY.          RECALL NOTICE          04/09/73

MR  S.                 THE FOLLOWING BOOKS,REQUIRED BY ANOTHER READER,MUST BE RETURNED IMMEDIATELY:-
         CHEMISTRY    *FABELINSKII,I./MOLECULAR SCATTERING OF LIGHT 68      QC436   27/02/73  69-071089


                                  PLEASE PLACE THIS SLIP IN THE BOOK WHEN RETURNING IT
                                       PLEASE RETURN THIS SLIP IN CASE OF QUERY.
```

Fig. 8.15. University of Southampton Library, recall note to borrower.

```
SOUTHAMPTON UNIVERSITY LIBRARY.           OVERBORROWING NOTICE                                    SLIP NUMBER:  1

7008422    4       YOUR LOAN ENTITLEMENT IS 5 BOOKS,  ON 07/02/75 YOU HAD ON LOAN THE FOLLOWING   9.
                                            PLEASE RETURN ANY 4 (LIBRARY REGULATION 3).

PISS M J
                        65144435        MANN,P.M./APPROACH TO URBAN SOCIOLOGY
    JUNIOR COMMON ROOM  67071414        NISBET,R.A./EMILE DURKHEIM.
                        67074985        PARSONS,T./SOCIAL STRUCTURE AND PRSONALITY
                        67098064        ALPERT,H./EMILE DURKHEIM & HIS SOCIOLOGY
                        69050705        DURKHEIM,E./DIVISION OF LABOR IN SOCIETY 53
                        70007105        PAHL,R.E./PATTERNS OF URBAN LIFE 70
                        71032627        HANDBOOK OF MEDICAL SOCIOLOGY,ED.H.E.FREEMAN 63
                        71105549        MULKAY,M.J./FUNCTIONALISM,EXCH.& THEORETICAL STRAT.71
                        72519871        GOODMAN,R./AFTER THE PLANNERS 72

              IN CASE OF QUERY, PLEASE RETURN THIS SLIP.
```

FIG. 8.16. University of Southampton Library, overborrowing note to borrower.

```
UNIVERSITAETSBIBLIOTHEK   BOCHUM


                                        4630  BOCHUM-QUERENBURG
                                        INSTITUTSGEBAEUDE    IB/1
FRL.                                    INSTITUTSGEBAEUDE    NB/1
DOROTHEA KROLL

                                        OEFFNUNGSZEITEN:
4630  BOCHUM-QUERENBURG                 MONTAGS - FREITAGS 9-22 UHR
                                        SAMSTAGS 9-12 UHR
LAERHEIDESTR. 10


                                        06.04.1972
                                          BEN.NR.:14097      TYP:P



SEHR GEEHRTES FRAEULEIN KROLL,


DAS FUER SIE VORGEMERKTE BUCH:
GA 28990
LIEGT IN DER LEIHSTELLE ACHT TAGE FUER SIE BEREIT.
WIR BITTEN, DEN BAND MOEGLICHST BALD ABZUHOLEN.

BUECHER DER SIGNATURGRUPPEN M, S, ZM, ZS, ER UND U SIND IN DER
NATURWISSENSCHAFTLICHEN ABTEILUNG DER UNIV. -STAATSBIBLIOTHEK
IM GEBAEUDE NB ABZUHOLEN ODER ZURUECKZUGEBEN.



                     MIT VORZUEGLICHER HOCHACHTUNG
                                I.A.
                            GEZ. LINDEMANN
```

FIG. 8.17. University of Bochum Library, letter to borrower.

REAL-TIME CIRCULATION SYSTEMS

Batch circulation systems have shown themselves to be reliable, economical and able to provide a range of outputs that no other type of system is able to match. Many different designs are in operation, giving a high level of satisfaction to library staff and to users. But, with the exception of those systems which include a small real-time trapping store, their single and important shortcoming is in the matter of currency.

Printed loans lists available to the circulation assistants show the items that were on loan when the loans file was last updated. They cannot take account of transactions since then. Special listings, such as borrower and author/title lists, may be even more out of date. Reservations remain a little unsatisfactory, particularly in respect of the identification of reserved books when they are returned to the library. Other checks and controls, for example, on the number of books which may be on loan to a user at any one time, cannot be made until after the event. And because circulation is the most rapidly moving area of library activity where currency is most important, some libraries have felt that only a real-time circulation system will fully meet their needs.

A small number of real-time loans systems are now operational, and it is possible to obtain a good idea of their salient characteristics. Perhaps the best known is the system, christened BELLREL, which has been operational in the Library and Information Systems Center of Bell Telephone Laboratories at Murray Hill, New Jersey, since March 1968.[14] Other real-time systems are operational at Bucknell University Library, Northwestern University Library, and Ohio State University Libraries. Reference 4 includes a detailed analysis of the characteristics of these systems. In the UK a small system is operational at the library in the Atomic Weapons Research Establishment at Foulness.[15]

An interesting system is at an advanced state of development in the University of Lancaster Library.[16] Termed "hybrid", it employs a mini-computer located in the library to give a real-time service in respect of recent transactions, items borrowed from a short loan or "reserve" collection, and of course all reserved or held items and delinquent borrowers. Such an approach has the twin advantages of costing much less than a full on-line real-time system, and improving on the standard batch system design only in its weakest areas, i.e. current transactions and reservations.

Library Aspects

The major differences between batch and real-time loans systems lie in aspects of systems design; they make use of quite different levels of computer service. The real-time system has the full power of a computer immediately available during library opening hours, whereas a batch system makes use of the computer only intermittently, so that it is only the system products that are immediately available during library opening hours. It is this instant availability of computing power that provides the important difference, as far as library services are concerned, between batch and real-time systems. And this computing power is seen in the form of a wide range of different responses the system is able to make to a variety of circulation transactions.

Consider first the operation of a standard batch loans system, without a trapping store. For a charge, or issue, transaction, the user comes to the loans desk with a book and his borrower's ticket. Ticket and book card are read by the data collection unit, the transaction is accepted, and the borrower leaves the library. But there could be a multitude of reasons why that loan should not take place. The book might be in a non-loanable collection. It might have been reserved by another reader. It might be wanted by the library for some reason, such as rebinding or recataloguing. There might be some reason why that borrower should not use the library's loans service. Some of these contingencies can be guarded against, for example by clearly marking all books in non-loan collections in some distinctive way. But if the circulation system is to provide safeguards against such eventualities, then although a batch system can provide them (and very effectively), it can only do so after the event.

A real-time system can provide immediate checks and reports on such a seemingly straightforward loan transaction. The library user brings his book and borrower's ticket to the loans desk as before, and book card and borrower's ticket are also read in the same way, but there the similarities cease. The computer can make immediate checks on the book number, the reader number and on both in combination together. Is this book in a non-loan collection? Is it reserved, and if so is it reserved for this borrower? Is the borrower's status OK? Are any fines outstanding? Is he permitted to borrow this category of book; has he exceeded his quota of items on loan at any one time? And so on. Answers to questions such as these can be provided, either positively or negatively, at the loans desk immediately.

Such features of a real-time system are, by nature, restrictive, and most borrowers would probably prefer the library not to be able to have the answers to such questions available immediately. But there are some positive features of a real-time system which serve to help rather than hinder the borrower. Most important of these is the facility for interrogating accurate and up-to-date files and obtaining immediate responses. An inquiry about the status of an item not on the library shelves can be answered in the sure knowledge that even if its status was changed only very recently, the loans file will fully reflect that change. If, for example, our imaginary reader came to the loans desk to borrow a book, the system, when checking on his status, might find that a book he had reserved had just been returned from loan, so that he could borrow it immediately.

In ways such as this, some small, some large, a real-time system will materially improve the operation of the circulation system. It will give "tighter" control of loans, and if the loans regulations have been wisely framed, this will give a better service to the library's users.

This does not, of course, take any account of the effort required to provide such improved service. To put the question bluntly, does it pay a library to install a real-time loans system in order to achieve improved reader service?

Each library must answer this question for itself in the light both of the value it sets on marginal improvements to service, and of the actual cost of a particular real-time system. At the present time, unit costs for real-time systems are approximately two to three times those of batch systems, and it is unlikely that such cost differentials could be justified on the grounds of improved reader services. There is a need, however, for a few libraries to develop experimental real-time loans systems so that, perhaps in a decade or so, when unit costs should be much more favourable, some well-proven systems will exist, which can be adopted widely without much difficulty.

System Aspects

Differences between batch and real-time systems can be considered under two main headings: the on-line linkage between the data-collection units and the computer, together with a facility for receiving responses from the system; and secondly, the file structure necessary for a real-time system.

On-line linkage

"On-line" means simply that a particular peripheral unit, such as a data-collection unit for a library circulation system, instead of writing transaction data to a punched or magnetic tape or to punched cards, writes this data to a file held in a suitable storage unit in the computer itself, such as a magnetic-disc file. To do this, the peripheral must be directly connected to the computer, and so is said to be "on-line". Real-time systems imply on-line data collection, and, fortunately, this is nowadays a perfectly straightforward procedure.

Most of the data-collection units used in batch-loans systems can be connected on-line, or "interfaced", with a computer. This causes no problem, provided, of course, that the computer itself has facilities for on-line working. But standard library data-collection units must be provided with a device to enable responses to queries to be received in the library. Most commonly, a teletypewriter is used, but Ohio State University Libraries use cathode-ray tube visual display terminals as well. In the UK, the Library of the University of Surrey is developing a real-time loans system using standard ALS data-collection units supplemented by a teletypewriter for system responses.[17]

File structure

A simple direct-access file structure has already been described (Fig. 4.6, p. 50), in which a record identification number served to indicate the record's location or address in the file. A similar technique must be used in the direct-access loans file of a real-time loans system. It is unlikely that, say, the book number can be used directly as an address in the file, but a simple modification of it might be suitable.

Take the case of a library where the maximum expected number of items on loan is 10,000. Then space in a direct-access memory store must be set aside for 10,000 loan records of stated size. Suppose also, for simplicity, that we divide that space into 1000 units, numbered 000 to 999, each of which is able to hold a maximum of ten loan records. Assume further that the library has 100,000 books available for loan, and that these have five-digit identification numbers ranging from 00000 to 99999. It is a straightforward matter to allocate book numbers to addresses in the direct-access memory—each addressable location has 100 books assigned to it. So the address may be calculated from the book number by dividing the book number by 100, or more simply, by dropping two digits (any two will do, provided that it is done consistently) from the book number.

This arrangement will work well until one of the locations in the memory store is asked to hold its eleventh loan record—100 books have been assigned to one location which can hold loan records for only ten books. A simple solution to this problem, which can occur frequently in real-time systems, is to store all such "eleventh records" in a special "overflow" area of the file, and to indicate in the correct locations, where any such overflow records are stored. Pointers are used for this purpose, in exactly the same way as in MARC records.

The above example has been kept simple by the use of simple numbers. But the principle of performing a mathematical computation on a book number to find an address in a direct access file can be applied to more complex situations, for example in systems using alphanumerical call numbers for book identification.

Access can be provided to the loans file by book number in this way. In order to provide access by borrower number, a separate index must be set up. Such an index is a direct-access file of borrower numbers, and is arranged in the same way as the file of book numbers. The record against each borrower number may either show directly those books on loan to that borrower, or may alternatively be a list of pointers to loan records in the book file.

A wide variety of alternatives is possible to this basic method of file handling, which differ largely in matters of detail. But there is one major alternative, which has been used in the Ohio State University Libraries system.[18] This is to store the complete library shelf list in direct-access memory, and to indicate in the shelf list record the loan status of an item. Such a system gives very sophisticated reader services, but is essentially a catalogue system to which a circulation module has been added. Real-time catalogue systems are discussed in Chapter 10.

REFERENCES

1. *Three systems of circulation control.* Library Technology Program, American Library Association, May 1967. (Library Technology Reports.)
2. WILSON, C. W. J. Comparison of UK computer-based loans systems. *Program*, Vol. 3, Nos. 3, 4, pp. 127–46 (Nov. 1969).

3. LINGENBERG, W. Comparison of computerised loans systems in the Federal Republic of Germany. *Program*, Vol. 5, No. 4, pp. 191–203 (Oct. 1971).
4. MCCANN, L., MCGEE, R. and KIMBER, R. T. Comparison of computerised loans systems in the United States. *Program*, Vol. 7, No. 1, pp. 24–37 (Jan. 1973).
5. MCGEE, R. *A literature survey of operational and emerging on-line library circulation systems*. University of Chicago Library Systems Development Office, February 1972. 66pp. (Available as Document No. ED 059 752 from ERIC Document Reproduction Service, Leasco Information Products Inc., P.O. Drawer 0, Bethesda, Maryland, 20014.)
6. YOUNG, R. C., STONE, P. T. and CLARK, G. J. University of Sussex Library automated circulation control system. *Program*, Vol. 6, No. 3, pp. 228–47 (July 1972).
7. *Die automatisierte Buchausleihe, Erfahrungen in der Universitätsbibliothek Bochum*. Bochum, 1967. 186 pp.
8. MCDOWELL, B. A. J. and PHILLIPS, C. M. *Circulation control system*. University of Southampton, 1970. 64 pp. (Southampton University Library Automation Project Report No. 1.)
9. FORD, P. and COLE, G. J. The University of Bradford issue system. *Program*, Vol. 6, No. 4, pp. 295–305 (Oct. 1972).
10. BEALE, C. B. and CARTER, M. Brunel University Library circulation control system. *Program*, Vol. 7, No. 4, pp. 238–48 (Oct. 1973).
11. YOUNG, R. C. University of Sussex Library. *Program*, Vol. 5, No. 1, pp. 8–11 (Jan. 1971).
12. RAO, P. V. and SZERENYI, B. J. Booth Library on-line circulation system (BLOC). *Journal of Library Automation*, Vol. 4, No. 2, pp. 86–102 (June 1971).
13. BOYD, A. H. and WALDEN, P. E. J. A simplified on-line circulation system. *Program*, Vol. 3, No. 2, pp. 47–65 (July 1969).
14. KENNEDY, R. A. Bell Laboratories' library real-time loan system, *Journal of Library Automation*, Vol. 1, No. 2, pp. 128–46 (June 1968).
15. EUNSON, B. G. UPDATE—an on-line loans control system in use in a small research library. *Program*, Vol. 8, No. 2, pp. 88–101 (April 1974).
16. BUCKLAND, M. K. and GALLIVAN, B. Circulation control: off-line, on-line or hybrid. *Journal of Library Automation*, Vol. 5, No. 1, pp. 30–38 (Mar. 1972).
17. HILL, A. R. *SLICE (Surrey Library Interactive Circulation Experiment) Report No. 3*. University of Surrey Computing Unit, March 1972. 21 pp.
18. GUTHRIE, G. D. An on-line remote access and circulation system. In *Proceedings of the 34th Annual Meeting of the American Society for Information Science, Denver, Colorado, 7—11 November 1971* (Communication for decision makers). Westport, Conn., Greenwood Publishing Corp., 1971, pp. 305–9.

CHAPTER 9

Ordering and Acquisitions

IN PREVIOUS chapters an understanding of the basic operation of each major library housekeeping system has been sought by comparison with the very simplest procedures which are encountered in preparing a list of serial holdings. A machine-readable file in some specified and convenient order is updated with new information and printed for consultation by librarians. Real-time systems allow access to a completely up-to-date file, and may be interrogated from remote locations.

Ordering and acquisitions systems in libraries control the purchase of new books. "Books" vary from simple items such as in-print monographs, through gifts, second-hand monographs, mutlivolume works, to massive treatises and compilations published in indefinite numbers of volumes over unspecified periods of time. Manual ordering systems maintain effective control through the use of a file of cards or slips, each representing one item on order. A record in the file means something ordered for the library and not yet received. Since the file is frequently in chronological order (i.e. arranged by order number) outstanding orders may readily be identified.

Before an order is placed, fairly accurate, though not necessarily complete bibliographical information is required. Since this is the same bibliographical information that is subsequently incorporated into a catalogue record, many libraries have established close links between order systems and cataloguing systems. In particular, order data may be added to by cataloguers to provide full cataloguing data.

Similar links exist between ordering systems and accounting systems. Accounts are encumbered by the total costs of items ordered, and when they are received in the library, payment is authorized and made.

Ordering and Acquisitions 175

In a computer-based ordering system, a machine-readable file of order records takes the place of the manual order file, and a series of quite straightforward listings provide library staff with the information and the controls they need.

BASIC SYSTEM CONCEPTS

Figure 9.1 shows the overall structure of a computer-based ordering system. Input to the system consists of records of new orders, items now received, alterations and corrections to existing records in the order file, items delayed or not available, etc. The main file of order records is arranged by order number, and is updated by the addition of the new information. The most important listings from the system consist of printed orders ready for dispatch to the booksellers, a list of all items currently on order (arranged by order number), and lists of new accessions. The order file may subsequently be sorted by author and title, to give a valuable author/title listing of items on order. Tests can be made of orders which have not been supplied within a stated time, and "chasers" or reminders sent to the booksellers concerned.

With the MARC bibliographic record service now covering new

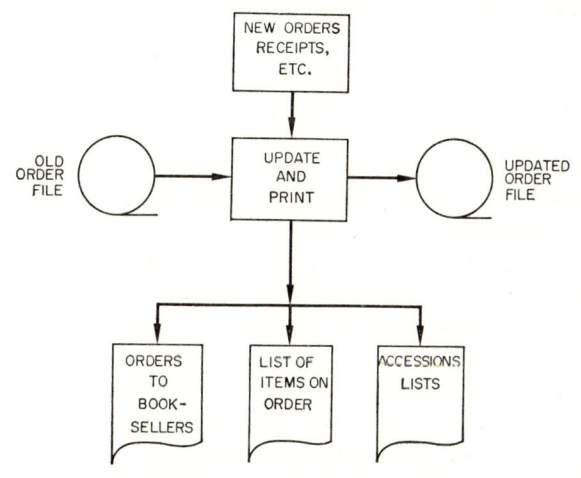

Fig. 9.1. Generalized flow chart for a computer-based ordering system.

British, American and some West European books, it is natural that libraries should seek to integrate MARC records in computer-based ordering systems. The MARC record service exists to avoid the necessity for individual libraries to keyboard bibliographical records; the argument being that it is simpler, cheaper and quicker to do this job centrally, once, and to make such machine-readable records widely and readily available. If this argument is true, and it undoubtedly is for many libraries, then, in principle at least, the earlier MARC records are introduced into a library's bibliographical procedures, the better. It makes good sense, therefore, to use MARC records in an ordering system.

It is assumed in the above argument that the right bibliographical records can be made available to individual libraries at the right time. Herein lies the problem.

Public libraries are well served by MARC. They tend to buy books as soon as they are published, or soon afterwards, and only the largest buy substantial numbers of books in languages other than the vernacular. So that for most public libraries, bibliographic records for a high proportion of their current orders will be found in files of current MARC records—for books published within the past year, for example. Some new orders will not have MARC records available for them, and in these cases, order records must be keyboarded in full.

But university and large research libraries purchase a high proportion of older and foreign books. So MARC records for many of their orders will not exist because only a small number of countries are supplying them anyway, and that over a comparatively short span of time. Both the US and UK MARC files are being extended backwards in time, so that this will rapidly help to solve one aspect of this problem —obtaining records for older books. Though even then, if prolonged machine searches are needed through large MARC backfiles to obtain records for older books, the point will soon be reached when it is more economical to keypunch the record locally from printed bibliographical data. Possible alternatives to local search include centralized search of large MARC files and subsequent transmission of MARC records to individual libraries for local processing (the British National Bibliography is doing this experimentally for the University of Liverpool Library), completely centralized processing of catalogue data

Ordering and Acquisitions 177

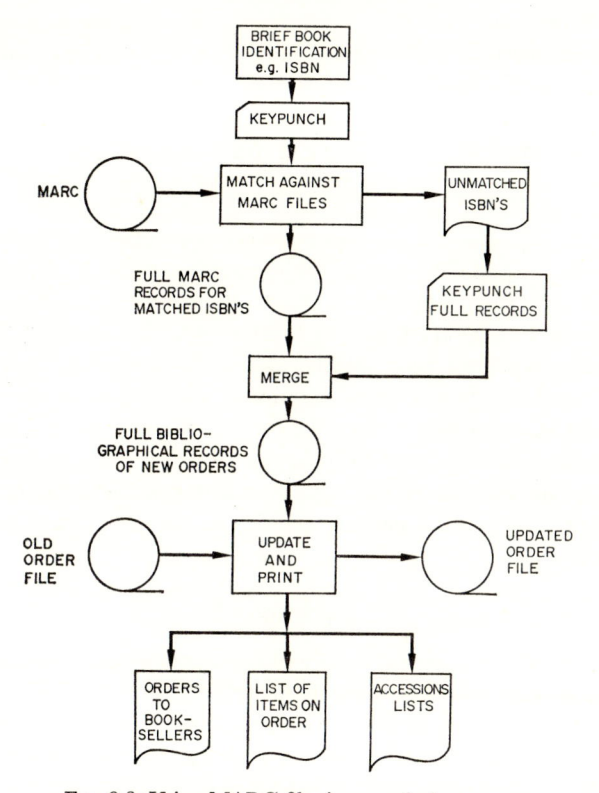

Fig. 9.2. Using MARC files in an ordering system.

for the local library (BNB is doing this experimentally for Brighton Public Libraries[1]), or a similar regional centralized processing centre, such as the Ohio College Library Center[2] or the Birmingham Libraries Co-operative Mechanization Project.[3]

Figure 9.2 shows schematically the process of searching a file of MARC records. Records sought are identified by ISBN or Library of Congress card number and matched records are written to a file for subsequent input to an ordering system. ISBNs which fail to match are listed, and full bibliographical records for these items must be keypunched. These records may be merged with the file of matched

MARC records and input to the order system with them, or may be input separately at a later stage. In any case, there will be a delay for these unmatched records.

DETAILED SYSTEM DESCRIPTION

Sources of Information about New Books

There are many sources of information about new and forthcoming books. National and commercial bibliographies, publishers' announcements, advertisements, notes and reviews in scholarly journals, library SDI services, etc. The amount of bibliographic information in these various sources differs quite widely, as does its accuracy, though with the very rapid acceptance of international standard book numbers by the book trade, every source may be expected to contain this one unique identifier. Subsequent procedures in the library ordering department depend on the amount of bibliographic information available in the first instance, and, to a certain extent, on the form in which it is presented.

MARC SDI

While special libraries commonly inform their regular users of newly published articles, reports, patents, standards, etc., relevant to their work and interests, public and university libraries have regarded such a specialized service as being beyond their capabilities. But the introduction of regular weekly MARC tape services by BNB and the Library of Congress has led a few libraries to implement computer-based selective dissemination of information (SDI) services for new books, based on these tapes. And the bibliographic information contained in such SDI notifications frequently forms the source of information about new books.

A typical MARC based SDI service is operated by the Oklahoma Department of Libraries.[4] Subjects may be specified either in terms of DC or LC classification numbers. A number of similar systems are operational in the US, Canada and the UK.[5] Figure 9.3 illustrates sample output from the Oklahoma service, and Fig. 9.4 reproduces the first page of one of the weekly listings received by the author from the DC-based SDI system operating at Queen's University, Belfast.

```
    01/29/73        LIBRARY & INFORMATION SCIENCE
VICKERY, BRIAN CAMPBELL.
    INFORMATION SYSTEMS  (BY) B. C. VICKERY.   (HAMDEN, CONN.)
    ARCHON BOOKS, 1973.
    P.
BIBLIOGRAPHY, P.
INFORMATION STORAGE AND RETRIEVAL SYSTEMS.
       * THIS BOOK IS TO BE PUBLISHED SOON
Z699.V494                       029/.9
72-014284                       0208013466
```

MARC - Oklahoma   Oklahoma Department of Libraries SDI User Information Service

```
    01/29/73        LIBRARY & INFORMATION SCIENCE

    STANDARDS FOR THE ENVIRONMENT (NORMER FOR MILJOKVALITET)  BY
    ANON. TRANSLATED FROM THE SWEDISH BY P. J. ELVIN.   GARSTON,
    BUILDING RESEARCH STATION, 1969.
    10 P.   30 CM.
(LIBRARY COMMUNICATION, NO. 1519)
ORIGINALLY PUBLISHED IN STATENS PLANVERK AKTUELLT, 1969, (3).
CITIES AND TOWNS--PLANNING.
ENVIRONMENTAL POLICY.

GARSTON, ENG.   BUILDING RESEARCH STATION.   LIBRARY.
    COMMUNICATION NO. 1519.
Z921.G33A3 NO. 1519+T166        690/.08A309.2/62
72-185507
```

MARC - Oklahoma   Oklahoma Department of Libraries SDI User Information Service

```
    01/29/73        LIBRARY & INFORMATION SCIENCE

    THE TEACHING OF PROGRAMMING AT UNIVERSITY LEVEL, PROCEEDINGS
    OF THE JOINT IBM/UNIVERSITY OF NEWCASTLE UPON TYNE SEMINAR,
    HELD IN THE UNIVERSITY COMPUTING LABORATORY, 8TH - 11TH
    SEPTEMBER 1970, EDITED BY B. SHAW.    NEWCASTLE UPON TYNE,
    UNIVERSITY OF NEWCASTLE UPON TYNE COMPUTING LABORATORY,
    1971.
    II-VI LEAVES, 153 P.   ILLUS.   30 CM.

ELECTRONIC DIGITAL COMPUTERS--PROGRAMMING--STUDY AND TEACHING
    (HIGHER)--CONGRESSES.

SHAW, B., ED.
INTERNATIONAL BUSINESS MACHINES CORPORATION.
NEWCASTLE-UPON-TYNE.   UNIVERSITY.
QA76.6.T4                       001.6/42/0711
72-191882                       0902383221
```

MARC - Oklahoma   Oklahoma Department of Libraries SDI User Information Service

FIG. 9.3. Sample output from the Oklahoma Department of Libraries MARC SDI Service.

```
QUEENS UNIVERSITY BELFAST    EXPERIMENTAL MARC SERVICE          BIBLIOGRAPHIC SERVICE          13/06/73        PAGE    1
*****************************************************************************************************************************

MR RICHARD KIMBER                                4218    SCHOOL OF LIB. & INFORMATION STUDIES
*****************************************************************************************************************


 LIBRARIES
**********


GREAT BRITAIN. DEPARTMENT OF EDUCATION AND SCIENCE. LIBRARIES DIVISION,                                          027.442746
     THE PUBLIC LIBRARY SERVICE. REORGANISATION AND AFTER. DEPARTMENT OF EDUCATION AND SCIENCE LIBRARIES
      DIVISION]
     LONDON. H.M.S.O.. 1973, 00.47. SBN 0112702651
     29P. 30CM. SD, LIBRARY INFORMATION SERIES. NO.2

VICKERY. BRIAN CAMPBELL,                                                                                          029
     INFORMATION SYSTEMS. [BY] B.C. VICKERY
     LONDON. BUTTERWORTHS. 1973, 06.00. SBN 040870456X
     [9],350P. ILL, FACSIMS, FORMS, PLAN. 23CM, BIBL.P.335-345. - INDEX

                                                                                                                  025.43
UNIVERSAL DECIMAL CLASSIFICATION. 621/621.0. MECHANICAL ENGINEERING IN GENERAL. NUCLEAR TECHNOLOGY
     ENGLISH FULL ED. (4TH INTERNATIONAL ED.)
     LONDON. BRITISH STANDARDS INSTITUTION. 1973, 01.25. SBN 0580075419
     13P. 30CM. SD, FOEDOERATION INTERNATIONALE DE DOCUMENTATION. PUBLICATIONS. NO.179, PIERCED FOR
      BINDER
     2699.08, 025.45:621/621.0

HUNNISETT. ROY FRANK,                                                                                             029.5
     INDEXING FOR EDITORS. [BY] R.F. HUNNISETT
     [LONDON]. BRITISH RECORDS ASSOCIATION. 1972, 01.50. SBN 900222026
     [1],145P. 25CM. PBK, ARCHIVES AND THE USER. NO.2, BIBL.P.145
```

FIG. 9.4. Sample output from the Queen's University of Belfast MARC SDI Service.

Bibliographies

In the case of conventionally printed bibliographies, and the other sources of bibliographic data, it is necessary in most cases for the information to be transcribed manually on to a proposal or order form for submission to the library order department. Exceptions to this practice occur when the bibliography or other printed list is itself marked to indicate which items are to be purchased, and then forwarded to the library.

The library order department will therefore receive requests for new books in a variety of forms, with the possibility that machine-readable records for some of the items will be available locally in the form of a file of MARC records. Subsequent processing of the order data will depend on whether MARC files are to be used as a source of full bibliographic data in machine-readable form, or whether all records will be keyboarded in full manually.

Creating Machine-readable Order Records

A simple record format for an ordering system has already been discussed in Chapter 5. This is a simple variable field structure using explicit tags. It is possible for some of the fields, for example the order number and ISBN fields, to be fixed length, and of course different tags may be used from the simple single-digit ones used for illustrative purposes in Chapter 5. For example, it is possible to use tags from the MARC format, labelling a personal author 100, the title 245, and so on. It is useful to introduce the MARC tags at this early stage if MARC records or the MARC format are to be used, or are planned to be used, at a later stage in ordering or cataloguing procedures.

If order records are to be keyboarded in full, then standard basic input procedures must be followed, to produce punched cards, paper tape or magnetic tape. In the ordering system operational at the University of Southampton Library, order records are keyboarded on a paper tape typewriter, which uses an auxiliary tape to introduce the correct MARC tags automatically.[6] Figure 9.5 shows the hard copy produced by this keyboarding operation (this is used as the actual order to be sent to the bookseller in the Southampton system). Figure 9.6 shows the paper tape produced at the same time printed out to

SOUTHAMPTON UNIVERSITY LIBRARY: ORDER

Author ☑ SHANANI, A.K. & NANDI, P.K.

Title ☑ Probability & Probability distributions

Vol. 1-6   Copies 1

Publisher George Allen & Unwin

sbn. 0 04 519009 7   Fund 1538
Date 1973

Price £2.50

Bookseller John Adams Bookservice

ACQUISITIONS SECTION, THE LIBRARY, UNIVERSITY OF SOUTHAMPTON, S09 5NH

S & O LTD 6-71/26858

221767

Please quote order number on all correspondence. All parcels, invoices and correspondence to be addressed to the Section.

Fig. 9.5a. University of Southampton Library order system: top copy of the multi-part order form completed on the tape typewriter.

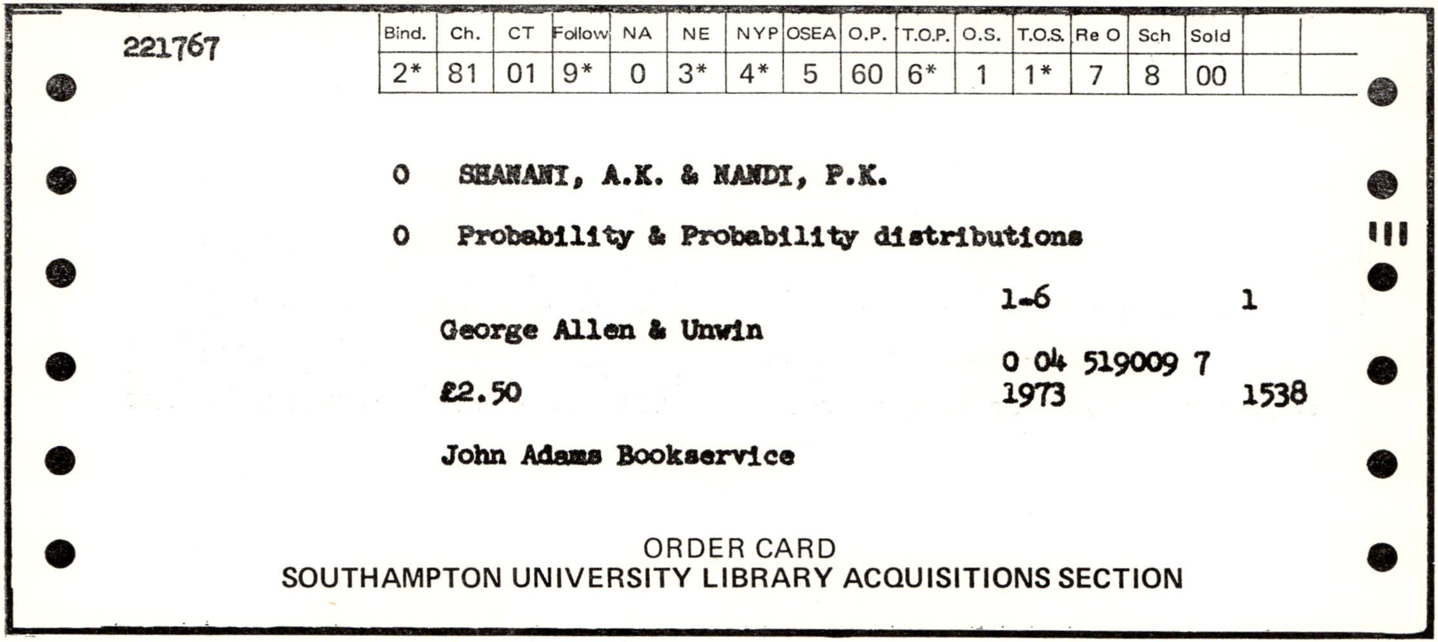

Bind.	Ch.	CT	Follow	NA	NE	NYP	OSEA	O.P.	T.O.P.	O.S.	T.O.S.	Re O	Sch	Sold
2*	81	01	9*	0	3*	4*	5	60	6*	1	1*	7	8	00

221767

o   SEAMANT, A.K. & NANDI, P.K.

o   Probability & Probability distributions

George Allen & Unwin   1-6

£2.50   0 04 519009 7   1
                               1973   1538

John Adams Bookservice

ORDER CARD
SOUTHAMPTON UNIVERSITY LIBRARY ACQUISITIONS SECTION

Fig. 95b. University of Southampton Library order system: bottom copy of the multi-part order form completed on the tape typewriter.

```
1221767     1000£A0SHANANT, A.K. & NANDI, P.K.          2400£A0Probability & Probability distributions
2450£D1-6    05101    2600£BGeorge Allen & Unwin        02000 04 519009 7
3500£A£2.50          2600£C1973    3500£B1538           5990£A01£BJohn Adams Bookservice
```

Fig. 9.6. University of Southampton Library order system: print of the paper tape produced by the tape typewriter, showing MARC tags introduced from the control tape.

Ordering and Acquisitions 185

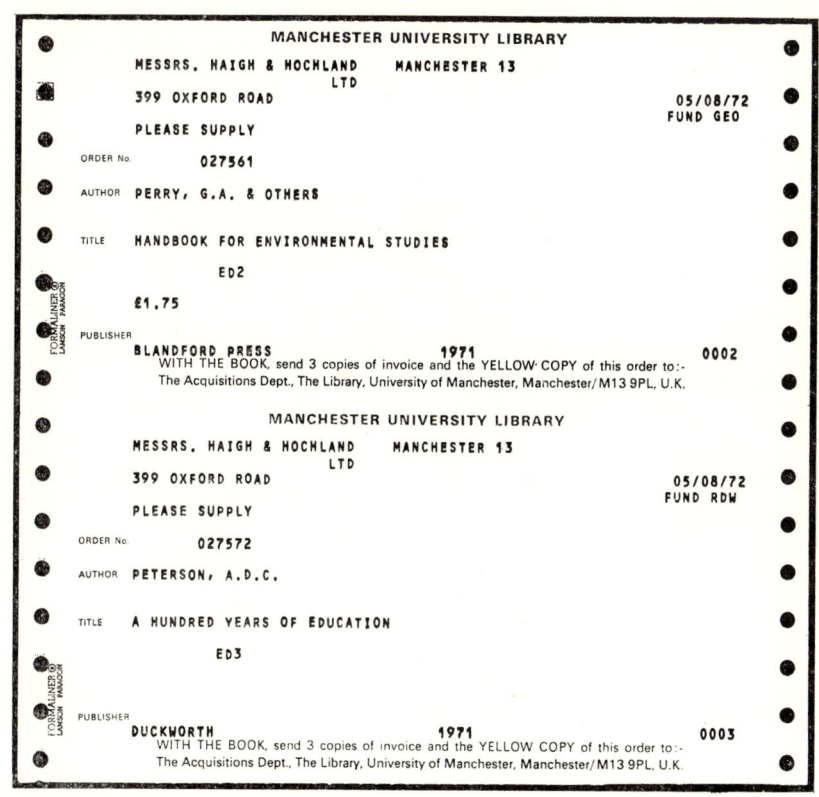

```
            MANCHESTER UNIVERSITY LIBRARY
    MESSRS. HAIGH & HOCHLAND      MANCHESTER 13
                       LTD
    399 OXFORD ROAD                              05/08/72
                                                 FUND GEO
    PLEASE SUPPLY

ORDER No.    027561

AUTHOR  PERRY, G.A. & OTHERS

TITLE   HANDBOOK FOR ENVIRONMENTAL STUDIES
                ED2
        £1.75

PUBLISHER
        BLANDFORD PRESS         1971              0002
        WITH THE BOOK, send 3 copies of invoice and the YELLOW COPY of this order to:-
        The Acquisitions Dept., The Library, University of Manchester, Manchester/M13 9PL, U.K.

            MANCHESTER UNIVERSITY LIBRARY
    MESSRS. HAIGH & HOCHLAND      MANCHESTER 13
                       LTD
    399 OXFORD ROAD                              05/08/72
                                                 FUND RDW
    PLEASE SUPPLY

ORDER No.    027572

AUTHOR  PETERSON, A.D.C.

TITLE   A HUNDRED YEARS OF EDUCATION
                ED3

PUBLISHER
        DUCKWORTH               1971              0003
        WITH THE BOOK, send 3 copies of invoice and the YELLOW COPY of this order to:-
        The Acquisitions Dept., The Library, University of Manchester, Manchester/M13 9PL, U.K.
```

FIG. 9.7. University of Manchester Library; book orders printed by line printer.

show the contents. This contains the MARC tags introduced by the control tape, which were prevented from printing on the order itself. At the University of Manchester Library, book orders are printed by line printer on special two-part stationery: Fig. 9.7 shows two sample orders produced in this way.

Figure 9.8 shows the procedures involved in creating a magnetic tape file of new order records in this way. But it should be pointed out that it is not only records of new orders which are input to the system in this way. The same procedure is followed for books that have been received and accessioned, for orders that will be delayed

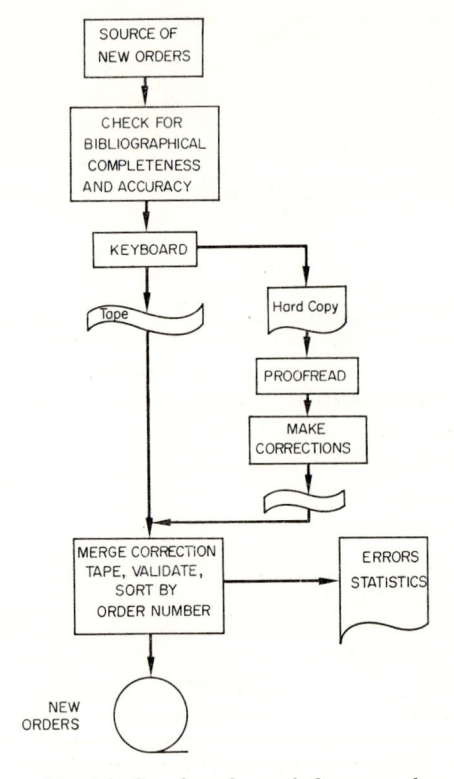

Fig. 9.8. Creation of records for new orders.

or cannot be filled. New orders are continually being made by the library, books are constantly being received, and machine-readable records are made of all such transactions. Since the main order file is updated (in a batch system) only weekly, for example, it is convenient to include all such other records in the magnetic-tape file of new orders. For this reason, it is necessary to include a sort routine in the computer program that prepares the file of new order records. This file therefore contains new records of all kinds, sorted by type within order number.

Obtaining Machine-readable Order Records from MARC Files

The advantage of being able to make use of MARC files of bibliographic records appears primarily in the simplicity with which new purchases may be identified. In the UK, Kent County Library is operating a MARC-based ordering system, in which books are identified for purchase simply by their ISBNs.[7] Librarians fill in requisition forms for new purchases, indicating for each item the branch library code number where the book is to be located, the code number of the bookseller from whom the books are to be supplied, the standard book number, and number of copies required (Fig. 9.9).

In the case of a county library such as Kent, most purchases are found in the MARC files, and books are bought across the whole subject spectrum covered by the MARC service. But many libraries, particularly research and special libraries, are interested only in a narrow range of subjects. The library at the Atomic Weapons Research Establishment, Aldermaston, has developed a technique appropriate to the needs of such libraries, whereby it selects from the full BNB and LC MARC tapes records lying within a specified range of subjects relevant to the interests of its users.[8] This is exactly the same procedure, but carried out on a larger scale, as is involved in preparing lists of new books relevant to the subject interests of individuals by an SDI system.

In the AMCOS system of the AWRE Aldermaston library, data for new orders is input to the system via an on-line teletype. For items for which MARC records exist in the AMCOS MARC files, orders are initiated by quoting the ISBN, number of copies required, and a two-digit code to indicate the nature of the order (firm order, or on approval). Similar two-digit codes are used to report to the system when items have been received by the library, etc.

Updating the Order File

Whether or not MARC files have been used to assist in the creation of records for new orders, the updating of the main order file is a comparatively standard and straightforward procedure. The main point of difference between various systems lies in the time when the actual orders to be sent to the bookseller are printed, whether they are

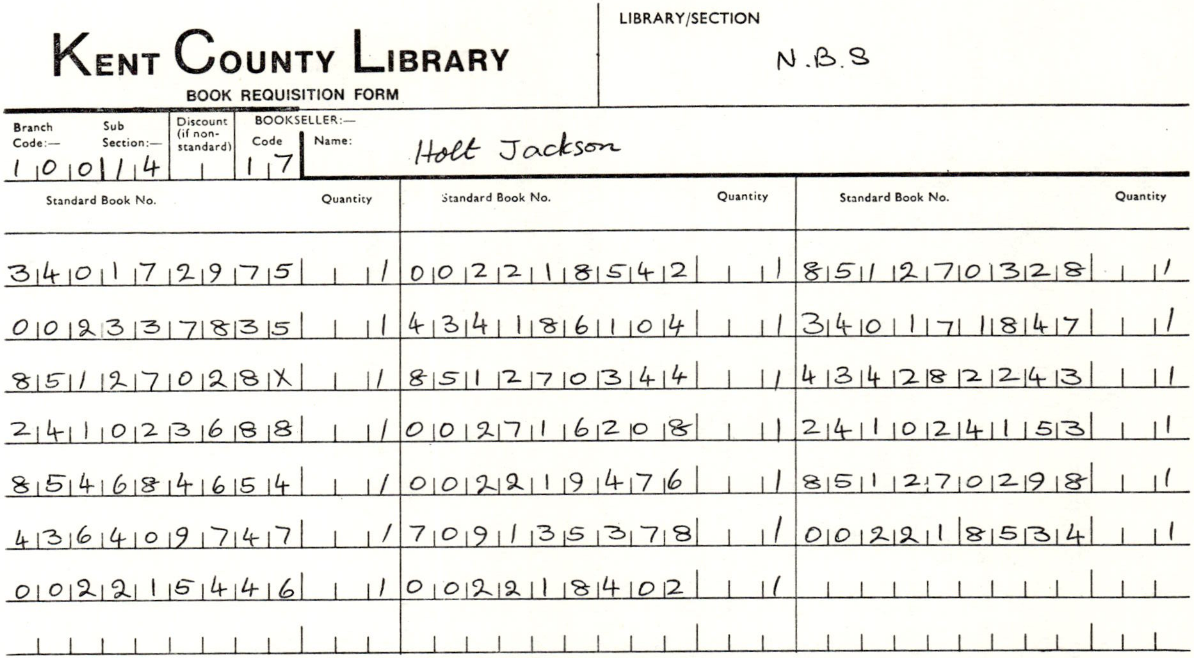

188 *Automation in Libraries*

Fig. 9.9. Kent County Library book requisition form.

prepared as a by-product of the data conversion operation (as at Southampton) or are printed by the computer as part of the file updating procedure.

Although most libraries purchase from a number of booksellers (the total may be in the region of several hundreds), a high percentage of orders are supplied from a comparatively small number of sources (of the order of a few dozen). It is therefore common practice to maintain a machine-readable file of booksellers' names and addresses as part of a computer-based ordering system. This file may be limited to only the most frequently used suppliers, or may include all those that have ever been used. In either case, it is possible (for those booksellers included in the file) to specify the supplier for each new item by means of a simple code number. Only the code number need then be given in each new order record, the full name and address being found by the system from the booksellers file.

The file of booksellers' names and addresses may be held at the beginning of the order file, so that the first part of the file updating procedure is to update this booksellers file. Additions may be made, and existing records altered or deleted.

The file of new order records shown at the bottom of the flow chart in Fig. 9.8 is arranged by order number. Since order numbers are normally assigned consecutively, i.e. chronologically, the first records in the new order file will relate to existing orders, and will include reports of books received, and booksellers' reports on delays to orders, and the unavailability of items.

For books that have been received, the status of the order record is altered accordingly. Depending on the particular procedure adopted, received books may or may not already have been accessioned. If they have, then the notification of a book's receipt can act as a signal to include a record of it in the next accessions register listing.

Reported delays in the supply of items may be added, in coded form, to the order record, and will appear in the printed list of items currently on order. Items which cannot be supplied may be listed in full to await a librarian's decision as to further action.

New orders will come at the end of the file of new orders, and are simply added to the on-order file, and orders for transmission to the bookseller printed as required.

Automation in Libraries

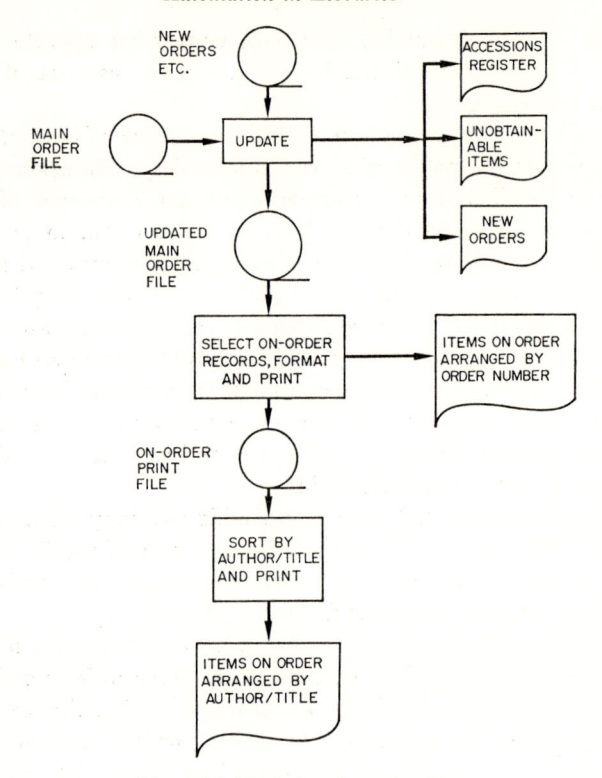

Fig. 9.10. Updating the order file.

The order file is printed in full, in order number order, and probably also arranged by author and title. To save space, records may be converted to a shortened format before printing; although, for example, the main order record may contain an author's full name and a work's complete title, perhaps with full MARC indicators and subfield codes included in the data fields, printed on-order records may contain an author's surname only, together with a limited number of characters of the title. Figure 9.10 illustrates the operation of these procedures.

A wide range of possibilities exist regarding the layout of the printed outputs from order systems, ranging from preprinted stationery on which the computer prints the variable data for each item concerned,

Ordering and Acquisitions 191

CHESHIRE COUNTY COUNCIL LIBRARIES AND MUSEUMS DEPARTMENT 91 HOOLE ROAD, CHESTER CH2 3NG TEL:- 0244 20055				BOOKSELLER NORMAN E. LUCAS LTD.			
				BOOK NUMBER	ORDER NUMBER	PRICE	COPIES
				0 500 45014 5	41281	£ 2.95	3
							ORDER DATE 06/09/73
AUTHOR GREEN, P							
TITLE A CONCISE HISTORY OF ANCIENT GREECE TO THE CLOSE OF THE CLASSICAL ERA. THAMES & H. 1973.							
ORDER TO BE RETAINED BY BOOKSELLER	BOOK TYPE N	BKSLR. CODE LUC	REM. 1	BCH. 1 DJ	2 R		
	PRICE £		COPIES	DST.			
REMARKS							

Fig. 9.11. Cheshire County Libraries, book order.

```
06/06/72                                                                                       PAGE NO      54
                              CURRENT TAPE LISTING OF BOOKS ON ORDER OR RECENTLY RECEIVED
* AVERINI, SHLOMO.           ISRAEL & THE PALESTINIANS.                              ORDR 016744    1008
         06/12/71            B/D 00003           14/01/72 £3.85     FU HIN  DP     13/03/72 AC 71-09240    B
  AVERY, MARY.W.             GOVERNMENT OF WASHINGTON STATE.                         ORDR 015297    1009
         22/11/71            B/D 00004                    $5.25    FU AMH  DP               AC
  AVESTA                     PAHLAVI YASNA AND VISPERAD                              ORDR 019686    1010
         24/01/72            B/D 00006                             FU PTH  DP               AC
* AVESTA                     YASNA 28 UBERSETZUNG VON W.LENTZ                        ORDR 019687    1011
         24/01/72            B/D 00006           23/02/72 DM 7.20  FU PTH  DP      22/05/72 AC 71-12070    B
  AVICENNA.                  AVICENNA'S TREATISE ON LOGIC.                           ORDR 023601    1012
         27/03/72            B/D 00008                    9.90FLS  FU NEB  DP               AC
  AVICENNA.                  DANESH-NAME ALAI.                                       ORDR 029118    1013
         15/05/72            B/D 00011                    £1.50    FU PER  DP               AC
* AVIDAN,D.                  SHIRIM HITSONIYIM                                       ORDR 009720    1014
         16/08/71            B/D 00079           07/11/71 $2.60    FU NEH  DP      24/01/72 AC 71-07712    B
  AVILA DE LOBERO, LUIS.     LIBRO DEL KEGIMEN DE LA SALUD..(ED BALTASAR HERNAN      ORDR 016067    1015
         29/11/71            B/D 00273 03/01/72 SO        250 PTAS FU LSA  DP               AC
* AVIS, F.C.                 E.P. PRINCE TYPE PUNCHCUTTER                            ORDR 005283    1016
         17/05/71            B/D 00246           01/01/72 £2.00    FU ABB  DP      31/01/72 AC 71-08930    B
* AVIS, F.C.                 EARLY PRINTERS CHAPEL IN ENGLAND                        ORDR 005282    1017
         17/05/71            B/D 00246           01/01/72 £2.25    FU ABB  DP      31/01/72 AC 71-08929    B
* AVTORKHANOV, A.            THE COMMUNIST PARTY APPARATUS.                          ORDR 012785    1018
         11/10/71            B/D 00001           20/03/72 £4.70    FU       DP FPE 08/05/72 AC 71-13293    B
* AXLINE,V.M.                PLAY THERAPY                                            ORDR 009721    1019
         16/08/71            B/D 00004           18/12/71 $8.00    FU RDU  DP      13/03/72 AC 71-09845    B
* AXTHELM, P.                THE CITY GAME.                                          ORDR 009860    1020
         23/08/71            B/D 00004           18/12/71 $6.50    FU QCS  DP      13/03/72 AC 71-10035    B
* AYALA ANGUIANO, A.         ARMANDO AYALA ANGUIANO.                                 ORDR 015496    1021
         29/11/71            B/D 00084           08/02/72 $16.00   FU LSA  DP      08/05/72 AC 71-13988    B
* AYALA, F.                  CAZADOR EN EL ALBA Y OTRAS UNAGINACIONES.               ORDR 015298    1022
         22/11/71            B/D 00009           28/12/71 PTAS50.00 FU LSA DP      07/02/72 AC 71-08900    U
  AYALA, F.                  EL RAPTO ED. P.Z.BORING.                                ORDR 023602    1023
         27/03/72            B/D 00003                             FU LSA  DP               AC
* AYALA, FRANCISCO.          EL JARDIN DE LAS DELICIAS.                              ORDR 010883    1024
         13/09/71            B/D 00009           24/11/71 PTAS 125.0 FU LSA DP     24/01/72 AC 71-07580    U
* AYALA, FRANCISCO.          EL LAZARILLO REEXAMINADO                                ORDR 019688    1025
         24/01/72            B/D 00091           21/02/72 PTAS 50.00 FU LSA DP     22/05/72 AC 71-12279    U
* AYALA, FRANCISCO.          LA ESTRUCTURA NARRATIVA.                                ORDR 016745    1026
         06/12/71            B/D 00009           22/01/72 ESC 50.00 FU LSA DP      13/03/72 AC 71-11339    U
```

FIG. 9.12. University of Manchester Library, main listing of books on order.

to formats which rely on the computer to print everything. Figure 9.11 illustrates the form of book order, complete with counterfoil, ready to be sent to the bookseller, that is produced by the system operational in Cheshire County Libraries.[9] Figure 9.12 shows the main on-order listing printed by the Manchester University Library system.[10]

Financial Control

One of the major functions of library ordering and acquisitions systems is to record and to control expenditure from the library's accounts. Funds are committed for spending when orders are placed,

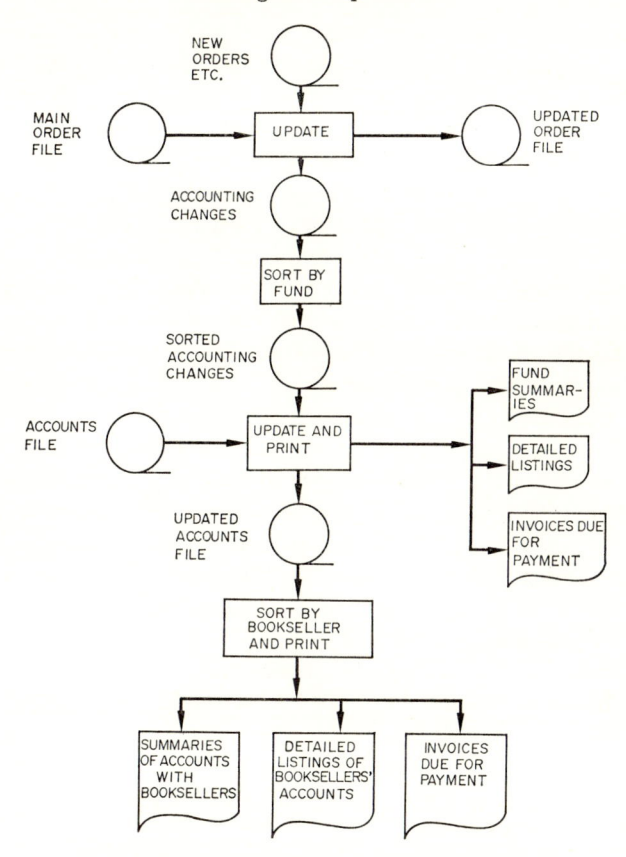

FIG. 9.13. Financial control in an ordering system.

and are actually spent when the items are received by the library. The design and operation of a separate library accounting system have already been considered in Chapter 6. But when order records are being created, either by manual keyboarding of the full bibliographic data or by picking up that data from a separate file of MARC records, the small amount of information necessary for accounting functions can very easily be included.

Figure 9.13 shows the accounting side of a typical ordering system. These aspects have, for the sake of simplicity, been omitted from previous order system flow charts, and for the same reason, Fig. 9.13 is simplified by omitting all except the major order system products.

The cost of each new item ordered is included in each order record together with the number of copies ordered, the supplier, and the library fund to which the item is to be charged. This data is contained in new order records that update the main order file, is held in the records in that file, and is available for use later as required.

When books are received, and the invoices are to hand, the estimated price, available at the time of ordering, can be converted to the actual price, and this is submitted to the system at the same time as the books' arrival in the library is reported.

The main order file is arranged by order number, and as it is updated, accounting changes are accumulated in a separate file, in order number order. These changes include new commitments, and amounts now due to be paid. This file is sorted into account number order, and used to update the main accounts file, which is held in account number order. The accounts file is printed to give summary statements of balance for each fund, detailed listings, and payments to be made from each fund.

The same data can usefully be presented from the booksellers' point of view by sorting the accounts file into bookseller order and printing, in the same way, summaries, detailed lists of transactions, and amounts now due for payment. These latter totals may be linked to a cheque-printing program, or payment may be made separately by a manual or semi-mechanized system.

REFERENCES

1. DUCHESNE, R. M. and DONBROSKI, L. BNB/Brighton Public Libraries catalogue project—"BRIMARC." *Program*, Vol. 7, No. 4, pp. 205–24 (Oct. 1973).
2. MARTIN, S. K. Library automation. *Annual Review of Information Science and Technology*, Vol. 7, p. 263 (1972).
3. BUCKLE, D. G. R. *et al.* The Birmingham Libraries' Co-operative Mechanisation Project: progress report. January 1972—June 1973. *Program*, Vol. 7, No. 4, pp. 196–204 (Oct. 1973).
4. BIERMAN, K. J. and BLUE, B. J. A MARC based SDI service. *Journal of Library Automation*, Vol. 3, No. 4, pp. 304–19 (Dec. 1970).
5. MAUERHOFF, G. R. and SMITH, R. G. A MARC II based program for retrieval and dissemination. *Journal of Library Automation*, Vol. 4, No. 3, pp. 141–58 (Sept. 1971).

6. Woods, R. G. *Acquisitions and cataloguing systems: preliminary report.* University of Southampton, 1971. 49 pp. (Southampton University Library Automation Project Report No. 2).
7. Dowswell, J. A. M. and Earl, C. A computer book ordering system for Kent County Library using Sbn's. *Program*, Vol. 5, No. 3, pp. 152–6 (July 1971).
8. Corbett, L. and German, J. AMCOS Project stage 2: a computer aided integrated system using BNB MARC literature tapes. *Program*, Vol. 6, No. 1, pp. 1–35 (Jan. 1972).
9. Berriman, S. G. and Pilliner, J. Cheshire County Library acquisitions and cataloguing system. *Program*, Vol. 7, No. 1, pp. 38–59 (Jan. 1973).
10. Hunt, C. J. A computerised acquisitions system in Manchester University Library. *Program*, Vol. 5, No. 3, pp. 157–60 (July 1971).

CHAPTER 10

Catalogues and Bibliographies

LIBRARY users may not be directly concerned with the introduction, use, or value of computer-based systems for serials accessioning and book ordering and acquisitions. They may be confronted with the tighter control of loans which an automated circulation system provides. But they cannot but be directly affected by any computer-based catalogue introduced by a library.

A library's first task is to assemble a collection of books and other materials well suited to the needs of its users. Then it must list and catalogue that collection and in other ways make it work as effectively as possible in meeting the information and other needs of its clientele. To list items in the collection, or items recently received, and to make the lists readily available, has been and remains the prime method of providing access to the collection. The order or arrangement of the list determines the form of question the user may pose to obtain a satisfactory answer.

Such interaction between library user and library collection as conducted through the intermediary of lists or catalogues is bounded or limited by the current state of the technology relevant to preparing lists, the library's ability to utilize such technology within the constraints of the available finance and personnel, and the user's ability to use effectively the lists and catalogues which the library can make available to him. All three of these aspects are currently in a state of rapid flux: rapid developments are taking place on a number of research fronts and the library user stands to gain in every respect.

The relevant computing technology for the production of library catalogues by computer concerns techniques for the rapid and high-quality typesetting of machine-readable data. The last few years have seen continual growth in phototypesetting techniques using computer-controlled typesetters, in particular on the "micro" side, with machines setting characters onto microfilm. The acronym COM (computer output microfilm) has been given to this process. On the bibliographical side, the technology has concerned systems for the creation of large files of bibliographical records in machine-readable form and for their distribution in various ways (MARC), and for the application of an internationally standardized numbering system for new books (ISBNs).

Libraries' ability to use any new technology has always been constrained by the money and men available. Here, the availability of financial and human resources has not matched the rapid growth of technology. Money for all aspects of libraries' activities has been, and continues to be, strictly limited, forcing library management to adopt systems, including cataloguing systems, which provide an optimum balance of cost and benefit. Such economic conditions will prevent the rapid growth of extravagant though perhaps technically advanced automated systems, yet at the same time encourage the replacement of labour-intensive manual systems by simple, straightforward and efficient computer systems.

Library catalogues must always effect a compromise between the niceties of bibliographic description and the inabilities of library users to comprehend them. Current trends are towards simpler forms of catalogue entry, and to a greater emphasis on education in methods of effective library use.

The end result of these changes should therefore be a greater use of more carefully chosen library collections, by better educated readers using simpler, cheaper, more convenient and typographically superior catalogues. Also, a wide range of forms of catalogue will be found, each, hopefully, appropriate to the characteristics of the library, collection and users concerned.

BASIC COMPUTER-PRODUCED CATALOGUES

Some of the earliest computer-based systems in libraries concerned the production of catalogues. In the United States, computer-produced catalogues were to be found in Florida Atlantic, Stanford and Chicago

University libraries by 1966. The University of Toronto had produced the first edition of its ONULP book catalogues by February 1965.[1] In the UK the public libraries in the London Boroughs of Barnet, Camden and Greenwich started their computer-produced catalogues in 1965. Not all of these systems are still operational, none have escaped the problems of a rapidly changing computer technology as discussed in Chapter 1, and the concept of book form catalogues of a whole library collection, printed on paper in upper case only has been improved upon since then. But such systems can still provide improved reader service at lower cost than equivalent manual systems producing book form or card catalogues. In particular they make it possible for a frequently updated catalogue to be produced in a number of copies for use in a number of different locations. Such locations may be branch libraries in a large public or county library system, or different floors or levels in a university or research library housed in a multi-storey building.

The basic concepts behind the production of these early catalogues have not changed, at least as far as catalogues produced by batch processing systems are concerned. On-line real-time catalogues embody quite new principles and are considered separately. Considerable progress, however, has been made in all of the many problem areas encountered in these simple catalogues. The problems and solutions to them are considered separately later in this chapter.

Overall System Design

The familiar pattern of file updating, printing, sorting and printing is once again found in systems for printing catalogues. The record is a bibliographic description or catalogue record for one item in the library collection, and the file is the catalogue of the library's holdings. It is printed on paper, reproduced in the number of copies that are required, and bound, probably in a modern "easy-binder" for convenience in use. Figure 10.1 illustrates the steps involved, and also another feature of such catalogues—the use of a cumulating supplement to the main catalogue.

The logic behind the catalogue supplement is simple. The user

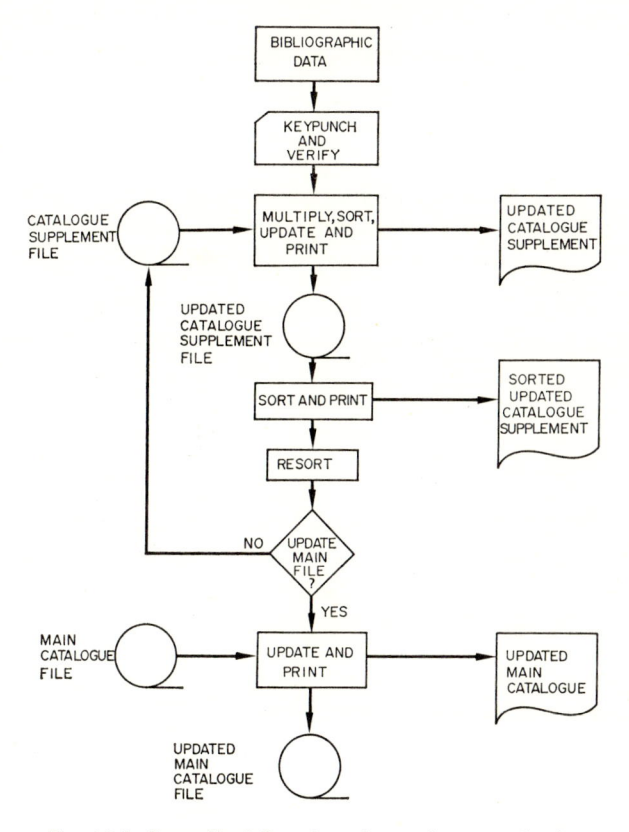

FIG. 10.1. Generalized flow chart for catalogue production.

wants a catalogue of the whole of the library's collection, so the catalogue must be up-to-date in order to include recently acquired material. A catalogue file is very large, and so is time consuming and expensive to print. The library cannot afford to update and print the main catalogue frequently (every week, for example), and so a small growing catalogue supplement is started. This can be updated and printed frequently and cheaply, leaving the main catalogue to be updated only seldom, perhaps two or three times each year.

Record Structure and Data Conversion

Fairly simple record structures are still encountered in some new catalogue systems. They may be based on the eighty-column card used for input, and may use fixed length data fields. Thus the following record structure is found in the system used by the University of Lancaster Library to print catalogues of the reserve or short loan collection.[2] One punched card is used for each bibliographic record, laid out as follows:

Data field	Columns
Author/title	1–58
Copy number	59–60
Classification number	61–71
Time in collection	72
Course	73–79
Spare	80

The value of fixed length data fields is found in the simplified programming and quicker computer processing that result. Choice of the fields which are identified, their size and the number of punched cards allotted to each input record are entirely matters for local determination.

A simple variable length record structure is sometimes used, as at the University of Bochum Library, where ten data fields are identified by single-digit numerical tags, as in the example of an order system record structure discussed in Chapter 5. But increasingly, record structures for individual systems are being based on the MARC format, in order to facilitate the interchange of bibliographic records. Thus the University of Southampton employs the MARC format in its Wessex Medical Library cataloguing system,[3] while the library of Loughborough University of Technology is using a simplified MARC-type record structure which is compatible with MARC, and termed MINICS (minimal input cataloguing system).[4]

Standard data-preparation techniques may be used to convert such bibliographical records to machine-readable form. If they are available, records from a MARC file can be employed, or in appropriate cases, brief bibliographical records may be obtained from book cards or other records used in a circulation system.

File Updating and Printing

It is usual for computer-produced book catalogues to be printed as a main catalogue plus a cumulating supplement. Thus, if a weekly updating run is made, each weekly batch of new catalogue records updates the small machine-readable supplement file. Each week the supplement grows larger and, of course, becomes more expensive to produce, and more cumbersome to use in the library. The point is eventually reached when it becomes more economical to merge the now large supplement with the main catalogue file, print the new main catalogue, and begin again the following week with a small supplement. A rapidly growing library will require new editions of the main catalogue more frequently than one which is growing only slowly, and a library should be able to afford new editions of its main catalogue more frequently during the first years of its lifetime. When its collections become larger, the frequency of production of updated editions of the catalogue should drop.

In a computer-based circulation system, one loan transaction gives rise to one record in the machine-readable file of loan records. In a cataloguing system, on the other hand, advantage is taken of the character manipulating ability of the computer to create as many records in the machine-readable catalogue file as there will be entries in the catalogue. Thus separate records will be created for the author, title and subject of an item, together with records for any additional access points which may be needed in the catalogue. Advantage may be taken at this stage to include different data in the different records that are created in this way. For example, full bibliographic details may be included in the record that will appear under the name of the author, whereas briefer details may be given in the subject and title entry records.

The first task of the update program, then, is to create multiple records as required from each input record, and to sort the input data into correct order for updating the catalogue supplement file.

In serials listing systems, where the contents of the file change only infrequently, it is common practice to use a unique identification number to sort each record into correct order. In cataloguing systems, where the frequency of updating the file makes a numbering system

Author	Title	Class	Cols	Page
LEVIN, BERNARD	PENDULUM YEARS: BRITAIN AND THE SIXTIES, CAPE, 1970.	309.142	A B C D E K L M N O X A C H	256 01 02
LEVIN, HARRY	MYTH OF THE GOLDEN AGE IN THE RENAISSANCE. FABER, 1970.	809.933		
LEVINE, DAVID	PENS AND NEEDLES; LITERARY CARICATURES BY DAVID LEVINE; SELECTED BY JOHN UPDIKE. DEUTSCH, 1970.	741.5973	D H	03
LEVITT, DOROTHY	WOMAN AND THE CAR: A CHATTY LITTLE HANDBOOK FOR WOMEN WHO WANT TO MOTOR; ED. BY C. BYNG-HALL. ETC., 1909? (1970 REPRINT)	629.2222	A	04
LEVY, BENN W.	MEMBER FOR GAZA: A PLAY BY BENN LEVY. EVANS, 1968.	822 LEV	A B	05
LEVY, HAROLD	HEBREW FOR ALL, 4TH ED. VALLENTINE, 1970.	492.4824	A	06
LEVY, MERVYN	DRAWING AND SCULPTURE. ADAMS AND DART, 1970.	731.1	A	07
LEWIN, G. F.	PHYSICS FOR ENGINEERS. BUTTERWORTHS, 1963.	530.02462	M	08
LEWIN, KURT	PRINCIPLES OF TOPOLOGICAL PSYCHOLOGY; TR. BY FRITZ HEIDER AND GRACE M. HEIDER. MCGRAW, 1966.	150	N	09
LEWIN, KURT	RESOLVING SOCIAL CONFLICTS; SELECTED PAPERS ON GROUP DYNAMICS; ED. BY GERTRUD WEISS LEWIN. HARPER, 1948. (ORANGE SERIES: THE SOCIAL SCIENCES)	301.15	B	10
LEWIS, C. D.	SCIENTIFIC INVENTORY CONTROL. BUTTERWORTHS, 1970. (OPERATIONAL RESEARCH SERIES)	658.787	A C Z	11
LEWIS, CLARENCE IRVING	COLLECTED PAPERS; ED. BY JOHN D. GOHEEN AND JOHN L. MOTHERSHEAD. STANFORD U.P., 1970.	191 LEW	N Z	12
LEWIS, CLINTON, IR	OXFORD ATLAS TERRAN. OXFORD U.P.,	115	N Z	13
LEWIS, D. B. WYNDHAM	THAT ADVENTUROUS MAN, CHARLES A. LINDUS, 1927.		A C	14
LEWIS, DAVID L.	MARTIN LUTHER KING; A CRITICAL BIOGRAPHY. ALLEN LANE 1970.	920 KING	A B C D M	15
LEWIS, JENNY LEWIS, JOHN	POETRY IN THE MAKING. SEE BRITISH MUSEUM GRAPHIC DESIGN, WITH SPECIAL REFERENCE TO LETTERING, TYPOGRAPHY AND ILLUSTRATION, BY JOHN LEWIS AND JOHN BRINKLEY. ROUTLEDGE, 1964.	655	N Z	16 17
LEWIS, JOHN	PRINTED EPHEMERA: THE CHANGING USE OF TYPE AND LETTERFORMS IN ENGLISH AND AMERICAN PRINTING. FABER, 1969.	655.1	L	18
LEWIS, JOHN WILSON	PARTY LEADERSHIP AND REVOLUTIONARY POWER IN CHINA SEE PARTY LEADERSHIP AND REVOLUTIONARY POWER IN CHINA			19
LEWIS, JOHN, B.1889	LEFT BOOK CLUB: AN HISTORICAL RECORD. GOLLANCZ, 1970.	655.58	A D E H M Z	20
LEWIS, LEOPOLD	BELLS. IN ROWELL, GEORGE : NINETEENTH CENTURY PLAYS			21
LEWIS, M. J. T.	EARLY WOODEN RAILWAYS. ROUTLEDGE, 1970.	385.5	N Z	22
LEWIS, MICHAEL	NAPOLEON AND HIS BRITISH CAPTIVES. ALLEN & UNWIN, 1962.	940.27	A C	23
LEWIS, NORMAN	HOW TO READ BETTER AND FASTER, 3RD ED. CROWELL, 1958.	028.8	C	24
LEWIS, OSCAR	PEDRO MARTINEZ; A MEXICAN PEASANT AND HIS FAMILY. SECKER & WARBURG, 1964.	301.35	B	25
LEWIS, PAUL	HUMAN BODY, BY PAUL LEWIS AND DAVID RUBENSTEIN. HAMLYN, 1970. (CHANLYN ALL-COLOUR PAPERBACKS)	612	A B C D E F G H	26
LEWIS, PETER	HUMBERSIDE REGION, BY PETER LEWIS AND PHILIP JONES. DAVID & C., 1970. (INDUSTRIAL BRITAIN)	338.0942	I K L M N O B	27
LEWIS, SINCLAIR	ESTE INMENSO MUNDO. BARCELONA: DESTINO, 1970.	863 LEW	A B C	28

FIG. 10.2. Sample page from non-fiction author catalogue, London Borough of Camden Public Libraries.

```
UNIVERSITY  OF  LANCASTER   SHORT   LOAN   COLLECTION.          24/03/72           SHEET 001
AUTHOR.                     TITLE.                      COPY     CLASSMARK       COURSE-CODE


D'ANTONIO W           REPUTATIONAL TECHNIQUE                    1    R6              POLI221
D'ENTREVES A          NATURAL LAW                               1    SAQ             HIST101
D.E.P.                NATIONAL MINIMUM WAGE                     1    TDR(EA)         ECON203
DAHL R                BEHAVIOURAL APPROACH                      1    R6              POLI221
DAHL R                MODERN POLITICAL ANALYSIS                 1    RRR.D1          POLI102
DAHL R                MODERN POLITICAL ANALYSIS                 2    RRR.D1          POLI102
DAHL R                MODERN POLITICAL ANALYSIS                 3    RRR.D1          POLI102
DAHL R                MODERN POLITICAL ANALYSIS                 4    RRR.D1          POLI102
DAHL R                MODERN POLITICAL ANALYSIS                 5    RRR.D1          POLI102
DAHL R                MODERN POLITICAL ANALYSIS                 6    RRR.D1          POLI102
DAHL R                PLURALIST DEMOCRACY IN AMERICA            1    RD(R).Y         POLI102
DAHL R                PLURALIST DEMOCRACY IN AMERICA            2    RD(R).Y         POLI102
DAHL R                POLITICAL OPPOSITION IN WESTERN DEMOCRACIES 1  RBO             POLI211
DAHL R                POLITICAL OPPOSITION IN WESTERN DEMOCRACY 1    RBO             POLI316
DAHL R                RULING ELITE MODEL                        1    R6              POLI221
DAHRENDORF R          CONFLICT AFTER CLASS                      1    KCND            SOCL202
DAHRENDORF R          SOCIETY AND DEMOCRACY IN GERMANY          1    RD(K)&          POLI316
DALE A                TAX HARMONISATION IN EUROPE               1    TU(CNW)         F.CL201
DALLIN A              SOVIET POLITICS SINCE KHRUSHCHEV          1    RD(N).Y         POLI312
DALLIN A              SOVIET UNION AT THE UN                    1    RIF(N)          POLI220
DALLIN D              SOVIET FOREIGN POLICY AFTER STALIN        1    MNQP.D          POLI102
DALLIN D              SOVIET FOREIGN POLICY AFTER STALIN        2    MNQP.D          POLI106
DANIEL N              ISLAM AND THE WEST                        1    HBE             HIST101
DANIELL J             EXPERIMENT IN REPUBLICANISM               1    NJF             HIST107
DANIELS R             STALIN REVOLUTION                         1    MNQQ            HIST106
DANTO A               ANALYTICAL PHILOSOPHY OF HISTORY          1    L4A             PHIL231
DANTZIG G             LINEAR PROGRAMMING AND EXTENSIONS         1    AYLL            OP.RDAK
DANTZIG G             LINEAR PROGRAMMING AND EXTENSIONS         2    AYLL            OP.RDAK
DARLING A             JACKSONIAN DEM. IN MASSACHUSETTS          1    L6              HISTS.7
DARLING F             WILDERNESS AND PLENTY                     1    DUNTA           POLI316
DARWIN C              EVOLUTION BY NATURAL SELECTION            1    EO              HISTS.8
DARWIN C              LIFE AND LETTERS OF CHARLES DARWIN VOL 2  1    E4.D2           HISTS.8
DARWIN C              THE ORIGIN OF SPECIES                     1    EO              H.SC
DASHKOVA E            MEMOIRS OF PRINCESS DASHKOVA              1    MNP.U           HIST303
DAVIES A              LINGUISTICS AND SPOKEN ENGLISH            1    YAB             ENGLCNC
DAVIES G              RESTORATION OF CHARLES 1                  1    MVQK            HISTS.4
DAVIES J              POLITICS OF POLLUTION                     1    DUHUP           POLI316
DAVIES M              ENFORCEMENT OF ENG. APPRENTICESHIP 1563-1642 2 MVM.E           HISTS.3
DAVIES M              ENFORCEMENT OF ENGLISH APPRENTICESHIP 1563-1642 1 MVM.E        HISTS.3
DAVIS D               SOME THEMES OF COUNTER-SUBVERSION         1    L6              HISTS.7
DAVIS R               COMMERCIAL REVOLUTION                     1    MVPR.F          HISTS.5
DAVIS R               HISTORY OF MEDIEVAL EUROPE                1    MR              HIST101
DAVIS R               HISTORY OF MEDIEVAL EUROPE                2    MR              HIST101
DAWSON C              MAKING OF EUROPE                          1    MR              HIST101
DE BEER G             CHARLES DARWIN                            1    E4              HISTS.8
DE CONDE A            AMERICAN SECRETARY OF STATE               1    RM(N).H         POLI221
DE FLEUR M            THEORIES OF MASS COMMUNICATION            1    KPP             POLI329
DE MAYO P             MOLECULAR REARRANGEMENTS VOL 1            1    COO             CHEMSB
DE RIVERA J           PSYCHOLOGICAL DIMENSION OF FOREIGN POLICY 1    RIF(N)          POLI221
DE TROKELOWE J        CHRONICA ET ANNALES                       1    MUS             HISTS.1
```

FIG. 10.3. Sample page from author list, University of Lancaster Library short-loan collection.

less practical, sorting must be carried out by machine on the basis of the characters in the record. This produces an arrangement which is largely similar to that found in library catalogues, and may well be acceptable in many situations. But statements of library filing rules consist largely of exceptions to straightforward alphabetical order, which machine sorting cannot reproduce. A subsequent section in this chapter is devoted to problems of filing in computer-produced catalogues, but there are a number of simple ways of getting round some of the problems.

In the first place, it must be emphasized that filing only becomes a real problem in very large catalogues. In most cases, straightforward

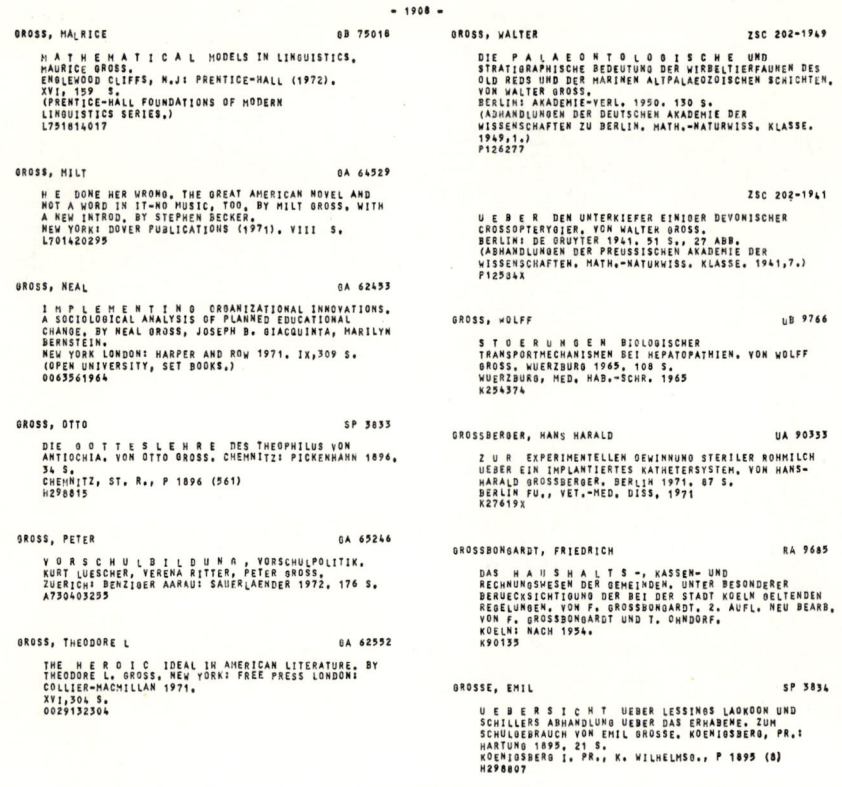

```
GROSS, MAURICE                                        GB 75018
    M A T H E M A T I C A L  MODELS IN LINGUISTICS,
    MAURICE GROSS.
    ENGLEWOOD CLIFFS, N.J: PRENTICE-HALL (1972),
    XVI, 159 S.
    (PRENTICE-HALL FOUNDATIONS OF MODERN
    LINGUISTICS SERIES,)
    L751814017

GROSS, MILT                                           GA 64529
    H E  DONE HER WRONG. THE GREAT AMERICAN NOVEL AND
    NOT A WORD IN IT-NO MUSIC, TOO, BY MILT GROSS, WITH
    A NEW INTROD. BY STEPHEN BECKER.
    NEW YORK: DOVER PUBLICATIONS (1971), VIII S.
    L701420295

GROSS, NEAL                                           GA 62433
    I M P L E M E N T I N G  ORGANIZATIONAL INNOVATIONS.
    A SOCIOLOGICAL ANALYSIS OF PLANNED EDUCATIONAL
    CHANGE, BY NEAL GROSS, JOSEPH B. GIACQUINTA, MARILYN
    BERNSTEIN.
    NEW YORK LONDON: HARPER AND ROW 1971, IX,309 S.
    (OPEN UNIVERSITY, SET BOOKS,)
    0063561964

GROSS, OTTO                                           SP 3833
    DIE  G O T T E S L E H R E  DES THEOPHILUS VON
    ANTIOCHIA, VON OTTO GROSS, CHEMNITZ: PICKENHAHN 1896,
    34 S,
    CHEMNITZ, ST. R,, P 1896 (561)
    H298815

GROSS, PETER                                          GA 65246
    V O R S C H U L B I L D U N G , VORSCHULPOLITIK,
    KURT LUESCHER, VERENA RITTER, PETER GROSS.
    ZUERICH: BENZIGER AARAU: SAUERLAENDER 1972, 176 S,
    A730403295

GROSS, THEODORE L                                     GA 62552
    THE  H E R O I C  IDEAL IN AMERICAN LITERATURE. BY
    THEODORE L, GROSS, NEW YORK: FREE PRESS LONDON:
    COLLIER-MACMILLAN 1971,
    XVI,304 S,
    0029132304

- 1908 -

GROSS, WALTER                                         ZSC 202-1949
    DIE  P A L A E O N T O L O G I S C H E  UND
    STRATIGRAPHISCHE BEDEUTUNG DER WIRBELTIERFAUNEN DES
    OLD REDS UND DER MARINEN ALTPALAEOZOISCHEN SCHICHTEN,
    VON WALTER GROSS.
    BERLIN: AKADEMIE-VERL. 1950, 130 S.
    (ABHANDLUNGEN DER DEUTSCHEN AKADEMIE DER
    WISSENSCHAFTEN ZU BERLIN. MATH.-NATURWISS. KLASSE.
    1949,1.)
    P126277

                                                      ZSC 202-1941
    U E B E R  DEN UNTERKIEFER EINIGER DEVONISCHER
    CROSSOPTERYGIER, VON WALTER GROSS.
    BERLIN: DE GRUYTER 1941, 51 S., 27 ABB,
    (ABHANDLUNGEN DER PREUSSISCHEN AKADEMIE DER
    WISSENSCHAFTEN, MATH.-NATURWISS. KLASSE. 1941,7,)
    P12584X

GROSS, WOLFF                                          UB 9766
    S T O E R U N G E N  BIOLOGISCHER
    TRANSPORTMECHANISMEN BEI HEPATOPATHIEN, VON WOLFF
    GROSS. WUERZBURG 1965, 108 S,
    WUERZBURG, MED, HAB.-SCHR. 1965
    K254374

GROSSBERGER, HANS HARALD                              UA 90333
    Z U R  EXPERIMENTELLEN GEWINNUNG STERILER ROHMILCH
    UEBER EIN IMPLANTIERTES KATHETERSYSTEM, VON HANS-
    HARALD GROSSBERGER. BERLIN 1971, 87 S,
    BERLIN FU,, VET.-MED, DISS, 1971
    K27619X

GROSSBONGARDT, FRIEDRICH                              RA 9685
    DAS  H A U S H A L T S -, KASSEN- UND
    RECHNUNGSWESEN DER GEMEINDEN, UNTER BESONDERER
    BERUECKSICHTIGUNG DER BEI DER STADT KOELN GELTENDEN
    REGELUNGEN, VON F. GROSSBONGARDT. 2. AUFL. NEU BEARB,
    VON F. GROSSBONGARDT UND T. OHNDORF.
    KOELN: NACH 1954.
    K90135

GROSSE, EMIL                                          SP 3834
    U E B E R S I C H T  UEBER LESSINGS LAOKOON UND
    SCHILLERS ABHANDLUNG UEBER DAS ERHABENE. ZUM
    SCHULGEBRAUCH VON EMIL GROSSE, KOENIGSBERG, PR,:
    HARTUNG 1895, 21 S,
    KOENIGSBERG I, PR,, K. WILHELMSG,, P 1895 (8)
    H298807
```

Fig. 10.4. Sample page from author catalogue, University of Bochum Library.

arrangement, first under author's surname, then initials or forenames, and then title of the work, is perfectly adequate. Initial articles in titles must be ignored for purposes of filing: they may safely be omitted from many library catalogues without loss of meaning or usefulness. In some cases, it is permissible to introduce spaces and other punctuation devices to achieve a desired order. Sometimes names, or their structure as defined by library cataloguing rules, may be altered slightly for the same purpose. If need be, in difficult cases, it may be necessary to introduce a special sort field into the bibliographical record. This contains the character string which the computer uses

PAGE 1270

LAUNCHED

Agreement on the rescue of astronauts, the return of astronauts and the return of objects launched into outer space. (Cmnd 3786) Foreign Office 1968, HMSO 1|3 6p 0101378602 341 246629 783 Copy 1 Library Shelf Cmnd Box

Table of earth satellites launched in the years 1957 to 1967. (RAE TR 68124). Quinn, E Ministry of Technology, 1968 46p 0aa001359X 629 783[083] aa001359 Library Shelf P 629

LAUNCHING

Agreement between Sweden, other member states of the European Space Research Organisation and the European Space Research Organisation on a special project concerning the launching of sounding rockets. (Cmnd. 5060) HMSO, 1972 £0 13 14p 0101506007 341 24*629 765 629 765*341 24 1563a72 Library Shelf Cmnd Box

Exchange of notes between the government of the United Kingdom of Great Britain and Northern Ireland and the European Space Research Organisation concerning the use of ESRO launching range (ESRANGE) by the United Kingdom for a special project. (Cmnd.3990). Foreign and Commonwealth Office HMSO, 1969 0|9 4p 0101399006 341 246629 7 085 26 629 7 085 26 Copy 1 Library Shelf Cmnd Box

NAVAL

De Naval engineering handbook. Gartmann, H , ed 3rd ed McGraw-Hill, 1970 120|- Various pagination 0070229092 621 621 4 621 5 336|71 Library Shelf 621 GAR

LAW

ABM, MIRV, SALT, and the nuclear arms race. Hearings before the Committee on Foreign relations, Subcommittee on Arms Control, International Law and Organization, Congress of the United States, 91st Congress, 2nd session held, March 16, April 8-9, 13-14, May 18,28, June 4, 29, 1970. USA Congress US Govt Printing Office, 1970 231- 624p 0aa003925X 341 676623 454 8 623 +54 88341 67 103|71 2 Copies Library Shelf Stack USA Congress

British patent system. Report of the committee to examine the patent system and patent law (cmnd 4407). Board of Trade HMSO,1970 23|- 234p 0101440707 608 2013|70 Library Shelf Cmnd Box

Businessman's guide to letter-writing and to the law on letters. Mitchell, E Business Books, 1970 70|- 224p 0220669752 651 2410|70 Library Shelf 65 MIT

Clean air - Law and practice. Garner, J F 3rd ed Shaw and Sons Ltd , 1969 £5 25 506p 0721900119 628 511*34 0578a72 Library Shelf 628 GAR

Comprehensive guide to factory law. A classified guide to the requirements of the Factories Act and other legislation affecting factories and allied premises, including offices and building sites. McKown, R 4th ed Godwin, 1969 50|- 163p 0aa0010S4X 658 382534 1937|70 Copy 1 Library 2654|68 Library FF 2609|68 SSGS 2308|68 SSGS 2463|68 Foulness Shelf 34 MAC

Digest of law and regulations affecting the superannuation of members of the civil service, governors of colonies and the judiciary. Treasury HMSO, 1965 70|- 715p 0aa003242X 658 325634 1318|70 Library Ref Shelf 65 TRE

Experience and trends in nuclear law. A selection of papers presented at the seminar on the development of nuclear law held, Bangkok, April 6-11, 1970, and the inter-regional training course on the legal aspects of nuclear energy held, Athens, December 7-18, 1970. International Atomic Energy Agency IAEA, 1972 169p 0aa005545X 34*621 039 621 039*34 Copy 1 Library Shelf 34 INT

FIG. 10.5. Sample page from main KWOC catalogue. Atomic Weapons Research Establishment Library, Aldermaston, Berkshire. The author catalogue at Aldermaston contains brief author, title, and location information only.

to sort the record into correct order. In most cases it will be the same as the data field itself, but in some instances, the sort field may be prepared manually, so that when operated upon by the straightforward alphabetical machine sort routines, it will result in the non-alphabetical library filing order that is desired.

A wide variety of formats for printed catalogues is possible, and some are illustrated in Figs. 10.2 to 10.5. Much can be done with standard line printers which have rather less than fifty different characters available in upper case only. A more pleasing result can be obtained with the use of an upper and lower case print chain which can be fitted to some line printers. But in either case, an array of catalogue entries on a printed page is generally regarded as being easier to scan than a conventional card catalogue, which may contain typewritten or printed cards of high typographic quality.

Card Form Catalogues

It has been assumed so far that the computer-produced catalogue will be printed first onto paper, and then reproduced in as many copies as necessary by an appropriate reprographic technique. It is, however, perfectly possible for a computer cataloguing system to print catalogue entries onto cards, ready for manual filing into a card catalogue in the usual manner.

The great advantage of producing cards from a computer cataloguing system is that they can be interfiled into the library's existing card catalogue: no change is necessary in existing cataloguing procedures. This can be of great benefit when, for other reasons, a conventional form of catalogue must be retained, at least for the time being, although the advantages of a computer system are sought immediately.

Whatever form of catalogue is adopted, if a machine-readable file of catalogue records is maintained (and such a file will be maintained in a card system, even though it will not be updated in the same way as the file for a book form catalogue system) then a catalogue in a different form may be produced from that file at a later date if desired.

The twin disadvantages of computer-produced card catalogues are that less information can be printed onto each card than can, for example, be typed, and that the slow, expensive, and error-prone task of filing cards is still retained. But on the other hand, the difficulty for the library reader in using a main catalogue plus a supplement, plus, in all probability, an earlier card catalogue, does not exist. A decision, therefore, between a card or book catalogue, will probably be based on service aspects, and if there is any advantage to be gained from having multiple copies of the catalogue available, then a book form catalogue will be chosen. Figure 10.6 shows a sample of computer-produced catalogue cards, showing the continuous-flow stationery that is used, and subsequently burst apart.

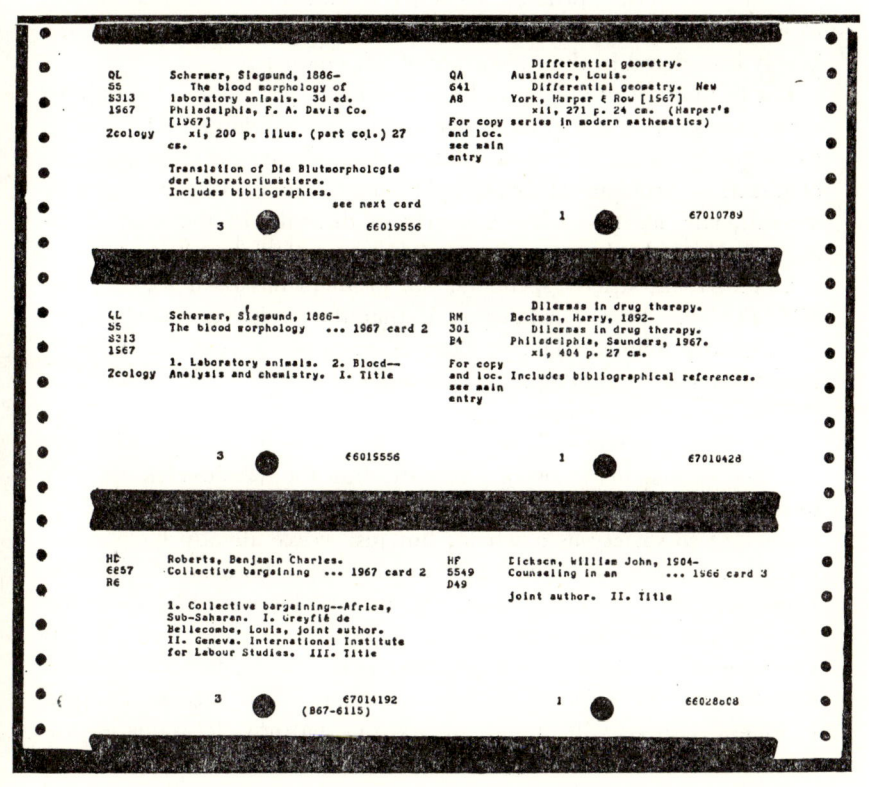

FIG. 10.6. Catalogue cards printed on continuous-flow stationery by line printer with extended character set, University of Toronto Library.

PROBLEM AREAS FOR COMPUTER-PRODUCED CATALOGUES

Mention has already been made of recent developments that have occurred in relation to computer-produced library catalogues, and of the benefits to readers which future developments should afford. To say this implies that in the past, computer-produced catalogues have not been all that they might have been, and that nowadays, computer-produced catalogues are not quite all that we might wish them to be. There remain certain problem areas in connection with such catalogues, to which adequate solutions have not yet been found. These are briefly considered in the remainder of this chapter.

But to think of problems and of solutions to problems is to simplify matters to such an extent as to give a slightly false picture. The library catalogue problem is not so clearly defined, as, for example, the engineering problem of building a supersonic passenger transport aircraft, nor, for that matter, nearly so difficult. In the case of the aircraft, the objectives are clearly defined, and when they have been achieved, then, strictly speaking, the problem has been solved. The difficulty with library catalogues is that the problems have not yet been clearly defined. The problem is certainly not concerned with how to prepare a catalogue by computer; the techniques involved in this are now almost commonplace.

The library problem is better seen by taking a different analogy, not the supersonic transport aircraft, but the whole civil aircraft industry. Of course, the library problems are smaller, simpler and less important to society as a whole; but just as we already have many excellent aircraft, so have we many excellent libraries. Supersonic transports are now flying regularly, just as, for example, there are some on-line real-time catalogue systems operating regularly. But at the time of writing, it is not yet clear either how supersonic aircraft will fit into the existing pattern of air travel, nor how real-time catalogue systems will fit into the existing pattern of catalogue production and use.

If all research and development on improved aircraft types and better catalogues were to cease, we should still travel by air and we should still use libraries and their catalogues. But somehow we feel that the world would be a poorer place to live in. Even though the problems are not clearly defined in either case, we are fairly sure of the general direction in which we should work. And once having an idea of the possibility of something better, creative man cannot but strive to improve what he already enjoys.

Five "problem areas" are therefore considered; Data conversion, Filing, Character sets and typesetting, Forms of catalogue, and On-line catalogues. It must be emphasized that not all of these areas are equally problematical; for example, there are few library catalogues which would not be more than adequately served by standard modern phototypesetters. On the other hand, despite the rapid development and wide acceptance of the MARC record services, few would accept that these represent the best way of communicating bibliographic records to libraries which need them.

Data Conversion

A fundamental problem remains in connection with the first and most basic step in producing catalogues by computer; that of creating or obtaining bibliographic data in machine-readable form for each book added to a library's collection. Note that this is not a critical problem in the sense that some key advance in data-conversion techniques is awaited before computer-based catalogues can become truly effective. Well-tried techniques of data-conversion exist, and are widely used in libraries all over the world, and herein lies the problem which gave rise to the basic idea behind MARC and, still unsolved, requires an improved MARC service or network for a satisfactory solution.

The logic is simple, that it is wasteful for individual libraries to prepare machine-readable catalogue records for books and other items added to their own collections. Viewed on a national or international scale, this premise can hardly but be true. Yet librarians have long been aware of the wastefulness inherent in individual libraries preparing manual catalogue records of items added to their collections, and although libraries in the US have moved very largely over to accepting and using a centralized cataloguing service, libraries in Europe still tend to do their own original cataloguing.

There have been, and there remain, two principal problems in the provision of centralized cataloguing services; the preparation of the catalogue data (and in particular the rapid preparation of catalogue data for new books), and the distribution of that data rapidly to libraries on demand. The first is a problem in organization; a central agency must obtain copies of, or information about, new publications well in advance of publication. The second is a problem in communication, and is directly affected by recent advances in telecommunications.

Viewed on a wide scale, then, the problem of data conversion for computer-based library catalogues concerns the creation of machine-readable bibliographic records of all books, reports, serials, theses, maps, tapes, slides and other items which libraries deem it their duty to collect, and making individual records quickly and cheaply available to any library on request. It is convenient to divide the whole problem into its various aspects and to consider each one separately.

NEWLY PUBLISHED MATERIAL

Libraries and their users are most interested in newly published materials, and the book remains the most popular medium for instruction and recreation that libraries are concerned with. The problem of creating and distributing machine-readable bibliographical records for new books is thus the most crucial aspect of the whole problem of data conversion.

This problem was tackled first by the Library of Congress which began an experimental MARC record service in October 1966, by distributing weekly cataloguing data on magnetic tape to sixteen libraries.[5] The experiment was successful, and it has been continued, with a change in the record format in 1968 to the present communications format. The number of recipients of the Library of Congress tapes has grown to about sixty, a similar service has been introduced by the British National Bibliography, and other countries such as France, Germany and Scandinavian countries, Italy, South Africa, Australia and Canada may follow suit in the near future.

Subscribers to the LC and BNB MARC tapes receive a magnetic tape each week, containing the week's cataloguing output of both institutions. The system works very satisfactorily, except for the delays occurring between the publication of new books and the receipt of

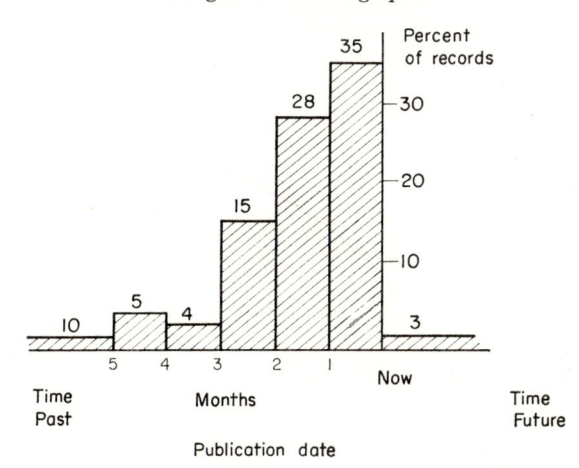

FIG. 10.7. Distribution of publication dates of 540 bibliographical records in one BNB MARC tape.

bibliographic records of them by libraries which subscribe to the MARC record service.

Coward[6] has discussed these delays, and his figures are presented as a histogram in Fig. 10.7. Analyzing 540 records in one BNB MARC tape whose publication dates could be ascertained from a trade bibliography, Coward found that 3 per cent of the records were for books that had not yet been published, 35 per cent were for books published during the past month, 28 per cent for books which had been published between 1 and 2 months previously, and so on. Looking at this data the other way round, and assuming that a sample of 540 records gives an adequate picture of the whole MARC record service, Fig. 10.8 shows the time taken for records of individual books to appear in the MARC record service. Imagine a sample of 100 newly published books, then bibliographic records for three of them will already have appeared in MARC, records for thirty-eight of them will appear in MARC within one month from now, records for sixty-six of them within 2 months from now, and so on. Bibliographic records for ten books will still not have been made available in 5 months time, and of these, there will in all probability be one or two still not included in MARC a year or so from now.

A.L.—H

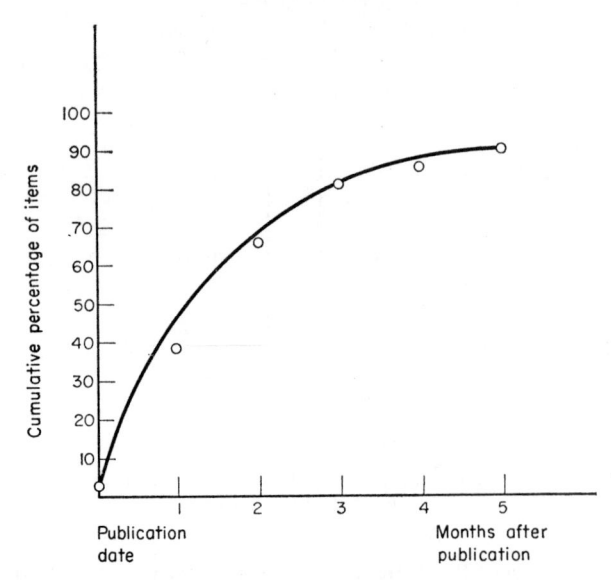

FIG. 10.8. Time taken (expressed in months after publication date) for bibliographic records for items to appear in the BNB MARC record service.

The shape of this curve will never be significantly altered. What the Library of Congress and the British National Bibliography are doing in their efforts to improve the currency of MARC is to obtain more books for cataloguing in advance of publication (thus sliding the whole curve bodily to the left) and to improve the arrangements for obtaining books from the publishers (thus making the curve slope more steeply upwards). The incorporation of the British National Bibliography as a division of the British Library will materially assist in achieving the latter objective.

OLDER MATERIAL

The MARC record service can cover a high percentage of libraries' current intake, but because of the many advantages of computer catalogues, libraries have turned their attention to the problems involved in preparing machine-readable records of their older holdings, and to replacing their existing card catalogues entirely with computer-produced catalogues. Some brave libraries, such as the Widener Library of Harvard University and the library of the University of Newcastle upon Tyne, have already converted their entire shelf lists to machine-readable form. But such projects, even though they each represent the work of many people over a period of several years, scarcely even scratch the surface of the problem as it appears when viewed in perspective, from an international and historical angle.

Ideally, one might postulate that bibliographical records should be available in machine-readable form for every book ever published throughout the world since, say, the invention of printing by movable type. Realistically, however, one might expect to be able to approach that goal over a period of time, but never quite reaching it. The curve illustrating the progress of such work would, incidentally, look something like that in Fig. 10.8.

The problem, then, is an international one, and in essence concerns the strategy that should be adopted in creating machine-readable records of older books. There is no intrinsic difficulty in setting editors and keypunchers to work in the world's major libraries; the mechanics of this would present no problem. But two drawbacks would immediately ensue. As Arms[7] has shown in his study of duplication in library holdings, there would be a high degree of duplication if, say, three or four national libraries were immediately to institute simultaneous programmes of retrospective catalogue conversion. Secondly, assuming that such large conversion programmes were successfully carried out, there remains the problem of matching individual library holdings with these large bibliographic files. The MARC record service works so well because each item on the file can be identified simply by a unique number—the ISBN. No other similar number exists for books published prior to 1968. Various national numbers extend further back in time, such as the Library of Congress card number, and the BNB number, and these can be used as identification numbers in so far as they will serve.

Two major national data conversion projects have been started. The Library of Congress RECON (retrospective conversion) project has started to prepare machine-readable records for English and foreign language monographs published before 1969, while the British Library is doing the same thing for all records in the printed *British National*

Bibliography, which includes all books published in Britain since 1950.

These two files, American and British, will be accessible by means of unique national bibliography numbers, but thereafter, as files of even earlier records begin to be considered, matching must begin to be by means of conventional bibliographic data fields. In other words, instead of specifying a sought record by means of its ISBN, LC card number or BNB number, its author and title must be quoted. This, of course, is how printed catalogue files are normally searched, but as is discussed below, in the section on on-line catalogues, the problems of matching are very much greater in a machine environment than in manual systems.

An important study in the machine matching of bibliographic records has been carried out by Jolliffe for a project to create a machine-readable catalogue of early books in the college and departmental libraries of Oxford and Cambridge Universities, the Bodleian Library, Cambridge University Library and the British Museum.[8] An interesting unique identifier or "footprint" was introduced in a test for this project, consisting of eighteen characters taken in pairs from the ends of lines, three lines to each of three predetermined pages. Also tested was a measure of degree of match between the words in two titles being compared, and a fifteen-character "search code" constructed from the date, title, author, edition and place of publication of a work.

The methodology of retrospective catalogue conversion has been the subject of study, especially with regard to the possibility of assigning tags automatically. Jolliffe wrote a suite of programs in 1967 to tag a small sample file of entries from the British Museum General Catalogue.[9] The programs were subsequently used by the Bodleian Library to tag machine-readable records prepared by optical character recognition techniques for entries in its pre-1920 catalogue.[10] The Library of Congress is similarly experimenting with procedures which assign tags to records on the basis of their strictly controlled format.[11] In the long term, it is expected that such automatic format recognition techniques should enable records to be tagged successfully with approximately 75 per cent accuracy, the remaining 25 per cent of cases being dealt with manually.

Filing Rules

Library filing rules are based on straightforward arrangement, word by word, according to the order of the English alphabet. Computer sort programs operate in the same way, so that fundamentally it is a straightforward operation to file a group of machine-readable catalogue records into correct sequence. In so far as the basic filing rule applies, there is no problem. Only when exceptions to the basic rule arise, does it become necessary to consider whether or not they will be included in an individual library sort program in order to produce a "library" arrangement rather than a more natural arrangement.

The *ALA Rules for Filing Catalog Cards* (2nd ed. 1968) constitutes the generally accepted authority on the subject, containing a daunting 230 pages of exceptions to the single basic rule. Strictly speaking, it would not be impossible to write a sort program incorporating all of these rules, provided that the machine-readable catalogue records had been tagged in a sufficiently detailed manner. There is no question of such a program ever being written, however, for the effort would just not be worth while in terms of the increased ease it might afford to the users of some larger catalogues. A compromise must be struck; the question is, where?

It is worth noting two trends in this connection; towards simpler cataloguing and greater user education in the techniques of library use. Taken together with an associated trend towards a general simplification and standardization arising from the use of computer methods in libraries, it seems safe to assume that most catalogue systems will include no more than a few small sophistications and enhancements to basic machine filing. After all, there are many reasons why a library user may fail to find a sought item in a library catalogue, and any departures from "strict" filing rules are likely only to prolong the search process rather than reduce the user's success rate significantly.

Davison [12] has written a very readable account of the problems of filing for computer catalogues. Hines and Harris [13] early made the suggestion that quite major concessions should be made to the computer, and that catalogue entries should be filed on the basis of the characters in them rather than "as if" they contained different characters. These proposals were not well received, but meanwhile the MARC tagging structure has been widely adopted, bringing with it the possibility of more complex filing. More recent proposals for computer-based filing rules have been made by a working party of the Library Association[14] and the Birmingham Libraries Co-operative Mechanization Project,[15] and are in effect compromises between the Hines–Harris proposals and the full ALA rules. Meanwhile any generally available program suite embodying any degree of sophisticated sorting is still awaited. Following are some examples of typical "exceptions" to straightforward alphabetical order, showing how they can be programmed for a computer catalogue.

INITIAL ARTICLES

An early exception to the basic filing rule concerns definite and indefinite articles occurring at the beginning of filing fields. The exception states that initial articles in the nominative case in all languages are to be disregarded in filing. Thus books with titles beginning

An introduction to . . .

are filed under "I" in the alphabetical sequence. In Dutch, the title

De witte huis

is filed under "W", because "de" is the masculine definite article in the nominative case. But the Latin title

De re poetica

is filed under "D", because here, "de" is a preposition meaning "about" or "concerning". Quite difficult decisions can sometimes be involved as to whether a word is or is not an article, especially in the cases of the more difficult foreign languages.

Such decisions could be made by a computer. A table could be inserted into the program listing all possible articles in each language, and if the language of the work were indicated explicitly in the catalogue record then the decision could be made on consulting the table. In practice, a much simpler approach has been adopted in the MARC format, which must be regarded as the framework within which any filing rules program must work. In the title field (Tag 245) and other fields where titles are to be found, the second indicator shows the number of characters at the beginning of the field which must be disregarded in filing. This indicator is set manually, and in the first two examples considered above it would have the value 3 (including the space after the two-character article as a character), while in the third example it would have the value zero.

ABBREVIATIONS

When an abbreviation occurs in a filing field, the ALA rule is that the abbreviation should be filed, not as it stands, but as it is spoken in the language concerned, i.e. as if written out in full. Thus
   Dr. Mabuse der Spieler
is a German language title, and is filed as if written
   Doktor Mabuse der Spieler
And
   St. Peter
is filed as it is spoken—
   Saint Peter
Numerals occurring in a title are treated in the same way. Thus
   Le XIXe siècle
is filed as it is spoken, in French, but with the omission of the definite article—
   Dix-neuvième siècle
The generally accepted solution to the filing of abbreviations is to set up a separate filing field within the bibliographic record. (MARC records do not include such a field because they are essentially designed for communicating bibliographic records rather than for processing them within one library.) Such a filing field contains the characters that are to be considered in filing, while the data field contains the characters that are to be printed.

ARRANGEMENT OF PERSONAL NAMES

Here the ALA rules become complicated because of the wide variety of forms in which personal names can appear in library catalogues. Considering only the simple case of Anglo-Saxon names with single surnames and one or more forenames or initials, the following arrangement results from strict adherence to the rules:

Smith, J.
Smith, John
Smith, John, of Malton, Eng.
Smith, John, pseud.
Smith, Sir John
Smith, John, surgeon and trading captain
Smith, John, 1563–1616

The operative rules here are that names must first be arranged alphabetically by surname, and within a given surname alphabetically by forename or initial. Thus "Smith, J." comes before "Smith, John". All the John Smiths come together, but first come those with neither dates nor designations, then those with designations (arranged alphabetically by designation), and finally those with dates, or designations and dates (arranged chronologically by the first date given). Thus "Smith, John, of Malton, Eng." comes before "Smith, John, pseud." which is in turn followed by "Smith, Sir John". Note that the "Sir" is treated in the same way as the other designations, except that it is printed before the forename "John" rather than after it.

The MARC tagging structure enables these parts of the name to be labelled specifically. Thus in the BNB MARC format, within tag 100 (personal name main entry) subfield £a contains the surname, subfield £h contains the forenames, subfield £e contains additions (such as "Sir") occurring between the entry element ("Smith") and other parts of the name, subfield £c contains dates, and subfield £f contains designations and other additions to the name.

With this high degree of detailed labelling of the parts of the data field it remains to specify to a sort program the order in which subfields should be considered in filing. In the above example, filing is first by subfield £a, then by subfield £h. Records with no other subfields (within each combination of subfield £a and £h) are grouped together; then come those with subfields £e and £f, arranged alphabetically but with subfield £e printed before subfield £h, and finally those with subfield £c, arranged numerically.

The same detail in labelling is found in all fields in MARC records which may be used as headings or entry points in a catalogue. A generalized sort program capable of grouping named subfields together for alphabetization, considering subfields in a specified sequence for alphabetization and printing subfields in any desired order would meet all the above requirements.

Character Sets and Typesetting

One of the early difficulties experienced in preparing library catalogues by computer concerned the limited range of characters then available on computer printers. Designed with the needs of mathematical and scientific computing in mind, such machines printed very rapidly, but paid a price for speed, in terms of rather poor printing quality and a restricted character set. Standard computer line printers still offer the user no more than the twenty-six characters of the roman alphabet in upper case, the ten decimal digits, plus about a dozen other punctuation marks, mathematical symbols, etc.

As many of the figures in this book show, it is possible to achieve a fairly high quality of printing from a well-adjusted line printer. The forty-five or fifty characters available are quite adequate for most normal library purposes, and if the rather large original printouts are reduced to two-thirds or half their original size, a pleasing final product can be obtained. A skilful use of white space in the layout of a catalogue or list can contribute materially to its ease of use.

Libraries have commonly been content to use typewriters to prepare catalogue cards. Typewriters have a normal set of about ninety characters, including the most common accents found in European languages. Non-roman scripts are transliterated anyway in most library catalogues, if only to make it possible to interfile entries for non-roman items in the main catalogue sequence. And, of course, in a manual card catalogue, the odd accent, diacritical mark or special character can be inserted by hand if the need arises.

It is possible to use tape typewriters for computer output, and thus retain the full typewriter character set, but these machines are very slow compared with line printers, operating at less than one-hundredth of their speed.

One computer manufacturer, IBM, seeing the need for a large character set in a number of computer applications, has introduced a special character set for one of its standard line printers. In the form of a chain which carries the characters, this replaces the standard print chain, the changeover taking only a few minutes so that a computer unit is not permanently tied to the slow speed of printing which the larger character set involves. Print speeds are reduced to about one-third of that possible with a standard print chain. Slow printing means expensive printing, and while the long IBM print chain offers 120 characters including the upper- and lower-case roman letters, the ten decimal digits plus a large number of punctuation marks, accents and diacriticals, it does not significantly increase the legibility of the printed output.

What is really needed is not so much a very large character set, but high-quality reproduction with a medium-sized character set. Taking the 145 different characters specified for the MARC record service as a basic requirement, this set should ideally be available in an ordinary roman typeface, an italic face and a bold face, with the possible addition of a larger size roman face. This makes a total of 600 characters.

Such requirements are well within the capabilities of modern computer-controlled phototypesetters, and at a price comparable to that of setting type by line printer. For example, a small paper-tape-driven phototypesetter is being used experimentally at the University of Southampton library.[3] Equipped with a set of exchangeable founts each of 180 characters, it easily meets the above requirements. Figure 10.9 shows an example of output from the machine.

West Sussex County Library have also produced a catalogue by means of a computer-controlled phototypesetter, and Fig. 10.10 shows a sample page.

Most computer-controlled phototypesetters are large, fast and expensive machines, but with a unit typesetting cost rather lower than that possible with a computer line printer. In other words, if the phototypesetter is used extensively, it produces higher-quality output than a line printer and at lower cost. The fastest machines, which offer the lowest unit costs, run at a rate of the order of ten times that of a standard line printer, and two things follow from this. Firstly, that library catalogues, large though they may be for line printers, are quite within the capacity of the fast phototypesetters. Secondly, that because of the large capital cost of these machines, their use will

ACHESON
  Medical record linkage, [by] E. D. Acheson
    London, 1967 (isbn 0 19 721343X)
  R 864   WML-U   68-092993

BOUFARD
  El niño hasta los tres años, por P. Boufard
    Barcelona, 1967
  WL 207   WML-GH   68-405061

CAIN
  Le symptôme psychosomatique, [par] J. Cain
    Toulouse, 1971
  WX 987   WML-U   71-123450

DEBRE
  El sueño del niño, por R. Debre
    Barcelona, 1967
  WL 211   WML-GH   68-415162

DELAMARE
  Dictionnaire français-anglais et anglais-français
  des termes techniques de médecine, [par] J.
  Delamare
    Paris, 1970
  WA 103   WML-GH   71-987652

GALLIEN
  Travaux du 4e. Symposium International
  d'Endocrinologie Comparée, Paris, 20-26 juillet,
  1964; publiés par L. Gallien
    Paris, 1965
  Papers in English and French
  WK 100   Physiol D   70-501014

GLASER
  Die jüngsten Siege in der Medizin, [von] H.
  Glaser
    München, 1966
  WA 437   WML-GH   67-304050

INTERNATIONAL SYMPOSIUM ON COMPARATIVE ENDOCRINOLOGY, 4th, Paris, 1964
  Travaux du 4e. Symposium International
  d'Endocrinologie Comparée, Paris, 20-26 juillet,
  1964; publiés par L. Gallien
    Paris, 1965
  Papers in English and French
  WK 100   Physiol D   70-501014

FIG. 10.9. Sample output from the Friden Justotext phototypesetter at the University of Southampton Library; experimental author sequence for the Wessex Library catalogue.

```
10. 7.73                              FRENCH                                                   LANGUAGE WORKS                                              PAGE  2

ALEXANDRE, PAUL                                                                                CHERBULIEZ, VICTOR
  VOIR LONDRES ET MOURIR ...PAR PAUL ALEXANDRE ET                                                SAMUEL BROHL ET CIE. PARIS, NELSON, 1930. 282P.
  MAURICE ROLAND. PARIS, LIBRAIRIE DES CHAMPS-ELYSEES,                                           P002060817 843.8CHERBULIE
  1956. 192P. P002051303X 843.91ALEXANDR                                                         HN
  HN
                                                                                               CHEVALLIER, GABRIEL
ANOUILH, JEAN                                                                                    CLOCHEMERLE: ROMAN. PARIS, J. FERENCZI, 1938. 301P.
  PIECES BRILLANTES. PARIS, EDITIONS DE LA TABLE RONDE,                                          P002057358 843.91CHEVALLI
  1960. 535P. P002085283 842.91ANOUILH                                                           TS
  CN
                                                                                               CLAUDEL, PAUL
AUGER, PHILIPPE                                                                                  VILLE. PARIS, MERCURE DE FRANCE, 1967. 158P.
  OBJECTS TROUVES. PARIS, EDITIONS DE MINUIT, 1970.                                              P002051613 842.91CLAUDEL
  184P. P002053560X 843.91AUGIER.P                                                               HN
  HN
                                                                                               CLAVEL, MAURICE
AYME, MARCEL                                                                                     TIRES DES ETOILES OU NE SAIT PAS QUEL ANGE. PARIS,
  EN ARRIERE. PARIS, GALLIMARD, 1950. 264P. INDEX.                                               GRASSET, 1972. 297P. P002060451 843.91CLAVEL.M
  P002060893 843.91AYME.MAR                                                                      BW
  HN
                                                                                               COCTEAU, JEAN
BALZAC, HONORE DE                                                                                MACHINE INFERNALE: PIECE EN 4 ACTES. PARIS, GRASSET,
  COUSIN PONS. PENGUIN, 1968. P002075946 843.78BALZAC.HO                                         1934. 191P. P002051564 842.91COCTEAU
  OS                                                                                             HN

  ILLUSTRE GAUDISSART ET LA MUSE DU DEPARTEMENT.                                               CROZET, CHARLOTTE
  NELSON, 1937. P002064808 843.78BALZAC.HO                                                       MARIANNE OU LES AUTRES. PARIS, GALLIMARD, 1972. 165P
  CW                                                                                             P002075253 843.91CROZET.C
                                                                                                 CW
BARJAVEL, RENE
  VOYAGEUR IMPRUDENT. PARIS, DENOEL, 1958. 318P. INDEX.                                        DANINOS, PIERRE
  P002081560 843.91BARJAVEL                                                                      CARNETS DU MAJOR W. MARMADUKE THOMPSON. PARIS,
  CN                                                                                             HACHETTE, 1954. 242P. INDEX. P002081598
                                                                                                 843.91DANINOS.
  VOYAGEUR IMPRUDENT: ROMAN. PARIS, DENOEL, 1958. 318P.                                          ZW
  P002051591 843.91BARJAVEL
  HN                                                                                           DAUDET, ALPHONSE
                                                                                                 ALPHONSE DAUDET: MARCHAND DE BONHEUR: RECUEIL DE
BAZIN, HERVE                                                                                     TEXTES EXTRAITS DE SES OEUVRES, PRECEDE D'UNE
  QUI J'OSE AIMER. BERNARD GRASSET, 1956. 315P.                                                  AUTOBIOGRAPHIE D'APRES LES SOUVENIRS ...  PARIS,
  P002081091 843.91BAZIN.HE                                                                      NELSON, 1932. 376P. P002060841 843.91DAUDET.A
  OS                                                                                             CW

BECKETT, SAMUEL                                                                                CONTES DU LUNDI. NELSON, 1873. 377P; ILLUS.
  MERCIER ET CAMIER. PARIS, EDITIONS DE MINUIT, 1970.                                            P002064901 843.8DAUDET.AL
  212P. P002077256 843.91BECKETT.
  CN                                                                                           DEKOBRA, MAURICE
                                                                                                 MADONE DES SLEEPINGS. PARIS, LIVRE DE POCHE, 1967.
BENOIT, PIERRE                                                                                   254P. P002051563 843.91DEKOBRA
  ATLANTIDE. ALBIN MICHEL, 1920. 240P. INDEX.                                                    HN
  P002081075 843.91BENOIT.P
  AW                                                                                           DESCLOZEAUX, MARC
                                                                                                 REFLET: ROMAN. PARIS, EDITIONS ALBIN MICHEL, 1964.
  CHATELAINE DU LIBAN. ALBIN MICHEL, 1924. 245P.                                                 190P. P002072360X 843.91DESGLOZE
  P002081105 843.91BENOIT.P                                                                      BW SS PN
  RS
                                                                                               DILLMONT, THERESE DE
  NOTRE-DAME DE TORTOSE: ROMAN. PARIS, ALBIN MICHEL,                                             DENTELLE RENAISSANCE EDITEUR PAR THERESE DE DILLMONT
  1939. 192P. P002051521 843.91BENOIT.P                                                          ALSACE: MULHOUSE. 76P. P002075865 746.2
  HN                                                                                             RV
```

Fig. 10.10. Sample page, West Sussex County Library catalogue.

inevitably be restricted to central agencies and commercial firms.

They therefore represent a significant development in the technology relevant to computer production of library catalogues. They offer a possible solution to the problem of printing new editions of complete catalogues (this is essentially a matter of cost), and they demand that libraries restrict themselves to projects that have been fully justified on cost grounds—because commercial firms must charge commercial rates.

So far, we have been considering only phototypesetting of full-size characters, associated with the printing of book form catalogues on paper for consultation and reading in the normal way. A recent development are machines which set characters onto film in micro-size. This technique essentially amounts to a method of printing onto microfilm, and is of extreme importance. Up to now, microfilm has always consisted of microcopies of full-size originals. This has meant that it has always been necessary to prepare a full-size original first. But now, the need for the original has disappeared, and the microfilm itself in effect becomes the original.

Although microfilm has not in the past achieved the degree of widespread use which many felt it deserved, the possibility of replacing the vast quantities of paper currently output from computers by microfilm is a very attractive possibility indeed. The name "Computer output microfilm" has been coined for the new technique, which is more generally known by its acronym of COM.

In the first place, COM replaces the paper originals, and is not an "extra", as microfilm has always been in the past. And secondly, it is easy and cheap to make a limited number of copies of a microfilm. Computer methods make it possible for multiple copies of library catalogues and lists to be produced, and this is a very significant advantage of mechanized over manual systems. But by "multiple" is meant, for most libraries, something between half a dozen and perhaps two or three dozen copies. Microfilm is ideal when such numbers of copies are involved.

Buckle and French studied the use of microfilm for manual and mechanized library catalogues in 1972[16] and suggested that there could be eight operational COM catalogue systems in the UK by the end of that year. They summarize the advantages of COM catalogues over book form catalogues printed by line printer, listing faster data transfer speeds (i.e. faster typesetting), upper- and lower-case character sets available, low cost of materials, and savings in volume, weight and postage for the finished catalogue. The one disadvantage of COM as a medium for library catalogues is that microfilm adds a further disincentive for the reader to use the catalogue.

Figure 10.11 shows a sample frame from the Birmingham Libraries Co-operative Mechanization Project COM catalogue, and Fig. 10.12 shows a frame from the COM catalogue prepared by BNB for Brighton Public Libraries as part of the experimental BRIMARC system.[17]

Birmingham University Library has been using COM catalogues for its new accessions since 1972. Fifty-nine separate copies of three catalogues are distributed throughout the library, and in order to provide the same degree of access for the old card catalogue, it also has been microfilmed, and forty copies made available. The reason for this comparatively large number of copies (subject catalogues and name catalogues are counted separately) lies in the need to allow for multiple access to the catalogue. Very many people can consult a large card catalogue at once, but since only one person can use a copy of a microfilm catalogue at one time, it is necessary to provide a large number of microfilm readers (Birmingham University uses thirty-five) and multiple copies of the catalogue.

Updating Computer-produced Catalogues

Brief reference has already been made to the problems of updating computer-produced catalogues; the expense of printing new editions of book catalogues, and the awkwardness of additional supplements. For this reason, card catalogues still find favour, in that the processes of manual filing can keep them completely up-to-date, and still provide a single file for searching. To find the same thing in completely non-manual systems, it is necessary to go to an on-line system of the kind discussed in the next section.

Card catalogues can be up-to-date but at the expense of rather tedious manual filing procedures. In many libraries, new cards are filed daily, in others the catalogue is updated weekly. Updating a card

BLCMP_UNION_NAME_CATALOGUE - AUG 73 PAGE 002086

Juniere, Paul
Aluminium: its applications in the chemical and food industries/ (by) Paul Juniere and M. Sigwalt. - London: Crosby Lockwood, 1964
Published in France under the title 'Les Applications de l'Aluminium dans les Industries Chimiques et Alimentaires, by Editions Eyrolles
*0004363 AU

Juniper, D F
Jackson, Roy
A manual of educational guidance/ (by) R. Jackson and D.F. Juniper. - London: Holt, Rinehart and Winston, 1971
0039100847 AU

Junius
The letters of Junius. - London: for J. Wheble, 1770
*1107355 BU

JUNIUS, Franciscus, 1545-1602
BIBLE. New Testament. Corinthians. Latin. Vulgate. 1578
S. Pauli Apostoli ad Corinthios epistolae duae/ ex Arabica translatione... per Franciscum Junium.... (Paris): apud Joannem Mareschallum, 1578
*1100330 BU

JUNIUS, Franciscus, 1589-1677
Francisci Junii... de pictura veterum, libri tres. Amstelaedami: apud Johannem Blaeu, 1637
*1114243 BU

Junta de Investigacoes do Ultramar
Mota, A Teixeira de
Fulas e Beafadas no Rio Grande no seculo XV (achegas para a etnohistoria da Africa Ocidental). - Lisboa: Junta de Investigacoes do Ultramar. (Agrupamento de estudos de cartografia antiga; 60)
Summary in French
*1049971 BU

Juran, Joseph Moses
Quality planning and analysis: from product development through usage/ (by) J.M. Juran, Frank M. Gryna, Jr. - New York; Maidenhead: McGraw-Hill, 1970
0070331715 BU

Jurek, Stefan F
Electrical machines for technicians and technician engineers. - (Harlow): Longman, 1972
0582426014 BL

JURY, E I
Theory and application of the z-transform method. New York; London: Wiley, 1964
64017145 AU

Just, Gottfried
Reflexionen zur deutschen Literatur der sechziger Jahre/ Herausgegeben von Klaus Gunther Just; Nachwort von Leo Kreutzer. - Pfullingen: Verlag Gunther Neske, 1972
3788500204 AU

Just, Klaus Gunther
Just, Gottfried
Reflexionen zur deutschen Literatur der sechziger Jahre/ Herausgegeben von Klaus Gunther Just; Nachwort von Leo Kreutzer. - Pfullingen: Verlag Gunther Neske, 1972
3788500204 AU

Just, Leo
Handbuch der deutschen Geschichte/ begrundet von Otto Brandt/ fortgefuhrt von Arnold Oskar Meyer/ neu hrsg. von Leo Just. Bd 1-. - Frankfurt am Main: Athenaion, 1935-
*1006246 BU

Just, Ward
Military men. - London: Joseph, 1972
Originally published, New York, Knopf, 1970
0718109767 BL

Just consequences: a survey of some contemporary health problems in relation to nutrition which suggests that there is a new pattern of diseases in Western Civilisation/ edited by Robert Waller.. London: Charles Knight, 1971
Symposium held at Attingham Park in 1971
0853141053 BU

Justema, Doris
Justema, William
Weaving & needlecraft color course/ (by) William & Doris Justema. - New York; London: Van Nostrand Reinhold, 1971 (i.e. 1972)
0442782322 BL BR

Justema, William
Weaving & needlecraft color course/ (by) William & Doris Justema. - New York; London: Van Nostrand Reinhold, 1971 (i.e. 1972)
0442782322 BL BR

FIG. 10.11. Sample frame from the COM union catalogue produced by the Birmingham Libraries Co-operative Mechanization Project.

£1 05 823 91J (B72-18385) ISBN 0 370 01268 2
Welch, Ronald. Tank commander. Oxford University Press.
£1 60 823 91J (B72-29541) ISBN 0 19 271349 3
–Welch, Stuart Cary. A king's book of kings: the
'Shah-nameh' of Shah Tahmasp. Thames and Hudson
£12 50 741 640955 (L72-27992) ISBN 0 500 23178 8
Welcome, John.
The Cheltenham Gold Cup: the story of a great
steeplechase. New revised ed. Pelham £2 75
798 45094241 (B73-05847) ISBN 0 7207 0647 5
Ten of the best: selected short stories. Faber £0 60 823 01
ISBN 0 571 08231 9
The Welcome collection: fourteen racing stories. Joseph
£2 60 823 91FS (B72-28146) ISBN 0 7181 1086 2
Welcome collection: fourteen racing stories. (Welcome,
John) Joseph £2 60 823 91FS (B72-28146)
ISBN 0 7181 1086 2
Well done 'Leander' (Harker, Jack Stanley) Collins £2 75
940 5459420924 (B73-16366) ISBN 0 00 211944 7
Well I never! (Berg, Leila) Macmillan £0 09 372 412
(B72-07759) ISBN 0 333 13130 4
Well met by witchlight. (Beachcroft, Nina) Heinemann.
£1 45 823 91J (B72-27515) ISBN 0 434 92850 1
Well-told lie. (Hobhouse, Christina) Macmillan £2 50
823 91F (B72-26168) ISBN 0 333 13224 6
Wellard, James. By the waters of Babylon. 3 Fitzroy Sq.,
W 1 Hutchinson £3 00 913 3503 (B72-18421)
ISBN 0 09 111060 2
Wellershoff, Dieter. Einladung an alle. Kiepenheuer &
Witsch unpriced 83391F (B79-00479)
Wellesley, Richard Colley, Marquis Wellesley. Two views of
British India. (Dundas, Henry, Viscount Melville)
Adams & Dart £3 50 915 40331 ISBN 0 239 00032 3
Wellings, Evelyn Maitland. Middlesex. Barker £2 25
796 35863094218 (B72-20321) ISBN 0 213 16403 5
Wellington
Vol 2: Pillar of state. (Longford, Elizabeth Pakenham,
Countess of) Weidenfeld and Nicolson £3 95 920
(B72-29639) ISBN 0 297 00250 3
Wells, Albert Laurence. The observer's book of sea fishes.
(Bagenal, Timothy Bracegirdle) Revised ed. F. Warne.
£0 50 597 092 (B72-21599) ISBN 0 7232 1509 x
Wells, Clifford Henry James. Introduction to molecular
photochemistry. Chapman and Hall £1 70 541 35
(B72-29876) ISBN 0 412 11250 7
Wells, Herbert George. The complete short stories of H G
Wells. Benn; St Martins Press. £1 50 823 91FS
Wells, Katharine Fuller. Kinesiology: the scientific basis of
human motion. 5th ed. Saunders £3 65 612 76
(B72-04975) ISBN 0 7216 9217 6
Wells, P A. Psychology and epistemology: towards a theory
of knowledge. (Piaget, Jean) Penguin £0 80 121
(B72-32122) ISBN 0 14 060011 6
Wells, Rosemary
International trading. Edward Arnold £0 90 658 8
ISBN 0 7131 1542 4
Law and business: recent legislation. (Swift, Moira K)
Edward Arnold £0 18 3400942 (B79-00695)
Wells, Tobias. What to do until the undertaker comes. Hale
£1 50 823 91F (B73-03821) ISBN 0 7091 3090 2
Wells, Tobias. For works of this author published under
other names see Forbes, Stanton
Welsh marches. (Millward, Roy) Macmillan £3 50 914 24
(B71-23636) ISBN 0 333 12607 6
Welsh Office. See Great Britain. Welsh Office.
Welsh walks and legends. (Styles, Showell). 21 Duffryn
Close, Cardiff CF2 6HT: John Jones Cardiff Ltd £1 20
398 2209429 (B72-18702) ISBN 0 902375 20 2
Welshpool & Llanfair Light Railway. (Cartwright, Ralph)
David and Charles £2 75 385 5094294 (B72-19397)
ISBN 0 7153 5500 7
Welty, Eudora. The optimist's daughter. Deutsch £1 75
823 91F (B73-07199) ISBN 0 233 96431 2
Welv, Bobs van. Mr Bumblemoose and the glad dog.
(Andreus, Hans) Abelard-Schuman £1 20 839 3136J
(B72-30860) ISBN 0 200 71925 4
Wembley: fifty great years. (Gee, Harry) Pelham £2 25
796 3340942185 (B72-22514) ISBN 0 7207 0593 2
Wen I-to. Red candle: selected poems. Cape £1 25 895 1:5
(B72-26247) ISBN 0 224 00701 7
Wenner, Jann. Lennon remembers: the 'Rolling Stone'
interviews with John Lennon and Yoko Ono. Talmy

FIG. 10.12. Sample frame from the BRIMARC COM catalogue.

catalogue includes the amendment and deletion of existing entries, which in most libraries are a very frequent occurrence. Manual filing is not an accurate procedure, with error rates of up to 5 per cent being not unusual. Computer filing, on the other hand, even though it may be according to a simplified set of filing rules, has the advantage of being 100 per cent consistent.

The efficiency of card catalogues must not be overlooked in a study of computer systems. They are just one example of the many cases where a degree of manual intervention can often be justified. A similar situation holds in connection with filing rules, where manual indication of filing position is preferable to long and complex programs to do the same thing. If the on-line catalogue is regarded as the realistic goal towards which all computer-based cataloguing development work should be directed, then to introduce a computer system which produces cards for an existing card catalogue can be regarded as a way of taking advantage of computer methods without the commitment to major catalogue changes that are implied in book form or COM catalogues.

It is well known, however, that there is a wide range of types of inquiry addressed to library catalogues, ranging from the call number of a prescribed text book to a complex bibliographical search. Some inquiries will be satisfied by a local library collection, or even a subset of a local collection, while others must be addressed to the library holdings of a nation or even a continent. But fortunately, there are many more simple searches than complex, and local collections satisfy most users' needs. This is why there has been a wide acceptance of the "undergraduate library" or "reserve" or "short loan" collection in many university libraries. These collections handle the large bulk of simple demands on the library, and their catalogues can be correspondingly simple.

The existence of this wide spectrum of types of library use and a similar range of catalogue requirements makes it realistic to think in terms of many catalogues of a library's holdings rather than one. In particular, a catalogue of the heavily used part of the collection (the undergraduate collection in a university library, and perhaps fiction in a public library) and a separate catalogue of the less heavily used collections. It may even be realistic to consider dividing the latter by date of publication, remembering that readers' queries tend to concentrate on newer books.

This means that, provided users are directed aright, a library with many catalogues, divided by degree and type of use of their holdings, may actually be easier to use than a library with a single card catalogue where everything in the library may be found in one sequence. Now a pattern of divided catalogues is produced naturally by computer systems to print book form catalogues. But experience has been that the division of the catalogues has resulted in inefficiency and frustration for the users, and some book catalogue systems have accordingly been abandoned. However, if the basis of division and the pattern of supplements are chosen to match the pattern of library use, users could be helped rather than hindered.

COM catalogues are cheaper to produce, update and duplicate than full-size book catalogues printed on paper, and afford the opportunity for experimentation in trying to achieve optimum catalogue structures.

COM technology has been linked to the use of ISBNs for book identification to produce a novel union catalogue in the London and South-eastern Region of Britain. Christened LASER, this system prints onto microfilm a numerical list of ISBNs together with numerically coded library locations for each. The data-processing techniques are very simple, and the final "catalogue" is very cheap, so that the concept of an updating supplement disappears; each new "edition" of the catalogue, which appears at 2-month intervals, replacing the previous one. The system is being extended to include the whole of the United Kingdom.[18] Figure 10.13 shows a sample frame from the LASER catalogue.

On-line Catalogue Systems

These may be regarded as the ultimate in cataloguing systems, wherein one centrally located file of bibliographic records is interrogated and updated by a number of remote consoles. Such a catalogue may record the holdings of one library and be searched by the users of that library, or it may be a union catalogue searched by users scattered widely throughout a region or state. There is no reason why

0-723-602-808	27	33	43	47	52	70						
0-723-602-816	21	27	29	40								
0-723-602-824	31	39	92									
0-723-602-832	27											
0-723-602-840	129											
0-723-602-859	36	129										
0-723-602-867	34	39	82	129								
0-723-602-875	21	25	33	34	36	60	67	82	87	91	92	111	116	118	128
0-723-602-883	129											
0-723-602-891	43	129										
0-723-602-905	11	21	27	29	31	34	45	69	74	111	116	118
0-723-602-921	40											
0-723-602-93X	11	21	38	52	82	129						
0-723-602-948	36	43	91	129								
0-723-602-956	129											
0-723-602-964	11	27	91	111	117	129						
0-723-602-972	129											
0-723-602-980	129											
0-723-602-999	25	52	129									
0-723-603-014	38	92	118	129	6							
0-723-603-022	21	27	30	33	34	36	40	112	118	125	126	129
0-723-603-030	25	34	40	47	92	111	112	118	129	21		
0-723-603-065	34	38	39	43	67	92	116	118	126	129		
0-723-603-073	56	60	92	125	129	21						
0-723-603-081	69	116	125	129	21	33	43					
0-723-603-111	129											
0-723-603-12X	116	129	21									
0-723-603-138	129											
0-723-603-146	109	129	6	21	27	31	34	68				
0-723-603-162	125	13	34	39	43							
0-723-603-170	62											
0-723-603-189	19	27	52									

FIG. 10.13. Sample frame from the LASER COM catalogue.

searchers may not access files held on-line in another country. The dividing line between library catalogues and "information-retrieval" systems becomes very thin when on-line systems are under consideration, and, in fact, both at the International Labour Office, Geneva, in the ISIS system,[19] and at Queen's University, Belfast, in the QUOBIRD system,[20] the same programs handle both books and "documents". This section considers such systems from the library service and technical viewpoints.

LIBRARY SERVICE ASPECTS

On-line catalogue systems enable the user to sit at a computer terminal, which will probably be situated some distance from the library, and carry out a search of the library's collection that is included in the on-line file. Figure 10.14 reproduces a search of the physics and applied mathematics departmental library in Queen's University, Belfast, from a remote teletype, and illustrates the kind of procedures involved in such a search.

It must be emphasized to begin with that this kind of search is not necessarily very quick; 5 minutes or even quarter of an hour passes rapidly in making a subject search of this kind. But time spent walking to the library to consult a conventional catalogue is eliminated, which is especially important if the search should end in failure.

Much of this search time is occupied by the teletype printing responses from the computer. Limited to fifteen characters per second, this can appear painfully slow when awaiting the results of a search. For this reason, the QUOBIRD system and most others tend to employ visual display terminals which permit a very rapid display of data on a

FIG. 10.14. Subject search of the Applied Mathematics Departmental Library, Queen's University, Belfast. (Each line written by the system begins with the characters AMPB (Applied Mathematics and Physics Books); all other lines were input by the author.) The subject of this search is rocket trajectories in space navigation, expressed as the logical product of three natural language search terms. Terms are input separately, and as each new term is submitted, the user is given the opportunity to examine the books indexed with the new term, with the previous terms, or with all terms so far given, coordinated either as a logical sum or as a logical product. Only one book is retrieved by the logical product of the three terms used in this search; its title and chapter headings are first printed, which together contain the sought terms, and finally, brief bibliographic details are provided.

```
AMPB: INTERACTIVE SUBJECT INDEX OF APPLIED MATHS BOOKS
AMPB: NAME AND DEPARTMENT
    : R KIMBER DEPT. OF LIBRARY STUDIES
AMPB: ARE YOU FAMILIAR WITH THE SYSTEM?
    : NO
AMPB: TYPE"?"IF YOU NEED MORE INFORMATION AT ANY STAGE.
AMPB: TYPE"X"IF YOU GIVE UP AND WISH TO STOP THE PROGRAM AT ANY TIME.
AMPB: TYPE"A"IF YOU WANT ANOTHER SEARCH AT ANY TIME.
AMPB: KEY?
    : ?
AMPB: TYPE A PHRASE,NO MORE THAN 8 WORDS.THIS (KEY) WILL BE USED AS A
AMPB: UNIT FOR COMPARISON IN A SEARCH OF TITLES AND SUB   HEADINGS
AMPB: KEY?
    : SPACE NAVIGATION
AMPB: KEY:    2 DOCS /   2 HDS
AMPB: R,H OR M?
    : ?
AMPB: R:  LIST OF REFERENCES REQUIRED
AMPB: H:  HEADINGS THAT CONTAIN THE KEYS
AMPB: M:  MORE KEY WORDS TO BE INCLUDED TO LIMIT OR INCREASE THE
          NUMBER OF DOCUMENTS RETRIEVED
AMPB: R,H OR M?
    : M
AMPB: KEY?
    : ROCKET
AMPB: NEW KEY:   8 DOCS /   8 HDS
AMPB: INTERSECTION:   2 DOCS /   4 HDS
AMPB: UNION:    8 DOCS /  10 HDS
AMPB: N,I,P OR U?
    : ?
AMPB: N:  THE DOCUMENTS FOR THE NEW KEYS
AMPB: I:  THE DOCUMENTS COMMON TO THESE AND PREVIOUS KEYS
AMPB: P:  THE DOCUMENTS FOR THE PREVIOUS KEYS
AMPB: U:  THE DOCUMENTS FOR BOTH THE NEW AND PREVIOUS KEYS
AMPB: N,I,P OR U?
    : I
AMPB: R,H OR M?
    : M
AMPB: KEY?
    : TRAJECTORY
AMPB: NEW KEY:   2 DOCS /   5 HDS
AMPB: INTERSECTION:   1 DOCS /   4 HDS
AMPB: UNION:    3 DOCS /   7 HDS
AMPB: N,I,P OR U?
    : I
AMPB: R,H OR M?
    : H
AMPB: TITLE:
AMPB: OPTIMAL TRAJECTORIES FOR SPACE NAVIGATION
AMPB: 2    MISCELLANEOUS OPTIMAL TRAJECTORY PROBLEMS
AMPB: 3    GENERAL THEORY OF OPTIMAL ROCKET TRAJECTORIES
AMPB: 4    OPTIMAL TRAJECTORIES IN A UNIFORM FIELD
AMPB: USEFUL?
    : YES
AMPB: R OR M?
    : R
AMPB: "OPTIMAL TRAJECTORIES FOR SPACE NAVIGATION"
AMPB:  BY LAWDEN,D.F.
AMPB: REF.NO.=            PUBLISHED BY BUTTERWORTHS           1963
AMPB: H OR M?
    : X
AMPB: THANK YOU AND GOOD DAY
AMPB: DELETED:- OK
    : £ENDJOB
MCS : MCS (CORE: 640)
MCS : CONNECT TIME  16:33  MILL TIME  3.578  DISC TRANSFERS    59
MCS : LOGOUT LINE    2    PUBL   ABED1234    14/55/38   09/01/74
```

cathode-ray-tube screen. The disadvantage of visual terminals is that if the results of a search need to be retained, then they must be written down by the user in longhand.

Depending on the indexes to the main file, searches may be constructed in a variety of different ways. Epstein and Veaner[21] describing the BALLOTS on-line interactive library automation system, include illustrations of searches by author's name, key words in the title, Library of Congress card number, etc., in logical combination. This facility to make searches by means of a logical combination of a number of search keys is, of course, common in information-retrieval systems, but quite new to library catalogues where, with conventional card or printed indexes for manual search, only the very simplest search logic could be employed. Hall and others describe the construction of complex queries in the on-line retrieval system at the UK Atomic Energy Authority Laboratory, Culham.[22] Up to thirty-two search terms may be specified using a visual display terminal, divided into four groups of eight terms, with the terms in each group taken together as a logical sum.

Complex searches of this nature are not often required for books, nor would on-line searches of a local library collection normally justify unit costs two or three times those of conventional cataloguing systems. However, at least two exceptions can be envisaged, wherein on-line cataloguing may be justifiable.

The first exception is an on-line real-time library technical processing system incorporating ordering and cataloguing functions. This is the idea behind the Ohio College Library Center (OCLC) system and the BALLOTS system. Both are designed for on-line use by a number of libraries and permit direct-access files to be interrogated in real-time by any of the co-operating institutions. For example, if one library having access to the Ohio College Library Center system wishes to order a set of catalogue cards for a book already in the system files, a search for the item is made, and when found the order for a card set is made. The cards are subsequently printed off-line in batch mode, and if desired, will contain the ordering library's specified alterations to the standard OCLC cataloguing. The BALLOTS system is similar in concept, permitting also the production of printed orders to booksellers as a result of an on-line file search and order command.

Systems such as this raise major questions as yet unanswered. What functions can and should such library networks carry out, and with what systems? What are library users' real needs and what is the value to be placed upon their being satisfied? What will be the future pattern of economic growth and employment in advanced technological societies?, because upon the answers to these questions depends the degree of financial support which will be given to advanced automated library systems.

COMPUTING ASPECTS

The basic ideas behind direct-access file structures and access to such files by means of associated indexes have already been discussed. The techniques used in organizing files for on-line catalogue systems are the same as those used for on-line loans systems, etc., only the contents of the records differ and the contents of the index files vary. But there is one major difference which has important implications for the design of on-line catalogue software; and this is the degree of certainty a searcher brings to his search statement.

When, in an on-line system, a query is made to determine the status of a book with a known identification or call number, that number can usually be quoted with complete certainty. The computer searches for that number in its files. If it is found, the contents of the corresponding record can be reported; if not, the item may be presumed to be not on loan.

But suppose a user puts a query to an on-line cataloguing system, for the book by P. White entitled "An introduction to physical chemistry". A number of possibilities exist. The book may be cited correctly in the query, the book may be in the library, and a match made by searching for the co-occurrence of the three keywords White, physical and chemistry, in one record. But supposing that the author's surname was really Whyte, and the book's title was "A historical introduction to physical chemistry", then a match would not ensue (one of the three necessary keywords is not present), and the user would receive a negative response, even though the book was actually in the collection.

A number of techniques exist for minimizing the occurrence of this kind of mismatch. None can totally solve the problem, and all introduce the concomitant risk of retrieving false records in addition to or instead of the correct one or ones. A situation exists where, as is common in information-retrieval systems, it is impossible always to find what is sought and to eliminate what is not sought. In fact, an on-line cataloguing system is really an information-retrieval system which happens to deal with records of books.

The standard approach to improve the possibility of matching and finding sought records is to generalize the search statement. (This is the exact analogy of the process of broadening subject search statements in order to increase recall in information-retrieval systems.) This is normally accomplished in catalogue systems by any of a number of methods of compressing or abbreviating the words concerned. The objective is to allow for possible errors without permitting the retrieval of "impossible" records. Possible techniques include the elimination of vowels, the deletion of the second letter of each double letter string, and the transformation or mapping of remaining consonants into equivalent groups based on their sounds.

For example, the two words "White" and "Whyte" would be compressed into the same three-character string "Wht" simply by deleting the two vowels in each (treating "y" as a vowel). Using this compression technique on the sample search considered earlier, the user would have found the book he was looking for.

Other matching techniques have included the selection of stated numbers of characters from author and title fields, and have been reported to yield success rates in the range 65 per cent to 100 per cent.

REFERENCES

1. KILGOUR, F. G. History of library computerization. *Journal of Library Automation*, Vol. 3, No. 3, pp. 218–29 (Sept. 1970).
2. GALLIVAN, B., BAMBER, R. N. and BUCKLAND, M. K. *Computer listing of a reserve collection*. University of Lancaster Library, 1972. 70 pp. (University of Lancaster Library Occasional Papers, No. 6, ISBN 0 901669 12 8).
3. WOODS, R. G. *Acquisitions and cataloguing systems: preliminary report*. University of Southampton, 1971. 49 pp. (Southampton University Library Automation Project Report No. 2).
4. WALL, R. A., ROBINSON, M. E. and LEWIS, D. E. *MINICS (Minimal-input cataloguing system): development report*. Loughborough University of Technology, 1973. (LUT/LIB/R6.)

5. AVRAM, H. D. and MARKUSON, B. E. Library automation and project MARC: an experiment in the distribution of machine-readable cataloguing data. In HARRISON, J. and LASLETT, P. (Eds.) *The Brasenose conference on the automation of libraries.* London, Mansell, 1967, pp. 97–127.
6. COWARD, R. E. MARC and local systems. *Program*, Vol. 5, No. 4, pp. 239–52 (Oct. 1971).
7. ARMS, W. Y. Duplication in union catalogues. *Journal of Documentation*, Vol. 29, No. 4, pp. 373–9 (Dec. 1973).
8. JOLLIFFE, J. Project LOC. In BALMFORTH, C. K. and COX, N. S. M. (Eds.) *Interface: library automation with special reference to computing activity.* Newcastle upon Tyne, Oriel Press, 1971, pp. 49–51.
9. JOLLIFFE, J. The tactics of converting a catalogue to machine-readable form. *Journal of Documentation*, Vol. 24, No. 3, pp. 149–58 (Sept. 1968).
10. BROWN, P. The Bodleian catalogue as machine-readable records. *Program*, Vol. 3, No. 2, pp. 66–69 (July 1969).
11. MARUYAMA, L. S. Format recognition: a report of a project at the Library of Congress. *Journal of the American Society for Information Science.* Vol. 22, No. 4, pp. 283–7 (July–Aug. 1971).
12. DAVISON, K. Rules for alphabetical filing by computer. In JEFFREYS, A. E. and WILSON, T. D. (Eds.) *UK MARC project; proceedings of the seminar on the UK MARC project organized by the Cataloguing and Indexing Group of the Library Association at the University of Southampton, 28–30 March 1969.* Newcastle upon Tyne, Oriel Press, 1970, pp. 62–69.
13. HINES, T. C. and HARRIS, J. L. *Computer filing of index, bibliographic and catalog entries.* Newark, N. J., Bro-Dart, 1966. 126 pp.
14. LIBRARY ASSOCIATION. Cataloguing and Indexing Group. Working Party on Computer Filing Rules. Filing by computer: report on the Working Party on Computer Filing Rules. *Catalogue & Index*, No. 27, Autumn 1972, 16 pp.
15. BIRMINGHAM LIBRARIES CO-OPERATIVE MECHANIZATION PROJECT. *Code of filing rules: Part A: General and manual version; Part B: Machine version.* Birmingham, 1971.
16. BUCKLE, D. G. R. and FRENCH, T. The application of microform to manual and machine-readable catalogues. *Program*, Vol. 6, No. 3, pp. 187–203 (July 1972).
17. DUCHESNE, R. M. and DONBROSKI, L. BNB/Brighton Public Libraries catalogue project.—"BRIMARC" *Program*, Vol. 7, No. 4, pp. 205–24, (Oct. 1973).
18. CHRISTOPHERS, R. A. The LASER union catalogue and a national ISBN interlending system. *Program*, Vol. 7, No. 2, pp. 89–95 (Apr. 1973).
19. ISIS (Integrated Scientific Information System); *A general description of an approach to computerized bibliographical control.* Geneva, International Labour Office, 1971. 115 pp.
20. HIGGINS, L. D. and SMITH, F. J. On-line subject indexing and retrieval. *Program*, Vol. 3, Nos. 3, 4, pp. 147–56 (Nov. 1969).
21. EPSTEIN, A. H. and VEANER, A. B. *A user's view of BALLOTS.* Stanford University, California, 1972, 31 pp. (A revised and updated version of the paper published in the *Proceedings of the 1972 Illinois Clinic on Library Applications of Data Processing.*)
22. HALL, J. L., NEGUS, A. E. and DANCY, D. J. On-line information retrieval: a method of query formulation using a video terminal. *Program*, Vol. 6, No. 3, pp. 175–86 (July 1972).

Index

Accessioning (serials) 124
Accounting systems 97, 115, 192
Acquisitions systems 174
  financial control 192
  MARC records in 176, 181
  record structures 66
Aldermaston, Atomic Weapons Research Establishment, Library 187, 205
Aslib Computer Applications Group, Circulation Working Party 150
Authority files 114
Automated Library Systems Ltd. 154
Automatic format recognition 214

BALLOTS system (Stanford University) 232
Barnet (London Borough) Libraries 198
Batch processing 97
Bell Telephone Laboratories Library, Murray Hill, N.J. 168
Bibliothèque Nationale 75
Binding (serials) 142
Birmingham Libraries Co-operative Mechanization Project 177, 224
Bochum University Library 150, 160, 200
Bodleian Library 214
Brighton Public Libraries 177, 224
British Museum Library 214
British National Bibliography 75, 177, 213
Bucknell University Library 168

California, University of
  Los Angeles 130, 134, 139
  San Diego 130, 132, 137
Cambridge University Library 214
Camden (London Borough) Libraries 198
Card-form catalogues 206, 227
Catalogues 36, 196
  book-form 197, 201
  card-form 206, 227
  COM (computer output microfilm) 223, 228
  data conversion 209
  file updating 201, 224
  on-line 228
  record structure 62, 68, 75, 200
  supplements 198
  typesetting 219
Check-in (serials) 134
Cheshire (England) County Library 192
Chicago University Library 197
Circulation control 35, 144
  book identification 150
  borrower identification 152
  data collection 146, 152
  real-time 167
  record structures 155
  reservations (holds) 145
  trapping stores 149, 154
City University Library (London) 115, 118
Claims (serials) 139
Compilers 53

Index

Computer output microfilm (COM) 57, 197, 223, 228
Computer science, growth of 9
Costing automated library systems 23, 43
Culham, UK Atomic Energy Authority Library 232

Data conversion 54, 58
 for catalogue systems 209
 for circulation systems 146, 152
DC subject index 115
Direct-access files 48
 updating 50
Directory (MARC format) 69, 79

East Anglia, University of, Library 104, 108
Exeter University Library 102

File conversion 58
File structures 47
 updating 49
Filing order
 catalogues 215
 serials holdings lists 107
Financing automated library systems 32
Fixed-field record structures 63
Florida Atlantic University Library 197
Flow charts 40
Foulness, Atomic Weapons Research Establishment, Library 168
Friden Justotext phototypesetter 221

Greenwich (London Borough) Libraries 198
Growth
 of computer science 9
 of libraries 33
 of library automation 8
 of library services 7

Harwell, Atomic Energy Research Establishment, Library 110
High-level programming languages 52

Indicator (MARC format) 78
Institutes of Education Libraries 106
Integrated systems 19

International Labour Office, Geneva, Library 230

Kent (England) County Library 187

Lancaster University Library 168, 200
LASER (London and South Eastern Region) catalogue 229
Laval University Library 139
Leader (MARC format) 76
Library Association, Cataloguing and Indexing Group, Filing Rules Working Party 216
Library automation
 costs 23
 financing 32
 growth 8
 objectives 2
 obsolescence 10
 planning 28
 reader services 26
 reasons for 17
 research 19
 staffing 14, 29, 32
 standards 11
 statistics 21
 user reactions 12
Library of Congress 7, 75, 213
 subject headings 115
Line printers 56
Loans systems 35, 144
 book identification 150
 borrower identification 152
 data collection 146, 152
 real-time 171
 record structures 155
 reservations (holds) 148
 trapping stores 149, 154
Loughborough University of Technology Library 115, 131, 137, 200
Low-level programming languages 53

MARC
 format 68, 75
 indicator 78
 leader 76
 subfield codes 78
 tags 78, 92
 record service 210
 currency 211

Index

SDI 178
Manchester University Library 185, 192
MASS format 92
MINICS (Minimal input cataloguing system) 200
MONOCLE format 92

Networks 28
Newcastle File Handling System 106
Newcastle upon Tyne University Library 213
Northwestern University Library 168

Oak Ridge National Laboratory Library 140
Objectives of library automation 2
Obsolescence of automated systems 10
Ohio College Library Center 177, 232
Ohio State University Libraries 168, 171
Oklahoma Department of Libraries 178
On-line processing 98
Optical character recognition (OCR) 55, 214
Ordering systems 174
  financial control 192
  MARC records in 175, 181
  record structures 66

Phototypesetting 220
Planning automated library systems 28
Plessey Telecommunications Ltd. 137, 154
Prediction (serials) 127, 130
Prestige through library automation 20
Programming 52
  languages 53
Punched cards 55, 63
  for serials check-in 134
Punched paper tape 55, 67

Queen's University, Belfast, Library 118, 178, 230

Reader services 26
Real-time processing 98
Reasons for automating 17

RECON (retrospective conversion) project 213
Record structures 46, 61
  cataloguing systems 62, 68, 75, 200
  circulation systems 155
  ordering systems 66
  serials accessioning systems 128
  holdings list systems 62, 107

San Francisco Public Libraries 136
Selective dissemination of information from MARC tapes 178
Serial files 47
  updating 49
Serials accessioning systems 124
  binding 142
  check-in 134
  claims 139
  prediction 127, 130
  record structure 128
Serials holding list systems 35, 97, 99
  filing 107
  record structures 62, 107
  subscription renewal 110
Southampton University Library 150, 156, 181, 200, 220
Staffing automated library systems 14, 29, 32
Standards in library automation 11
Stanford University Library 197
  BALLOTS system 232
Statistical analysis of library operations 21
Subfield codes (MARC format) 78
Subject indexes 114
Surrey University Library 171
Sussex University Library 154
Systems analysis 38
  analysts 30
  design 44

Tags (MARC format) 78, 92
Technology of librarianship 6
Timing library processes 42
Toronto University Library 298, 207
Trapping stores (loans systems) 149, 154
Typesetting for library catalogues 219

UDC subject index 115
Unit costs 23, 43
  changes in 25
User reaction to library automation 12

Value of library services 21

Variable field record structures 66, 68, 75

Wessex Medical Library 200
West Sussex County Library 220
Widener Library, Harvard University 213
Woodstock Agricultural Research Centre, Sittingbourne, Kent, Library 110